D1631407

THE FIELD GUIDE TO TYPOGRAPHY

TYPEFACES IN THE URBAN LANDSCAPE

IRT THAN ANYONE
CLUB'S HISTORY
RESERVE AND WARTIME GAMES AS WELL AS FIRST-TEAM
ILL HE NEVER SCORED AS MANY AS HE SHOULD HAVE DONE
GOT HIS AUTOGRAPH ONCE AND CONGRATULATED HIM ON
HAT DAY. 'IT DOESN'T FEEL RIGHT', HE TOLD ME, 'AND IT WON'T
VINO
TECA
S.PIETR
only
T
S
R
Q
P
N
M
Wideopen
Gosforth & North Rd
Gosforth & North Rd
American Apparel
MILTON
60 CHISWELL STREET
MADRID
MOLA

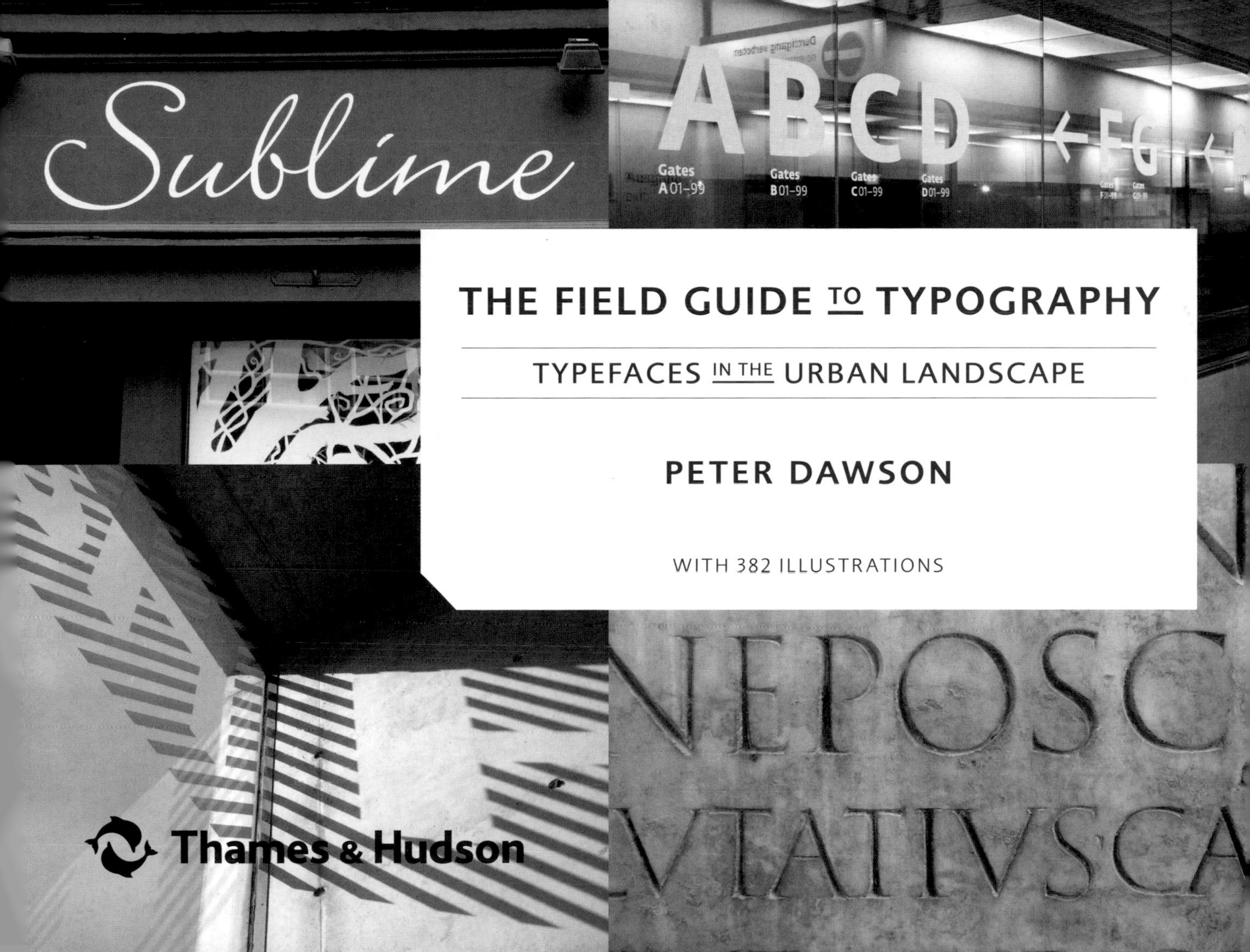

THE FIELD GUIDE TO TYPOGRAPHY

TYPEFACES IN THE URBAN LANDSCAPE

PETER DAWSON

WITH 382 ILLUSTRATIONS

Thames & Hudson

To my parents, John and Evelyn

First published in the United Kingdom in 2013 by
Thames & Hudson Ltd, 181a High Holborn,
London WC1V 7QX

Reprinted 2013

Book design and layout: Peter Dawson, Louise Evans www.gradedesign.com

British Library Cataloguing-in-Publication Data
A catalogue record for this book is available from the British Library

ISBN: 978-0-500-24144-8

Printed and bound in China

CONTENTS_

THE FIELD GUIDE_

SANS SERIF 118

DISPLAY 230

SCRIPT 326

SYMBOLS & DINGBATS 354

FOREWORD_

STEPHEN COLES

Type enthusiasts acquire their odd passion through various channels, be it writing and language, or lettering arts like calligraphy, or simply a penchant for the most basic element of graphic design. My road to fontdom travelled a more circuitous route. As a young boy, I was a birdwatcher. While my peers were playing ball, I was scouring my neighbourhood for uncommon species. I volunteered at an aviary, caring for every winged thing, from rescued magpies to the zoo's prized Andean condor. The regular attendance at our local Audubon Society meetings consisted of a couple dozen grey-haired ladies and me, the 12-year-old blonde kid in the corner.

Birders, it turns out, have a lot in common with type geeks. They are acute observers (of course), but they are also preoccupied with identification, classification, anatomy and minute details that distinguish different breeds. Documentation is also part of every birdwatcher's life; the 'life list' – a record of every species they've ever seen – is an essential companion. (It could be interesting if designers kept a life list of all the typefaces they've ever used. Some of our lists would be much longer than others.)

Later, I learned that it wasn't so much the biology or behaviour of birds that interested me most. It was something else: a fascination with everyday things. The ordinary stuff that surrounds us is usually considered mundane, but it is actually full of variety, and intrigue, and clues that shed light on our environment and ourselves. These everyday things can be parts of the natural world, like birds, plants, insects or clouds. Or they can be part of the manmade world, the designed world that most people don't consider – door knobs, silverware, the guardrail on a roadway. And perhaps the most elemental and omnipresent aspect of everyday design is type.

Peter Dawson's *Field Guide* is not unlike the trusty books I carried on my birding trips. Once armed with photographs of typefaces in the wild, along with their natural histories and defining characteristics, anyone – even those without much typographic knowledge – can discover that what fascinates them most are the things that most people ignore.

Stephen Coles is a writer and typographer living in Oakland and Berlin. After six years at FontShop San Francisco as a creative director, he now publishes the acclaimed online resources fontsinuse.com, typographica.org and a tribute to modernism, midcenturymodernist.com. He consults with various organizations on type selection. Stephen is author of the book *The Geometry of Type* and is a regular contributor to *Print* magazine.

Birds and typefaces live parallel lives. While many people take these omnipresent denizens of our environment for granted, there are others who can't help but observe, classify, and identify them. If you picked up this book, you are likely one of these obsessed few. Welcome.

KEY_

1 Clarendon
2 Akzidenz Grotesk
3 Antique Olive
4 Helvetica
5 Century Expanded
6 FB Garamond Display
7 ITC Souvenir
8 Goudy Old Style

INTRODUCTION_

What is that typeface? This is a common and recurring question heard among design professionals, the budding typographic enthusiast and the general public alike.

As modern society and technology reinvents and expands the ways in which we communicate, we are increasingly confronted with a vast array of messages, be they printed, online or surrounding us in the built environment. The words we want and need to read (and on occasion don't wish to read) are now styled in such an array of differing typefaces that interest and enthusiasm in all things typographical is at an all-time high. The number of fonts available, in all styles and categories, is now well over 150,000, and rising by the day. The task of navigating this ocean of letterforms, separating and identifying one typeface from another, can be bewildering.

The Field Guide to Typography identifies and provides context to over 125 typefaces commonly used and seen today. In this book, I hope to help the 'spotter' identify the familiar – and not so familiar – typefaces that we see around us in our day-to-day lives. The book will also explain the thinking behind their design, the stories of their development, and the impact they have had on people, organizations, communities and even countries. Taken as a whole, it is a comprehensive celebration of our ever-expanding typographic world.

Each typeface has varying permutations, known as fonts. These include Light, Roman and Bold – or even Extra Light and Extra Bold – often with Condensed and Extended variants thrown into the mix. And that's before we've discussed the overall 'classifications' of typefaces. It is a vast and complex picture. So where do we begin?

A basic appreciation of the origins of typefaces can aid our understanding, providing strong clues to their design and appearance. Many of the typeface designs we see today have been created from or influenced by, or are revivals of, historical references, with the majority born from principles and forms created centuries ago by our Roman ancestors.

Their appearance has also been influenced by a wide variety of other factors. Key to many are technological developments, from the earliest letterforms carved in stone, through to the invention of movable type with the Gutenberg Press in the mid-fifteenth century, and on to the advent of the computer and the early digital experimentation starting in the 1960s with OCR (Optical Character Recognition) typefaces. The 1980s brought us DTP (desktop publishing) and the advent of the Macintosh computer, which revolutionized and expanded the way type

OPPOSITE: New York's Times Square, where visitors are confronted with a vast array of messages and the right choice of typeface provides not only clear communication but also context for the message.

New
"BEST NEW COMEDY"
WINNER! BEST MUSICAL
MEMPHIS
AWAKE
DON'T BELIEVE THE LIBERAL MEDIA!
TellTheTruth2012.org
DON'T BELIEVE THE LIBERAL MEDIA!
FRIDAYS
TOSHIBA
TDK
SONY
Hankook
Kodak
Kodak
MARQUIS
New
Coming Soon

AM
OR
DE DEUS
x
o
TODOS
OS
SANTOS
AJUDAM
VOZ

DELI

Arrivals
Aankomst
Departures
Vertrek

FOX
AUTHOR

could be drawn and created. Innovations in printing presses, paper manufacturing and the mixing of ink have also played a major part in type evolution. As technology has moved on, so have the abilities and skills required to design a typeface. The parameters dictated by the medium allowed for a wider freedom of creative expression and opportunity for designers.

Within the design community, trends have certainly played their part in innovating type design, either through creative experimentation or by happy accident. Additionally, art movements have provided inspiration and been a driving force. Along with the Art Deco and Art Nouveau movements, the German Bauhaus School pioneered and rationalized modernism in all areas of design including type design and typography. The International Typographic Style, more commonly known as the Swiss Style, emerged in the 1950s and still has great influence to this day.

Finally, let's not forget instances of a designer answering a client's brief to deliver a typeface for a specific function. Through the ages, commercial organizations large and small have relied on the printed word to communicate their products, message and/or services to a wider market. This, too, has contributed to the development of typeface design. One example is the bold and heavy 'Fat Face' and Wooden Block types (now known as Egyptian or Slab Serif typefaces) produced for use in posters and flyers in the late eighteenth and early nineteenth century.

OPPOSITE: The number of fonts that are now available, in all styles and categories, is well over 150,000, and rising by the day.

Today, many companies and charities commission bespoke, contemporary typefaces to reflect their personality and brand to the consumer.

Despite the diverse impact of history, design and application, one constant that we will always come across – since the dawn of our recognized letterforms – is the passion (and often frustration!), love and skill that go into a font's development. The creation of a typeface family for a specific task requires an understanding of a great number of issues. A designer who is asked to create a typeface that has to work on both an airplane livery and on a handheld PDA – or, even grander, a typeface for use on an entire national road network's signage system – faces an even greater challenge. To explore this aspect of typefaces, the book includes interviews with some of the world's leading type designers, sharing their insights into this highly skilled and exhaustive craft.

The selection of typefaces included within the book was, of course, much deliberated upon and subject to several limitations. There are plenty of 'designer favourites', but a more varied collection – old and new, common and uncommon – has been chosen in order to reflect the diversity of our rich typographic world. Within the Serif section alone, we have long-established classics from the fifteenth century alongside a number of less well-known contemporary designs. As the decades pass, these will also become iconic as their employment becomes more widespread. The good, the bad and the ugly are all here – the much loved as well as the equally loathed. And just as typefaces communicate messages to us in a literal sense, so all of the typefaces shown here have their own stories to tell.

HOW TO USE THIS BOOK_

The Field Guide to Typography is a collection of over 125 typefaces – classic and contemporary, common and unusual – found in our modern urban environment and on the day-to-day objects we come into contact with.

Lightly based on traditional field guides, each spread focusses on one typeface and provides budding 'font spotters' with all the information they need to be able to recognize it in the real world.

The typefaces are divided into five categories for easy reference – Serif, Sans Serif, Display, Script and Symbols and Dingbats – with sub-categories in the side tab. Each spread provides photographic examples, a short history, key identification features, and a 'Not to be confused with' element that acts as a cross reference to similar-looking typefaces.

TYPEFACE PROFILES

1 Side tab provides typeface name and category for easy navigation.

2 The name of the typeface, along with the designer/s, the foundry it originated from, if relevant, and year of design.

3 A short history of the typeface, its design and common uses. Highlighted features include designer and typeface.

4 Sidebar headings include: Category, Classification, Distinguishing Marks, and 'Not to be confused with'.

5 Photograph caption provides useful additional information.

6 Photographic representations of the typeface in use.

7 'Field Facts' feature box providing little-known nuggets of information.

TYPEFACE COMPARISONS

1 Colour coding for side tab alters, distinguishing comparison spread from typeface profiles.

2 Overview of the two typefaces including a brief history.

3 Page reference to locate full typeface profile.

4 Key glyphs of both typefaces are overlaid to highlight the differences in design.

5 Notes explaining the variation in a letterform's structure.

6 Colour-coded key indicating typeface design.

HELVETICA

192_193 SANS SERIF · GROTESQUE

1

Helvetica

2

MAX MIEDINGER, EDUARD HOFFMANN · HAAS TYPE FOUNDRY · 1957

Helvetica is possibly the most widely used (and certainly the most famous) typeface in the world, adored and loathed in equal measures by designers and typographers everywhere. The neutral appearance, distinctive clean lines and clear legibility of Helvetica make it an easy spot to even the most relaxed font-spotter.

A true 'global' typeface, Helvetica was developed in 1957 by Swiss type designer **Max Miedinger** and **Eduard Hoffmann** of the **Haas Type Foundry** with the intention to create a new Sans Serif typeface to compete with the established Akzidenz Grotesk (p. 122). When launched, the typeface was originally called Neue Haas Grotesk, but when Linotype later adopted the typeface, they not only revised the design to work on their system but renamed it Helvetica (a derivation of 'Swiss') so as to appeal to a wider international market. In 1983, the original cut was redesigned and relaunched by Linotype as Neue Helvetica, a much larger, self-contained and structured font family (51 fonts in 9 weights) which adopted the numbering system employed by Univers (p. 224) to designate width, weight and stroke thickness.

3

Helvetica has been employed by many international organizations, including American Airlines, Apple, BMW, Lufthansa, Microsoft, the New York Subway and Panasonic to name but a tiny fraction.

4

CATEGORY: Sans Serif
CLASSIFICATION: Grotesque
COUNTRY OF ORIGIN: Switzerland
DISTINGUISHING MARKS: Moderate x-height; horizontal or vertically cut terminals at 90° angles; double-storey 'a'; square dot over letter 'i'; monocular 'g'; near circular rounded shapes; mildly curving leg on 'R'; low stroke contrast
FURTHER SIGHTINGS: A truly universal typeface, easily spotted in most environments
NOT TO BE CONFUSED WITH: Akzidenz Grotesk (p. 122); Arial (p. 128); Univers (p. 224)

5

OPPOSITE, CLOCKWISE FROM TOP LEFT: From big business to transport, clothing to luxury brands, Helvetica is everywhere. New York Subway signage system; US homeware store Crate & Barrel's delivery truck; American Apparel clothing store; airport wayfinding in Asia.

Subway
New Yo
6
7
Crate&Barrel
E57-E62
E51-
Gates
American Apparel
FIELD FACTS_
In 2007, Helvetica became the only typeface to become a movie star. The self-titled film, directed by Gary Hustwit and released to international acclaim, celebrated Helvetica's 50th anniversary with commentary by leading graphic designers from all over the world about the phenomenon that also led to Helvetica being voted number one in FontShop Germany's "Best Fonts of All Time."

ARIAL VS HELVETICA

130_131 SANS SERIF · TYPEFACE COMPARISON

1

Arial vs Helvetica

[p. 128] [p. 192]

3

Arial is famous for existing only as a replica, employed by a company who wanted to avoid licensing the real deal: **Helvetica.** So it's no wonder these two are similar. Arial even matches all Helvetica's character widths and spacing – which accounts for some of its awkward, forced shapes. Still, despite all its mimicry, Arial does have a different pedigree. It is mostly based on older English Grotesques, rather than the Swiss/German tradition of Helvetica. This results in letterforms that are slightly more open, less cold and calculated. But these minor differences are nearly imperceptible to the untrained eye. An easier way to tell these two apart is by knowing their natural habitat. Helvetica is used (sometimes even worshipped) by professional designers. Arial is a computer default, invoked without a second thought by Microsoft Office users. So you're much more likely to see Helvetica in the logo of an international brand, and Arial in an office memo.

2

6

Gas QRrt 3 Arial
Gas QRrt 3 Helvetica

4

Gas QRrt 3

In light to regular weights, Helvetica's 'a' has a tail that faces laterally. Arial's tail is stunted and sits flat on the baseline.

5

Helvetica has a bearded 'G'. Arial lacks that spur.

All of Helvetica's strokes end flatly, either parallel or perpendicular to the baseline. Arial's curved strokes have a slightly angled terminal.

The tail in Helvetica's 'Q' is straight. Arial's has a slight curve.

With its vertically oriented leg, Helvetica's 'R' is a signature glyph. Arial's diagonal leg flops downward.

Helvetica's 'r' faces sideways. Arial's faces downward.

The top of Helvetica's 't' is flat. Arial's is angled.

Helvetica's '3' is nearly symmetrical. The upper bowl in Arial's '3' is noticeably smaller.

THE ANATOMY OF TYPE_

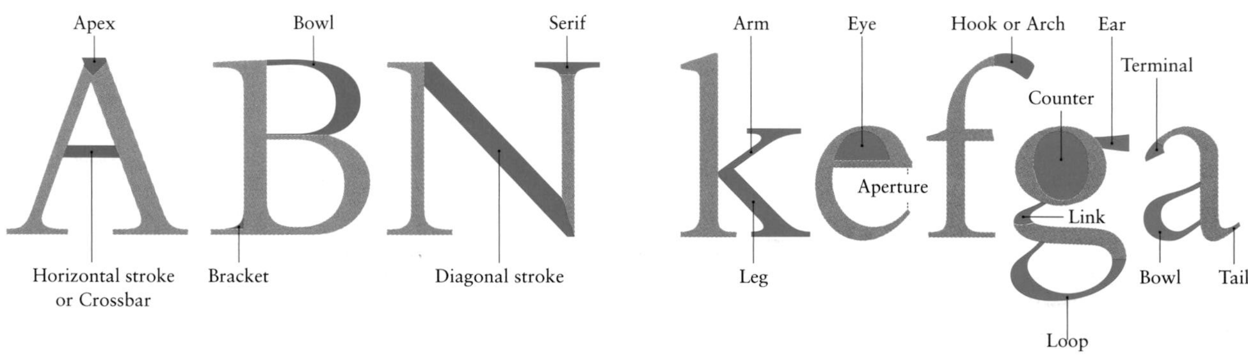
Apex
Bowl
Serif
Arm
Eye
Hook or Arch
Ear
Terminal
Counter
Aperture
Link
Horizontal stroke or Crossbar
Bracket
Diagonal stroke
Leg
Bowl
Tail
Loop

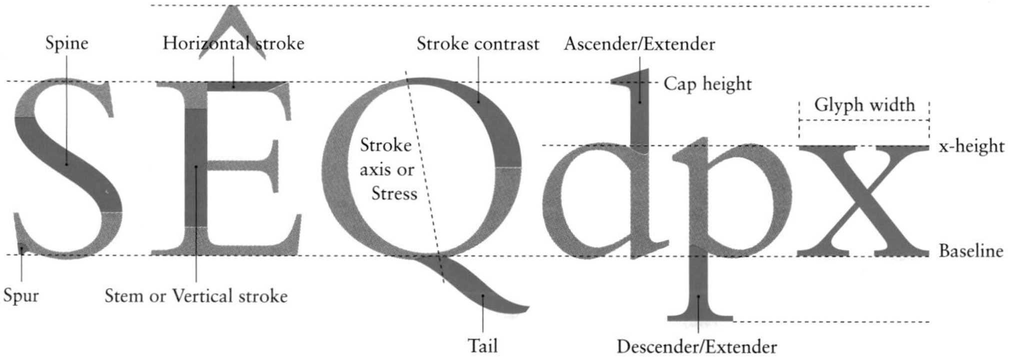
Spine
Horizontal stroke
Stroke contrast
Ascender/Extender
Cap height
Glyph width
x-height
Stroke axis or Stress
Baseline
Spur
Stem or Vertical stroke
Tail
Descender/Extender

GLOSSARY_

Antiqua
Serif types with calligraphic Old Style letterforms.

Ball terminal
A circular form at the end of a stroke.

Bitmap
Character or form defined by pixels set within a grid.

Blackletter
A form of heavy calligraphic script employing broad-nibbed strokes. Seen from the Middle Ages onwards.

Bold
A heavier variation of the Regular weight of a typeface.

Calligraphy
Letterforms written by hand (with a writing implement).

Capital (Cap) height
The height of capital letters from the baseline to the capital's top.

Character
Used to describe any individual letter, number, punctuation mark or symbol within a typeface.

Colour (typographic)
The density of tone seen when a block of text is set on a page. Usually referred to in shades of grey.

Condensed
Typeface design with a narrow character width.

Constructivist
Twentieth-century art and architectural movement. Major influence on Bauhaus.

Contrast
The difference between the thick and thin strokes of a character.

Cursive
Type reminiscent of, or imitating, handwritten letterforms.

Didone
A Serif family that possesses very high stroke contrast with unbracketed serifs.

Dingbat
Non-alphabetical typeface consisting of symbols, shapes or other pictorial elements.

Display type
Typefaces designed for title or headline applications rather than for reading texts.

Drop shadow
Offset replication of letterform positioned behind character to provide the impression of three dimensions.

Egyptian
Serif typeface with low stroke contrast and large, heavy, squared serifs.

English round hand
Calligraphic, connecting script. Often elaborate and having a degree of refinement over other Script typefaces.

Expanded
A font with an 'expanded' character set containing non-aligning numerals, fractions and other characters.

Extended
A typeface whereby the letterforms are 'stretched' on the horizontal axis with wider character widths than the Regular.

Family
Generic description of a collection of fonts of varying weights and styles sharing a common design approach and construction features.

Fat Face
Bold Serif typefaces. Appearance of letterforms close to Moderns/Didones but heavily exaggerated.

Fleuron
Decorative typographic ornament, often a flower or botanical symbol.

Font
A collection in a digital file (or a set of metal types) of all the letterforms, punctuation marks, numerals and font metrics of a single typeface design and weight (e.g. Light, Bold).

Fraktur
A form of decorative Black letter type.

Glyph
A single character, mark or icon.

Grotesque
From the German *grotesk*; a classification of Sans Serif typefaces.

Humanist
A classification of typefaces based on calligraphic letterforms with moderate stroke contrast; can be applied to both Serif and Sans Serif.

Ink trap
Design feature where corners and elements of letterforms are removed to allow for the spread of ink when printed.

Italic
A sloped, script version of a Roman typeface; a bespoke design incorporating distinctive and individual letterforms.

Junction
Point at which the end of one stroke in a letter meets another stroke.

Legibility
The quality of one letter being recognizable from another.

Ligature
Two characters joined to form one letterform – e.g. 'fi'.

Light
A reference term for a weight of type with thinner strokes.

Lining figures
Numeral characters of common size and position on the baseline (also 'Regular').

Litho(graphic) printing
Printing onto paper from etched metal plates.

Minuscule
The small or lower-case letters of the alphabet based on hand-drawn letterforms from the seventh century.

Modern
A classification of Serif typefaces with high stroke contrast and vertical stress.

Monoline
A letterform's stroke having a constant width. Seen mainly in a number of Sans Serifs.

Monospaced
Typeface where each character occupies the same amount of space regardless of its width. Commonly seen in typefaces based around typewriters.

Non-aligning figures
Numeric characters of varying height and position on the baseline. Also referred to as 'Old Style' numerals.

Oblique
Slanted Roman letterforms; not to be confused with italic.

OCR
Optical Character Recognition. Type to be scanned and read by machine.

Old Style
A classification for Serif types that appear with low stroke contrast, an angled stress and angled serifs.

OpenType
Cross-platform font format by Microsoft and Adobe.

Photo-composition
Prior to digital typesetting, typefaces existed on glass negatives and were exposed to light-sensitive paper by shining light through them to create hard copy versions. Also referred to as 'cold type'.

Point
A standard typographic unit of measure equal roughly to 1/72nd of an inch (0.351 mm).

PostScript
Adobe's page description programming language that allowed for vector-based layouts and typefaces to be accurately rendered. Now largely replaced by OpenType.

Proportional figures
Numbers with spacing based on their individual character widths for better readability within running text.

Punch/Punchcutter
A steel die faced with an individual letter in relief hand-carved in. This die was then 'punched' into a softer metal with other punches to create page layout and form printing blocks.

Readability
The definition of being able to read and absorb typeset text when composed.

Regular
A classification term for a standard weight of typeface.

Roman
Regular, upright style of letter.

Running text
Continuous typeset body text, as seen in textbooks.

Sans Serif
A typeface with no serifs.

Semi-bold
A weight of type. Lighter than Bold, heavier than Medium.

Slab Serif
Typefaces where serifs are 'squared' and equal (or close) to the stroke weight.

Slope
Oblique simulated Roman letterforms, not to be confused with italic.

Small caps
Capital designed letterforms but with a height roughly that of lower-case letters.

Stress
The direction of a letterform's stroke contrast, either vertical or angled.

Stroke
The line that forms the letterform.

Style
Reference terms that can be applied to the varieties of the same typeface, such as Light, Roman, etc.

Tabular figures
Numbers that share a common width so when employed in columns they can be aligned to be easily read.

Thicks and thins
A term to describe the contrast in the stroke of a letterform.

Titling
A style of typeface designed for large settings, typically lighter, with finer details.

Transitional
A group of typefaces that bridge the distance between Old Style and Modern Serifs.

Typeface
The aesthetic design of a font possessing a collection of all the character elements that share the same design characteristics.

Weight
Definition for the lightness or thickness of the letter forms design.

CLASSIFICATION TYPES_

Although there is no 'official' system in place for typeface classification there is a recognized agreement of understanding in the design community of referencing the various styles that have been created. Invariably, the period of their creation within type and printing development and their distinctive visual appearance dictates how they are classified. Opposite there is an overview of how the types have been classified within *The Field Guide to Typography*, although alternative and more exacting methods of differentiation do exist that drill down further into the nuances of the letterforms' make-up.

The key distinction between Serif and Sans Serif is evidently clear, with the Serif typefaces all possessing 'serifs' which complete the strokes at the terminals with a flared, pronounced ending (bracketed serif) or a rectangular, squared-off form (Slab Serif). From these core Serif types, the variations in design can greatly vary and within the book you will see how they differ when compared against each other.

Within the Display classsifications there are a number whose characteristics are shared with the Serif and Sans Serif types but these particular typefaces are positioned within this section as they are deemed unsuitable for employment with larger extents of text and are primarily created to work as headline and titling fonts. 'Ornamented/Novelty' fonts come in many guises, from 'Art Nouveau' types to 'Futuristic' and 'Distressed'.

SERIF

Bodoni [p. 40]
Modern/Didone

Lubalin Graph [p. 84]
Geometric Slab

PMN Caecilia [p. 44]
Humanist Slab

Albertus [p. 24]
Inscribed

Garamond [p. 74]
Old Style

TRAJAN [p. 112]
Roman Inscribed

Clarendon [p. 54]
Slab Serif/Egyptian

Baskerville [p. 32]
Transitional

SANS SERIF

Avant Garde [p. 132]
Geometric

Franklin Gothic [p. 174]
Gothic

Helvetica [p. 192]
Grotesque

Bliss [p. 150]
Humanist

DISPLAY

Blur [p. 254]
Amorphous

Bodoni Poster [p.256]
Modern/Didone

Cooper Black [p. 262]
Old Style

Arnold Böcklin [p. 238]
Ornamented/Novelty (Art Nouveau)

Aachen [p. 232]
Slab Serif/Egyptian

BANK GOTHIC [p. 240]
Square Gothic

STENCIL [p. 316]
Stencil

ZEBRAWOOD [p. 324]
Tuscan

SCRIPT

Brush Script [p. 334]
Brush Script

Bickley Script [p. 330]
English Round Hand

Edwardian Script [p. 338]
French Round Hand

Comic Sans [p. 336]
Handwriting

Fette Fraktur [p. 340]
Blackletter (Fraktur)

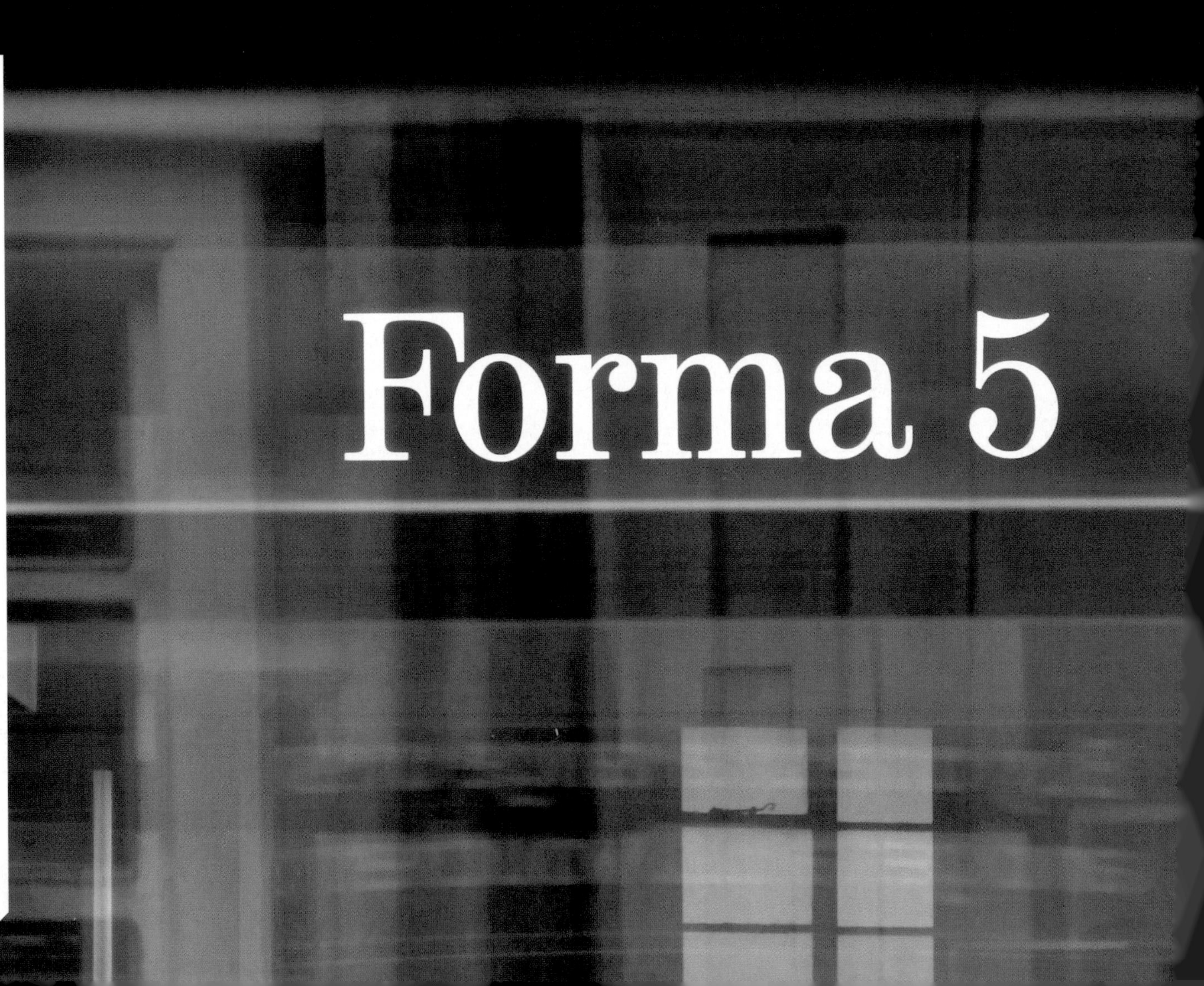

Forma 5

Serif

OPPOSITE: Century *(see* p. 52) in use as retailer branding for designer furniture shop Forma 5, London, UK.

FIELD FACTS_

Albertus's designer Berthold Wolpe worked at Faber and Faber from 1941 right up until his retirement in 1975, by which time it was estimated he had designed well over 1,500 book covers and dust jackets.

In 1980, a retrospective show of Wolpe's work was held at London's Victoria & Albert (V&A) Museum. Wolpe died in 1989, at the age of 84.

Albertus

BERTHOLD WOLPE · MONOTYPE · 1932–1940

CATEGORY: Serif

CLASSIFICATION: Inscribed

COUNTRY OF ORIGIN: Germany

DISTINGUISHING MARKS: Bold simple strokes with subtle, minimal flaring terminals; asymmetrical crossbar on 'E' and 'F'; descender on upper case 'J'

FURTHER SIGHTINGS: The Bitstream foundry version is referred to as Flareserif 821

NOT TO BE CONFUSED WITH: Friz Quadrata (p. 70); Optima (p. 220)

OPPOSITE: Albertus employed on street signage within the 'City of London' district.

Named after the thirteenth-century German philosopher and theologian Albertus Magnus, Albertus was inspired by letterforms that had been carved into bronze.

Commissioned by Stanley Morison of the **Monotype Corporation** type foundry, German typographer and type designer **Berthold Wolpe** initially began designing Albertus as titling capitals in 1932, launching in 1935. Over time, the typeface evolved, with a lower-case Roman set being added, followed by an italic and a lighter weight in later years. The family was completed in 1940. An extremely popular typeface due to its ease of use and strong legibility, Albertus is often used for display purposes on items such as book covers, packaging and signage systems.

Berthold Wolpe originally started out as an apprentice metal engraver at the Klingspor foundry in Offenbach (later a strong influence on Albertus's visual aesthetic). He then went on to study at Offenbach's Kunstgewerbeschule (school of arts and crafts) before moving to England in 1935. When World War II broke out he was sent, along with many other German nationals living in Britain, to an internment camp in Australia. He returned in 1941 and joined the production department of book publisher Faber and Faber. As well as designing several other typefaces, it was there that he established his reputation as a leading book jacket designer of the time, employing Albertus and hand-lettering in many of his cover designs.

ITC American Typewriter

JOEL KADEN/TONY STAN · ITC · 1974

With a touch of nostalgia, ITC American Typewriter is a tribute to those early letter-writing machines, the predecessors to our digital age. Whether used to format the classic business letter or employed in a more varied, contemporary manner, ITC American Typewriter has, since its release, been used in a whole host of different applications. Its success can be attributed to the friendliness and immediacy of its presentation.

It was launched by **International Typeface Corporation** (ITC) in 1974 to celebrate the 100th anniversary of the office typewriter. The brief was to create a typeface family that, while emulating the classical appearance of typewriter letterforms, nonetheless broke away from their monospaced appearance to create a proportionally spaced font. This meant creating letterforms that vary in width like a conventional text typeface rather than employing a standard space for all characters – a feature that allowed the typeface to work much better in text settings, increasing its readability.

Never created to be formatted for metal type, its first use was in photocomposition machines. Only later was it produced as the digital font that is now a standard on all PC operating systems.

CATEGORY: Serif

CLASSIFICATION: Slab Serif

COUNTRY OF ORIGIN: USA

DISTINGUISHING MARKS: Pronounced rounded serifs and terminals, appearance of typewriter letterforms

FURTHER SIGHTINGS: OfficeMax; Dorset Cereals; 'I love NY'; Budgens food retailers, UK

NOT TO BE CONFUSED WITH: Clarendon (p. 54); Courier (p. 64);

OPPOSITE: For US retailer OfficeMax, the use of ITC American Typewriter Bold as their logotype is an ideal choice to communicate their area of expertise and range of business products.

FIELD FACTS_

The design of American Typewriter was based on the typewriter patent by Christopher Latham Sholes in 1868. A newspaper publisher and a politician in Wisconsin, USA, he initially tried to develop a typesetting machine following a strike by compositors at his printing press. His early attempts were in fact to create a numbering machine that could index the pages of a book. His successful efforts acted as a spur and, with the help of an amateur inventor, Carlos Glidden, and fellow printer Samuel W. Soule, he developed the patent of the typewriter. In 1873, they approached the Remington Arms Company (then E. Remington & Sons) who purchased the patent from them.

Introducing a new font
Inspired by
PLANTIN
Moretus Museum Archives
in Antwerp
A 16th Century *Typeface* with contemporary proportions
Designed for Newspapers
museum
Publications
Magazin
Available *in 5 weig*

Read more here: http://blog.eyemagazine.com/?p=7260

A2/SW/HK
Designed by Henrik Kubel, 2011
TYPE
To be released in 5 weights this Autumn
by London based type studio
www.a2-type.co.uk

FIELD FACTS_

Henrik Kubel is a partner in London-based design studio A2/SW/HK, which he co-founded with fellow designer Scott Williams in 2000. As a result of their extensive award-winning portfolio of work for the likes of Tate Modern, *Wallpaper** magazine, Royal Mail and Penguin Press, they embarked on creating A2-TYPE in 2010. The foundry was set up to license and sell the wide range of specially crafted typefaces A2/SW/HK had created for client-based projects over the previous decade.

Antwerp

HENRIK KUBEL · A2-TYPE · 2011

CATEGORY: Serif

CLASSIFICATION: Contemporary Serif

COUNTRY OF ORIGIN: Belgium/UK

DISTINGUISHING MARKS: Large x-height; large counters on lower case 'a' and 'e'; increased angle of italic at 19°; pronounced ink traps; open counter on upper-case 'P'; pronounced ear on double-storey 'g'

FURTHER SIGHTINGS: Ideal for applications where authority and elegance are both required

NOT TO BE CONFUSED WITH: Plantin (p. 100)

OPPOSITE: A2-TYPE promotional design for their sixteenth-century influenced typeface, Antwerp.

A contemporary design inspired by sixteenth-century typefaces, this recent family of text typefaces was inspired by the many archives of type on display in the Plantin-Moretus Museum, Antwerp, Belgium.

In 2010, Danish graphic designer Henrik Kubel was awarded the prestigious three-year artist and designer working grant from The Danish Art Foundation. As part of his grant and his studies at the Expert Class Type Design course at the Plantin Institute of Typography, Kubel developed the concept and design of Antwerp over a ten-month period, applying the many years of type design experience he had gained while designing bespoke typefaces for commercial graphic design projects.

He worked traditionally, creating initial sketches from his research before transferring to a digital medium (using Fontlab software) to complete the design. Antwerp encompasses many of the qualities of Dutch typography of the early period but with a larger x-height than its ancestors to aid legibility and reflect twentieth-century aesthetics and requirements.

The resulting typeface, with its broad range of weights (Light, Regular, Medium, Semibold and Bold, all with italic styles), is particularly elegant and warmer than some of its contemporaries, making it ideal for use in print and on-screen reading applications.

Archer

HOEFLER & FRERE-JONES · 2008

Created exclusively for American cookery and interior design guru Martha Stewart's *Living* magazine, this elegant Slab Serif combines the geometry of a Slab design with a softer, humanist quality, making it ideal for texts that require a lighter and accessible tone of presentation.

Eminent New York type foundry Hoefler & Frere-Jones's Archer typeface was commissioned to meet the extensive demands of modern editorial and publishing requirements. In a magazine such as *Living*, the content is highly varied, ranging from tables and diagrams to calendars, reading texts and headlines, all of which require a typeface that is flexible and possesses enough typographic variation to create differentiation between the many hierarchies of information. In addition, the typeface's appearance had to be one of innocence and friendliness, inviting the reader into the subject matter and conveying the Martha Stewart brand as credible and straightforward.

Hoefler & Frere-Jones's innovative design incorporates details drawn from typewriter faces, such as ball terminals and slab serifs, to create a note of 'honesty' within the design. Married with the mathematical purity of a geometric approach, the Slab Serif design is not only hard-working and legible but also warm and approachable.

CATEGORY: Serif

CLASSIFICATION: Geometric Slab

COUNTRY OF ORIGIN: USA

DISTINGUISHING MARKS: Ball terminals on lower-case 'a', 'f', 'g', 'j', 'r' and 'y'; slab serif on descenders of 'p', 'q'; open, rounded counters; horizontal slab serif on apex of upper-case 'A'; long ascenders; short descenders; low x-height

FURTHER SIGHTINGS: *San Francisco Chronicle*; *Passion for Business* magazine; Central Park development in Sydney, Australia; Wells Fargo; Quaker Oats

NOT TO BE CONFUSED WITH: ITC Lubalin Graph (p. 84); Rockwell (p. 102)

OPPOSITE: Archer used in the identity, and as signage, for The Craft Beer Co., UK.

FIELD FACTS_

Slab Serifs derived from early wood-carved type, which was employed for the printing of large display types. Due to the difficulties of carving wood and of attempting to convey the intricate shapes of Serif type, the typefaces that were cut in this medium possessed 'slab serifs', squared off serifs close to the stroke weight in thickness.

FIELD FACTS_

Design studio Emigre's founder and designer Zuzana Licko used Baskerville as the basis for her Mrs Eaves typeface in 1996 (*see* p. 88). The typeface is named after John Baskerville's housekeeper, Sarah Eaves, who married Baskerville following the death of her husband.

Baskerville

JOHN BASKERVILLE · 1757

CATEGORY: Serif

CLASSIFICATION: Transitional

COUNTRY OF ORIGIN: England

DISTINGUISHING MARKS: Moderate contrasting thick and thin strokes; large x-height; circular curves; rounded terminals; flat top stroke on lower-case 'a'; decorative tail on upper-case 'Q'; long straight leg on upper case 'R'; vertical stress

FURTHER SIGHTINGS: Kate Spade designer clothing; McQueens florist identity; WHSmith stationers; Kindle Paperwhite readers

NOT TO BE CONFUSED WITH: Caslon (p. 50); Garamond (p. 74); Mrs Eaves (p. 88)

OPPOSITE: From fashion houses to stationers, and public houses and flower shops in-between, Baskerville's timeless authority lends an air of grace and elegance to any organization.

A quintessentially English Serif design, Baskerville has long been deemed a classic typeface thanks to its elegance, refinement and the perfection of its letterforms. However, upon its release both designer and typeface came under heavy criticism.

John Baskerville's passion for writing and printing are evident in his eponymous design, one of the most outstandingly beautiful typefaces created. Baskerville's type designs were intended to improve upon letterforms created by his contemporary, William Caslon. Employing a more refined cut to the serifs, an increased contrast in the letters, with thinner stroke weights and more circular curves, Baskerville achieved a consistent character shape across the letters and increased legibility. Despite this, these design innovations were rejected by many critics because they were deemed to 'hurt the eye'!

As he was a perfectionist, Baskerville's designs took an age to come to fruition. Setting up his printing business in 1750, he worked with John Handy to punchcut his designs; his first complete book wasn't printed until 1757. Delays were caused by his experimentation with the structures of the printing presses, the inks he used, the papermaking and, of course, type design.

In 1978, designer John Quaranda created the ITC New Baskerville revival typeface, which is a version often seen used today.

Baskerville vs Times New Roman

[p. 32] [p. 110]

Each of these faces serves an important role in typographic history. **Baskerville** is the quintessential Transitional Serif, originating in the eighteenth century as a reaction to the very calligraphic forms of the type that preceded it, yet not as constructed and high contrast as the Didones that followed. **Times New Roman** belongs to this same stylistic category, but was born roughly 150 years later for the *Times of London* newspaper. It is therefore more modern and crisp in appearance, with a taller, narrower lower case. Both are designed for text, but Baskerville is more of a long-reading book face, while Times was designed specifically for the cheap paper and shorter texts of news.

Sage

Baskerville has a ball terminal on the 'g'. Its loop is open, a signature feature of the typeface.

Times's serifs are much sharper and longer in length.

Baskerville has a much lower, traditional book face x-height. Times's is tall and narrow, designed for larger type in smaller spaces.

Baskerville has a vertical stress. Times's is angled and has much more stroke contrast.

Sage CEGJQ Baskerville

Sage CEGJQ Times New Roman

CEGJQ

Baskerville's bottom horizontal stroke is much longer than the upper strokes, giving it a kind of underbite.

Baskerville's 'J' descends below the baseline.

Baskerville is one of the few text typefaces with a serif on the bottom of its 'C'.

The vertical stroke in Baskerville's 'G' is relatively short, while Times's 'G' is unusually long.

Baskerville has a very decorative, swashy tail on its 'Q'.

FIELD FACTS_

Legendary German typographer and book designer Jan Tschichold was a fan of Bell and used it in many of the books he designed, even referring to it in his work on modernist graphic design, *Typographische Gestaltung* (Typographic Design).

Bell

RICHARD AUSTIN · 1788

Described by Stanley Morison as the 'first English typeface', Bell was influenced – much like Baskerville before – by the typeface designs emanating from Europe at the time.

Much as John Baskerville was impressed and influenced by the European style of typeface cutting, from figures such as Firmin Didot in France and Giambattista Bodoni in Italy, so was John Bell, who ran his own foundry and newspaper, *The Oracle*.

Bell commissioned the former engraver and then punchcutter **Richard Austin** to create a typeface that possessed sharp serifs and the highly contrasting thick and thin stroke weights of the French style but still retained traditional bracketed serif features. The resulting creation was described as 'Scotch Roman', a class of typeface popular at the beginning of the nineteenth century that was widely used for both text and heading.

When launched, however, typeface tastes were changing drastically – in part due to the development of lithographic printing – and sadly it fell out of favour in Europe. In the USA it became very popular and was used widely in publishing and press settings, enjoying a revival in 1932 by the Monotype Corporation.

CATEGORY: Serif

CLASSIFICATION: Transitional

COUNTRY OF ORIGIN: England

DISTINGUISHING MARKS: Fine hairlines; strong verticals; double-storey lower case 'a'; double direction stroke on 'Q'; ball terminal on upper case 'J'; high stroke contrast

FURTHER SIGHTINGS: A rare spot as little used but traditionally employed as a classical text face for reading books

NOT TO BE CONFUSED WITH: Baskerville (p. 32); Galliard (p. 72); Minion (p. 86)

OPPOSITE: A rare sighting of Bell, not commonly used today despite its classical appearance and highly legible letterforms.

Bembo

FRANCESCO GRIFFO/STANLEY MORISON · MONOTYPE · 1495–1501/1929

Dating back to 1495, Bembo was originally designed and cut by Venetian type designer and punchcutter Francesco Griffo for his employer, the renowned Italian Renaissance printer Aldus Manutius. It was one of the first of the Old Style Serifs to be created.

The typeface was first used in a short book by the young and respected Italian classical scholar Pietro Bembo (later Cardinal Bembo) entitled *Petri Bembi de Aetna Angelum Chalabrilem liber*, which described his visit to Mount Etna.

Griffo's work has influenced many typeface designers since the fifteenth century. The Roman typefaces he created moved away from the heavier, less refined hand-drawn approach of many of the Serif typefaces being cut at the time to a more elegant, calligraphic look that we see in most modern Serifs today.

Many of the older typefaces that were originally cut in metal have been rediscovered, revived and refined so that modern technologies can employ them. In 1929, **Monotype**'s **Stanley Morison** oversaw – as part of Monotype's restoration of historical typefaces – the recreation of the typeface and named it Bembo. Since then it has become widely used and is a favourite for typography in books because of the balanced consistency of its stroke weights, and its legibility, warmth and lightness.

CATEGORY: Serif

CLASSIFICATION: Old Style

COUNTRY OF ORIGIN: Italy/USA

DISTINGUISHING MARKS: Reduced variation between thick and thin stroke weights; calligraphic quality to its letterforms; ascender height that exceeds cap height; upper-case 'R' presented in two forms – with straight tail and curved tail; double-storey lower-case 'a'; diagonal centre strokes on upper-case 'W' cross over

FURTHER SIGHTINGS: Many books, both illustrated and text only

NOT TO BE CONFUSED WITH: Baskerville (p. 32); Garamond (p. 74); Minion (p. 86)

OPPOSITE: Bembo employed as the display typeface at London's National Gallery, UK.

THE
NATIONAL
GALLERY
WELCOME
ADMISSION
FREE
GALLERY

LADY
GAGA
PRESENTS
THE MONSTER BALL TOUR
AT MADISON SQUARE GARDEN
SATURDAY, MAY 7 9PM
mediacy

Bodoni

GIAMBATTISTA BODONI · 1790

CATEGORY: Serif

CLASSIFICATION: Modern/Didone

COUNTRY OF ORIGIN: Italy

DISTINGUISHING MARKS: High contrast with thick and thin strokes; hairline thins; hairline unbracketed serifs; tail of 'Q' centred at baseline; vertical stress; moderate x-height; long extenders

FURTHER SIGHTINGS: Lady Gaga branding; *Vogue* magazine; Nirvana logotype

NOT TO BE CONFUSED WITH: Baskerville (p. 32); Didot (p. 66)

OPPOSITE: Bodoni's mix of classic appearance with high fashion connotations means even the likes of Lady Gaga adopt it for use.

The typeface of choice for the 'fashionista', Bodoni has long been employed by fashion journals and houses, with its contrasting thick/thin letter strokes and sharp serifs reflecting an elegance, refinement and style.

The many modern revivals of Bodoni's typeface that have been created all draw from two of the original's core characteristics: the extreme contrast between the thicks and thins of the line strokes and the possession of sharp, fine serifs. As printing methods improved and cutting techniques for type evolved in the late eighteenth century, the refinement of letterforms continued apace. Giambattista Bodoni, along with his respected contemporaries Fournier, Didot and Baskerville, pushed the design of the letterforms towards increased definition and contrast. The 'calligraphic' approaches that had existed before were replaced with structure and a geometric purity.

Bodoni's outstanding skills in printing and type design (drawing heavily from the achievements of Didot in the latter) took the letterforms to a higher level of technical precision. Heinrich Jost's 1926 revival for the Bauer Type Foundry is regarded as one of the finer interpretations of Bodoni's designs. His work stands out as the most popular of the typeface designs employing this defined approach.

FIELD FACTS_

On 1 April 1977, the British newspaper *The Guardian* ran as an April Fools' joke a special report on the fictional island of San Serrife, which employed typographical naming conventions throughout for its locations and history. In the feature, the make-believe capital was listed as Bodoni and served by the Bodoni International Airport.

Museum für
Kommunikation
Frankfurt

POLLEN
STREET
SOCIaL

LANCIA
5.20
2400 V.I.S.

OPPOSITE: Bodoni's elegance and fashion and beauty associations make it an ideal choice as the primary design element for Spanish design consultancy Pepe Gimeno – Proyecto Gráfico's packaging designs for RNB's hand cream range.

ABOVE: Identity signage for the Museum of Communication, Frankfurt, Germany.

TOP RIGHT: Bodoni as window signage for a bar/restaurant in central London. Note the addition of the dropped 'a' set in Neue Helvetica 25 Ultra Light.

RIGHT: The engine block of a Lancia employing Bodoni for the car manufacturer's title.

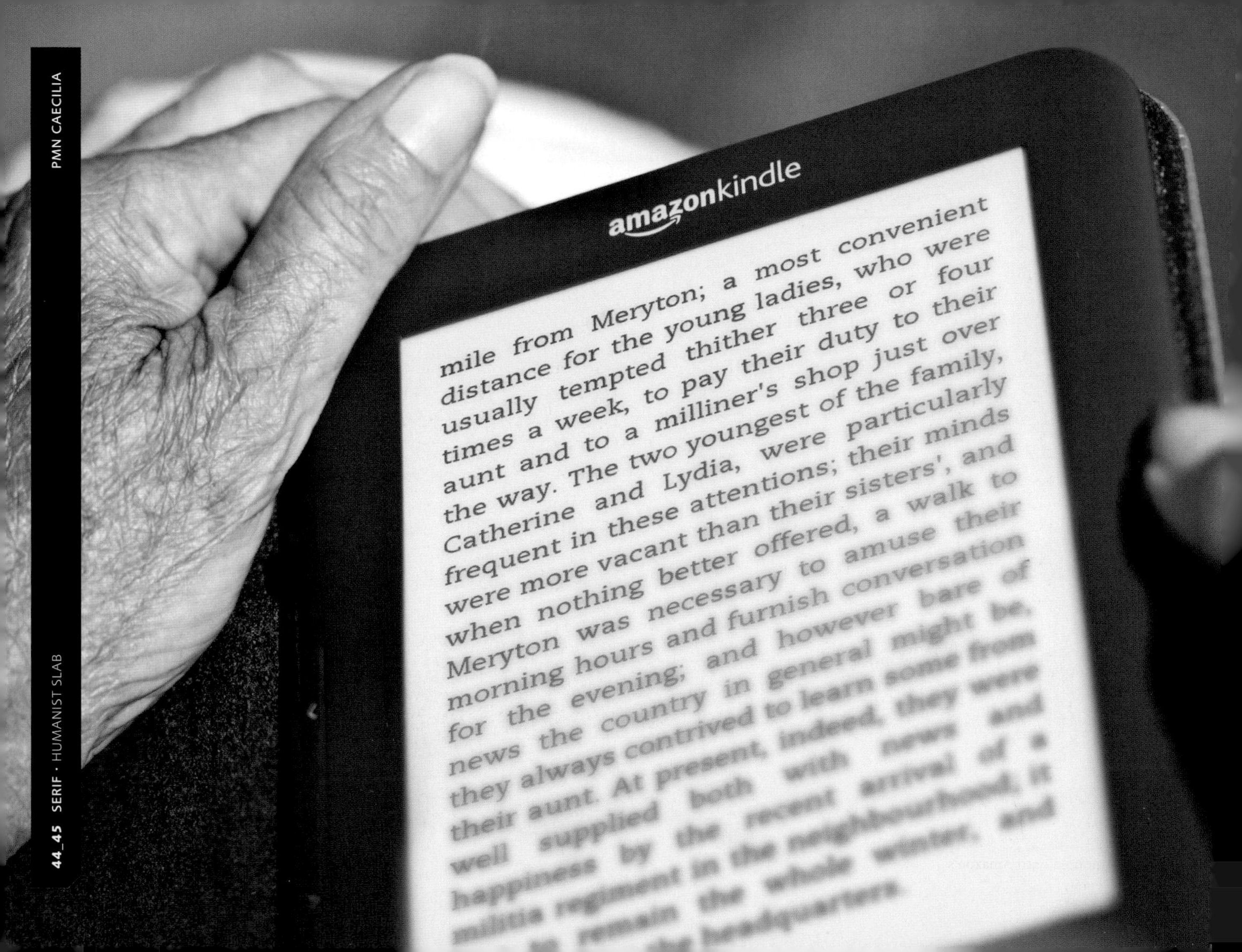

amazonkindle
mile from Meryton; a most convenient
distance for the young ladies, who were
usually tempted thither three or four
times a week, to pay their duty to their
aunt and to a milliner's shop just over
the way. The two youngest of the family,
Catherine and Lydia, were particularly
frequent in these attentions; their minds
were more vacant than their sisters', and
when nothing better offered, a walk to
Meryton was necessary to amuse their
morning hours and furnish conversation
for the evening; and however bare of
news the country in general might be,
they always contrived to learn some from
their aunt. At present, indeed, they were
well supplied both with news and
happiness by the recent arrival of a
militia regiment in the neighbourhood; it

PMN Caecilia

PETER MATTHIAS NOORDZIJ · LINOTYPE · 1990

CATEGORY: Serif

CLASSIFICATION: Humanist Slab

COUNTRY OF ORIGIN: Holland

DISTINGUISHING MARKS: Subtle change in stroke widths; large x-height; open counters; large round dots; curved leg on upper-case 'R'; unbracketed serifs; upturned tail on lower-case 't'; long descender on lower-case 'j'; angled stress

NOT TO BE CONFUSED WITH: Clarendon (p. 54); Courier (p. 64); Neutraface Slab (p. 90); Rockwell (p. 102)

A warm, friendly Slab Serif typeface, PMN Caecilia's low contrast in stroke weights and even texture when set in paragraphs mean it is ideal for low-resolution screen-based display, hence its adoption and inclusion on the early Amazon Kindle and Nook Touch readers.

While studying in 1983 at Koninklijke Academie van Beeldende Kunsten in The Hague, Dutch type designer **Peter Noordzij** made his initial sketches for the design of Caecilia but it wasn't until 1990 that the full family was realized and launched by **Linotype**. The concept behind the design was for the letterforms to flow as if handwritten, with a gently varying stroke weight and consistent serifs. This created a more humanist aesthetic which viewers would find easier to read whether on printed or screen-based media.

The typeface itself possesses a large range of weights, from light to heavy, and an extensive character set, ideal for the Kindle and Nook Touch to display most Latin alphabet languages, including an expert family of old-style non aligning figures and small caps. Its comprehensive and precise design allows it to be used for a wide range of applications and over other Slab Serifs, it has the advantage of being more readable. The PMN prefix is the designer's initials, while Caecilia is named after Noordzij's wife.

OPPOSITE: PMN Caecilia's Humanist Slab design makes for a great reading face so no surprise it was adopted onto Amazon's Kindle reader.

Calvert

MARGARET CALVERT · MONOTYPE · 1980

Originally drawn for the Tyne and Wear Metro system in Newcastle, UK, Margaret Calvert's eponymous design was just one of a number of projects she created for Britain's transport infrastructure.

A timeless Slab Serif, one of the more distinctive aspects of Calvert's appearance is the use of half serifs on certain characters ('A', 'X' and 'M', for example), which lends it a more humanist and softer quality than other Slab Serif designs. Its clear structure and contemporary appearance make it ideal for a modern display and also signage application, and the use of yellow and black as a colour palette on the Tyne and Wear Metro system make communications clearer and much more immediate.

Graphic designer and typographer Margaret Calvert is renowned for having contributed, with colleague Jock Kinneir, to the design of the majority of UK road and traffic warning signs over the 1950s and 1960s. In addition, she designed the typeface Transport used on the very same road signage and the Rail Alphabet typeface (a refinement of Akzidenz Grotesk, p. 122) employed on the British railway system. Earlier work included a collaboration with Kinneir to design the signage system for Gatwick Airport in the south of England.

CATEGORY: Serif

CLASSIFICATION: Geometric Slab

COUNTRY OF ORIGIN: England

DISTINGUISHING MARKS: Constructed feel; more humanist; less mechanical character shapes; slab serifs with half serifs; double-storey 'a'; horizontal terminals on 'a' and 'e'; vertical stress; minimal stroke contrast

FURTHER SIGHTINGS: Royal College of Art; Tyne and Wear Metro System, UK

NOT TO BE CONFUSED WITH: Clarendon (p. 54); ITC Lubalin Graph (p. 84); Neutraface Slab (p. 90); Rockwell (p. 102)

OPPOSITE: Newcastle upon Tyne brand communications consultancy, Gardiner Richardson, use Calvert to striking effect in their rebranding of the Tyne and Wear Metro identity system.

FIELD FACTS_

On 3 January 2010, Calvert's designer Margaret Calvert appeared on the BBC's *Top Gear* programme to be interviewed by co-presenter James May about the design process of Britain's road signage system with Jock Kinneir. Their Transport typeface has been employed on the majority of the UK's road and traffic warning signs since the 1950s.

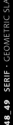

Stands D to N
Metro, Taxis
M
Jackson Street
Toilets, Information
i
Carpets
Rugs
Laminates
Roll Stock

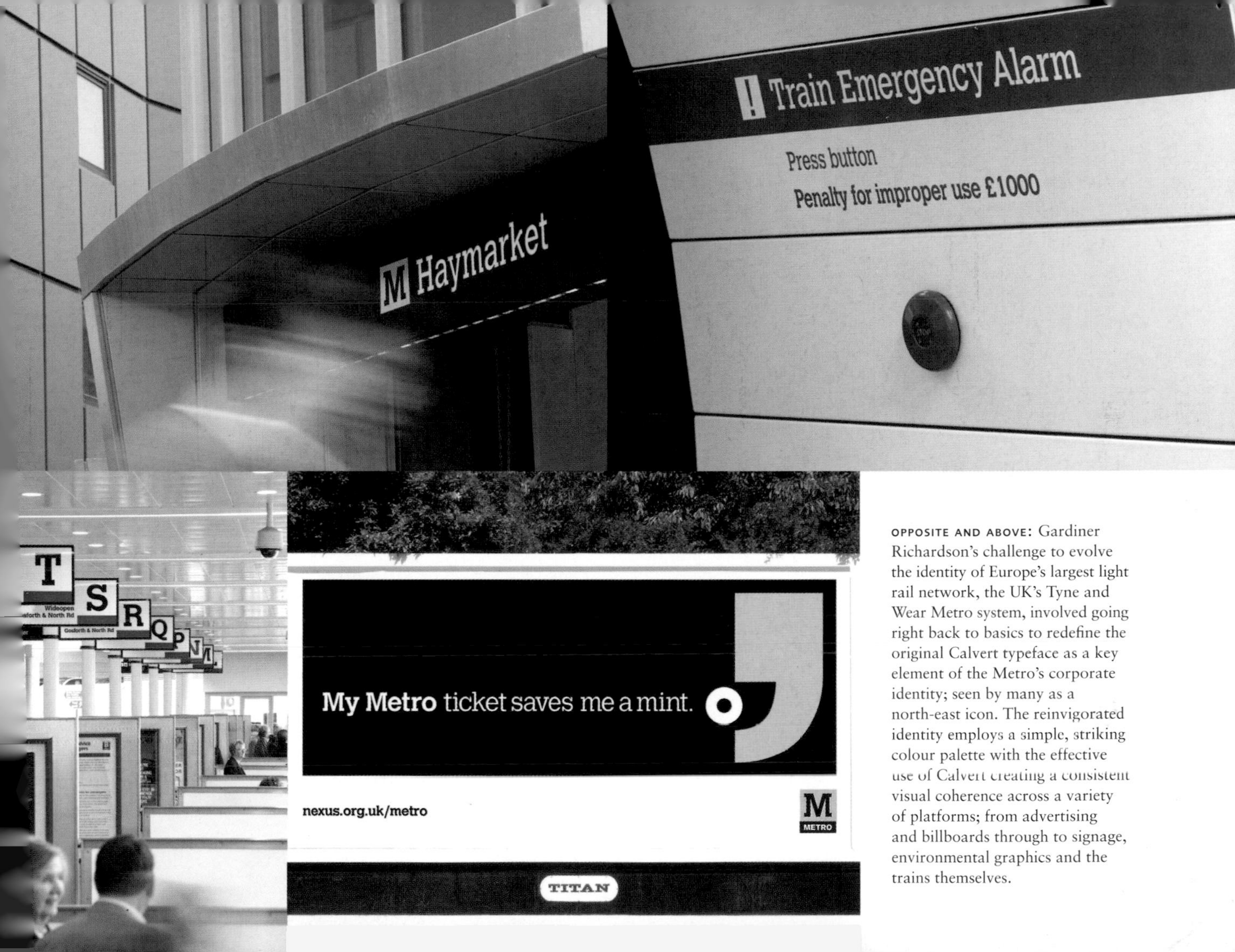

OPPOSITE AND ABOVE: Gardiner Richardson's challenge to evolve the identity of Europe's largest light rail network, the UK's Tyne and Wear Metro system, involved going right back to basics to redefine the original Calvert typeface as a key element of the Metro's corporate identity; seen by many as a north-east icon. The reinvigorated identity employs a simple, striking colour palette with the effective use of Calvert creating a consistent visual coherence across a variety of platforms; from advertising and billboards through to signage, environmental graphics and the trains themselves.

IN CONGRESS, JULY 4, 1776.

A DECLARATION

BY THE REPRESENTATIVES OF THE UNITED STATES OF AMERICA, IN GENERAL CONGRESS ASSEMBLED.

WHEN in the Courſe of human Events, it becomes neceſſary for one People to diſſolve the Political Bands which have connected them with another, and to aſſume among the Powers of the Earth, the ſeparate and equal Station to which the Laws of Nature and of Nature's God entitle them, a decent Reſpect to the Opinions of Mankind requires that they ſhould declare the cauſes which impel them to the Separation.

WE hold theſe Truths to be ſelf-evident, that all Men are created equal, that they are endowed by their Creator with certain unalienable Rights, that among theſe are Life, Liberty, and the Purſuit of Happineſs—That to ſecure theſe Rights, Governments are inſtituted among Men, deriving their juſt Powers from the Conſent of the Governed, that whenever any Form of Government becomes deſtructive of theſe Ends, it is the Right of the People to alter or to aboliſh it, and to inſtitute new Government, laying its Foundation on ſuch Principles, and organizing its Powers in ſuch Form, as to them ſhall ſeem moſt likely to effect their Safety and Happineſs. Prudence, indeed, will dictate that Governments long eſtabliſhed ſhould not be changed for light and tranſient Cauſes; and accordingly all Experience hath ſhewn, that Mankind are more diſpoſed to ſuffer, while Evils are ſufferable, than to right themſelves by aboliſhing the Forms to which they are accuſtomed. But when a long Train of Abuſes and Uſurpations, purſuing invariably the ſame Object, evinces a Deſign to reduce them under abſolute Deſpotiſm, it is their Right, it is their Duty, to throw off ſuch Government, and to provide new Guards for their future Security. Such has been the patient Sufferance of theſe Colonies; and ſuch is now the Neceſſity which conſtrains them to alter their former Syſtems of Government. The Hiſtory of the preſent King of Great-Britain is a Hiſtory of repeated Injuries and Uſurpations, all having in direct Object the Eſtabliſhment of an abſolute Tyranny over theſe States. To prove this, let Facts be ſubmitted to a candid World.

HE has refuſed his Aſſent to Laws, the moſt wholeſome and neceſſary for the public Good.

HE has forbidden his Governors to paſs Laws of immediate and preſſing Importance, unleſs ſuſpended in their Operation till his Aſſent ſhould be obtained; and when ſo ſuſpended, he has utterly neglected to attend to them.

HE has refuſed to paſs other Laws for the Accommodation of large Diſtricts of People, unleſs thoſe People would relinquiſh the Right of Repreſentation in the Legiſlature, a Right ineſtimable to them, and formidable to Tyrants only.

HE has called together Legiſlative Bodies at Places unuſual, uncomfortable, and diſtant from the Depoſitory of their public Records, for the ſole Purpoſe of fatiguing them into Compliance with his Meaſures.

HE has diſſolved Repreſentative Houſes repeatedly, for oppoſing with manly Firmneſs his Invaſions on the Rights of the People.

HE has refuſed for a long Time, after ſuch Diſſolutions, to cauſe others to be elected; whereby the Legiſlative Powers, incapable of Annihilation, have returned to the People at large for their exerciſe; the State remaining in the mean time expoſed to all the Dangers of Invaſion from without, and Convulſions within.

HE has endeavoured to prevent the Population of theſe States; for that Purpoſe obſtructing the Laws for Naturalization of Foreigners; refuſing to paſs others to encourage their Migrations hither, and raiſing the Conditions of new Appropriations of Lands.

HE has obſtructed the Adminiſtration of Juſtice, by refuſing his Aſſent to Laws for eſtabliſhing Judiciary Powers.

HE has made Judges dependent on his Will alone, for the Tenure of their Offices, and the Amount and Payment of their Salaries.

HE has erected a Multitude of new Offices, and ſent hither Swarms of Officers to harraſs our People, and eat out their Subſtance.

HE has kept among us, in Times of Peace, Standing Armies, without the conſent of our Legiſlatures.

HE has affected to render the Military independent of and ſuperior to the Civil Power.

HE has combined with others to ſubject us to a Juriſdiction foreign to our Conſtitution, and unacknowledged by our Laws; giving his Aſſent to their Acts of pretended Legiſlation:

FOR quartering large Bodies of Armed Troops among us:

FOR protecting them, by a mock Trial, from Puniſhment for any Murders which they ſhould commit on the Inhabitants of theſe States:

FOR cutting off our Trade with all Parts of the World:

FOR impoſing Taxes on us without our Conſent:

Caslon

WILLIAM CASLON · EARLY EIGHTEENTH CENTURY

CATEGORY: Serif

CLASSIFICATION: Transitional

COUNTRY OF ORIGIN: England

DISTINGUISHING MARKS: Medium ascenders/descenders; moderate x-height; long extenders; bracketed serifs; capital 'A' possesses scooped-out apex; moderate contrast; near-vertical stress; long tail on 'Q' continues stroke

FURTHER SIGHTINGS: Penguin *Scores* series; *The New Yorker* magazine

NOT TO BE CONFUSED WITH: Baskerville (p. 32); Minion (p. 86); Plantin (p. 100); Times New Roman (p. 110)

OPPOSITE: The birth of a nation. William Caslon's types were employed on the very first printed versions of the United States Declaration of Independence back in 1776.

Nearly 300 years old, Caslon remains one of the most popular typefaces of all time. Historic in its own right, it has been employed in many great works of literature and documents of historical importance, including in 1776 the American Declaration of Independence.

William Caslon was by trade a gunsmith and engraver when in the early 1720s he began to design and cut type. His first typefaces were Arabic but soon he was designing Roman type, drawing influence from the Dutch 'old face' designs that were popular in England at the time. Upon its release, his type was immediately popular not only in England but across the world. Caslon's simplicity, reliability and legibility were much favoured by the likes of Benjamin Franklin in the American colonies and later by the Irish playwright George Bernard Shaw.

Because of its success, Caslon has spawned many copies and as technology developed over the years, with a hot metal then phototypesetting and now digital process, a great many revivals carrying the Caslon name have been created, all possessing the core design features of Caslon's original creations.

Century

MORRIS FULLER BENTON · 1900

Century's outstanding legibility and ease of use has ensured it remains a leading typeface of choice in numerous contexts, from legal papers to museum signage and everything in-between.

It was in 1894 that Century's story started with the design of Century Roman by Morris's father Linn Boyd Benton. Commissioned by publisher Theodore Low De Vinne, Century was designed for use in De Vinne's *The Century Magazine* in the USA. Its key design characteristics include a decreased contrast between the strokes (as a reaction to the trend then of printing with more contrasting typefaces such as Bodoni and similar), a larger x-height and interestingly a slightly condensed width to maximize its character count when set in paragraphs. Benton succeeded in creating a typeface that is incredibly legible and with increased presence on the page when printed.

Some time after the ATF (American Type Founders) was formed in 1892 from a number of US foundries, Lynn Boyd Benton's son, **Morris Fuller Benton**, took on the challenge of redesigning and refining Century as part of a reorganization of the then extensive ATF type portfolio. He went on to extend Century and create a full family of variations holding the name, what is since regarded as one of the first fully considered typeface 'families'. Century was a huge success and over the years has been licensed out to a great many foundries and is as popular now in digital form as it was in its original hot metal format.

CATEGORY: Serif

CLASSIFICATION: Transitional

COUNTRY OF ORIGIN: USA

DISTINGUISHING MARKS: Moderate x-height; moderate contrast; short descenders and extenders; slightly condensed form; use of ball terminals on a number of letters (for example, 'c', 'f', 'g' and 'j'); curved leg on upper-case 'R' possessing an upturned tail; vertical stress

FURTHER SIGHTINGS: Supreme Court of the United States

NOT TO BE CONFUSED WITH: Baskerville (p. 32); Clarendon (p. 54); Walbaum (p. 114)

OPPOSITE: Possessing a combination of heritage and formality, Century's appearance makes it ideal for period typography where authority is required, such as museum displays.

CALIFORNIA
SINCE 1864
STATE PARKS

CALIFORNIA STATE
RAILROAD MUSEUM

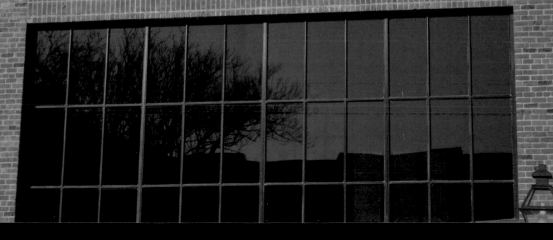

FIELD FACTS_

Edouard Hoffman, who founded the Haas Type Foundry and directed the revival of Clarendon in the 1950s, was also responsible for the creation of Helvetica with Max Miedinger. Originally called 'Neue Haas Grotesk', it was later renamed Helvetica by Haas and their parent company Stempel, as an approximation of the Latin name for Switzerland 'Helvetia'.

Clarendon

ROBERT BESLEY · 1845

CATEGORY: Serif

CLASSIFICATION: Slab Serif

COUNTRY OF ORIGIN: England

DISTINGUISHING MARKS: Bold appearance; ball terminals; bracketed and pronounced serifs; short extenders; moderate stroke contrast; curved leg on upper-case 'R' with upturned tail; large x-height; vertical stress

FURTHER SIGHTINGS: Sony logo; Wells Fargo; El País; National Parks Service

NOT TO BE CONFUSED WITH: Courier (p. 64); ITC Lubalin Graph (p. 84); Neutraface Slab (p. 90); Rockwell (p. 102)

OPPOSITE: From boutique fashion stores to corporate identities and wayfinding, Clarendon's sturdy yet friendly appearance has meant its use as a titling font is widespread.

Employing square serifs, referred to as 'slab serifs', this classic, more refined Egyptian typeface was created to partner traditional lighter Serif typefaces as a way of bringing definition to text containing hierarchies, such as in dictionaries and encyclopedias.

Named after the Clarendon Press in Oxford, the original Clarendon was created by **R. Besley & Co**, a type company that was formerly known as the Fann Street Foundry. A hugely popular typeface, deriving its looks from wooden display type, **Clarendon** is often used as a typeface for headings and display work. However, the fact that its lighter weights can be employed for text applications adds to its flexibility.

Clarendon was revived and refined by Edouard Hoffmann and Hermann Eidenbenz at the Haas Type Foundry in 1953. This consolidated Clarendon's popularity and spawned many imitations by other foundries. It is characterful in appearance and, although it has been well over 150 years since its origination, it retains a contemporary aesthetic.

Rudy VanderLans, Zuzana Licko • Emigre

BERKELEY, USA

Founded in 1984 by Rudy VanderLans and Zuzana Licko, coinciding with the birth of the Macintosh computer and its entry into the graphic arts field, Emigre was one of the first independent type foundries to establish itself centred on personal computer technology.

Emigre holds exclusive licences to over 300 original typeface designs created by leading designers from around the world. As well as their own font designs, their roster includes types from Jonathan Barnbrook, Christian Schwartz, Xavier Dupré, and John Downer. Emigre was also the publisher of the critically acclaimed design journal *Emigre* magazine from 1984 to 2005.

Q: You both studied graphic design and visual communications but made the transition to designing your own typefaces, establishing Emigre Fonts. Could you explain how this came about?

A: When we started *Emigre* magazine in 1984, we had no budget for typesetting which was very expensive and involved third-party typesetters. We used a typewriter and a Xerox copy machine. Then, the Apple Macintosh was introduced, and we quickly figured out that you could design your own bitmap fonts and use them to set text. Mind you, this was all before PostScript and laser printers, so it was very primitive but it allowed for much greater experimentation with type than the typewriter had allowed. As we used these typefaces in our magazine, readers started asking about their commercial availability, and a light went on above our heads. That was the start of the Emigre type foundry.

Q: The Emigre Fonts collection reflects a wide spectrum of approaches and styles and several have a distinct 'technology' aesthetic to them. Where do you get your ideas from and is there a systematic process in creating them or does each typeface demand a different working approach?

A: Initially, we were simply working within the restrictions of bitmap fonts. We were basically building fonts with little blocks. When postscript was introduced, and fonts were defined by an outline, we explored Geometric fonts that were based on simple combinations of circles and straight lines. Since memory space

OPPOSITE LEFT: Oakland, designed by Zuzano Licko originally in 1985, its lo-resolution bitmap appearance reflected the introduction of the Macintosh computer and the creation of the means to design type digitally. In 2001, the four variants of Oakland were incorporated into their Lo-res font family.

OPPOSITE FAR RIGHT: Press advert for Emigre Fonts presenting a selection from their collection of over 300 typefaces.

Emperor

OAKLAND

Emigre

ABCDEFGH
IJKLMNOPQR
STUvwxyz
abcdefgh
ijklmnopqr
stuvwxyz
0123456789

OAKLAND

THE
EMIGRE
TYPE
CATALOG
Now in full color!

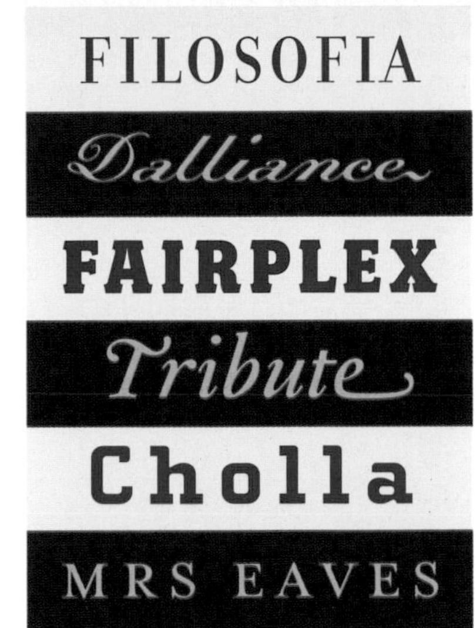

FILOSOFIA
Dalliance
FAIRPLEX
Tribute
Cholla
MRS EAVES
PRIORI
Emigre Fonts

LICENSED and DISTRIBUTED by EMIGRE
FREE CATALOG WITH FONT PURCHASE
Emigre
www.emigre.com

THE EMIGRE FONTS LIBRARY

LITTLE BOOK OF LOVE LETTERS

EMIGRE TYPE CATALOG

SELECTIONS FROM VOLUME I & II

TEXTS BY DAVID BARRINGER

was very limited in those early days of the computer we had to be smart about how to draw fonts with the least amount of data points. Now that memory space is no longer an issue and the tools to design fonts are very sophisticated, our imagination is the only limit. Now we are exploring purely formal issues, trying to find unexplored territory, which is becoming more and more difficult to do.

Q: You have long been known as supporters of, and innovators with, the computer in design. Could you explain how the computer features in your graphic design work and especially your type design today?

A: Without the computer there would be no *Emigre* magazine or Emigre Fonts or type design as we know it today. The computer features very heavily in our design work. It's our most important tool. We rarely work outside of the computer. But the aesthetic of the computer has become less pronounced over time as the technology has become very sophisticated and is now able to mimic any media.

OPPOSITE: Examples of Emigre font catalogue covers incorporating the typefaces Base 9 Sans Bold (left) and Fairplex Wide Black Italic (right), both by Zuzana Licko.

Q: Do you work together when designing a typeface? Or do you operate independently of each other?

A: Zuzana is in charge of the design and production of the typefaces, and I do all the design and production of the promotional material to market the typefaces. But we provide each other with feedback. For instance, when Zuzana is working on the fonts, I'm test-driving the beta versions as they're being developed. This way I get acquainted with them and can give Zuzana feedback on what works and what doesn't. It's also when I start thinking about the design of the promotional materials. So there's a very tight integration between the two disciplines.

Q: How do you go about naming your typefaces?

A: Sometimes it comes from their form, like Modula, which is a very modular design, and sometimes it comes from the backstory of the font, like Mrs Eaves, which was named after the mistress of John Baskerville who designed the classic font that Mrs Eaves was based on. But naming a font is mostly a marketing issue. There are hundreds of thousands of fonts out there, and the name has to be unique. And it has to be able to work in all languages in terms of pronunciation and meaning. And it helps if it can be memorable.

Q: Emigre Fonts licenses a number of other notable designers' typefaces in addition to your own. What are the criteria for selecting typefaces to market within your collection and how do these partnerships with other type designers come about?

A: We've always been highly selective. Our library is a curated selection of fonts. We've always tried to keep the library as small and manageable as possible, offering a wide variety of styles without too many similar-looking fonts. Partnerships with other designers usually come about when fonts are submitted to us for consideration. When we started out releasing digital typefaces in the late 1980s, there were so few people designing type on the Macintosh, they would eventually come to us since we were one of the few foundries set up to commercially produce and distribute fonts. Now that the font market is completely saturated we almost exclusively release fonts designed by Zuzana Licko.

Q: Having designed typefaces for over two decades, what changes have you seen to typeface development over the years?
A: The biggest change we have seen is the amount of competition. There are literally hundreds of websites that sell fonts. When we started there were only a handful.

Q: What's the strangest use you have seen of one of your typefaces?
A: Probably a tattoo using one of our fonts.

Q: To the budding typeface designers out there, what advice would you give them when creating their own font?
A: Have fun! Don't be shy. Please realize that you're young only once, and that's a great opportunity to experiment, to do something out of the ordinary. It's the one time in life that you can claim innocence and get away with anything and in the process perhaps create something extraordinary.

OPPOSITE TOP LEFT: Press advert for Mr Eaves typeface family.

OPPOSITE BOTTOM LEFT: Detail showing the differing letterform design of both Mr Eaves and Mrs Eaves (*see* p. 88).

OPPOSITE FAR RIGHT: Front cover for *Emigre No.70: The Look Back Issue*, a 512-page selection of reprints that traces Emigre's development from its early bitmap design days in the mid-1980s through to the experimental layouts that defined their designs.

Mr Eaves Sans
Mr Eaves XL Sans
Alpha
BRAVO
Charlie
delta
Echo
foxtrot
golf
Hotel
INDIA
Juliet
kilo
LIMA
mike
november
OSCAR
FREE CATALOG WITH EACH TYPE PURCHASE
MR eaves
MADE BY EMIGRE
Mr Eaves XL Modern
Papa
Quebec
ROMEO
Sierra
Tango
UNI-
form
Victor
whiskey
Xray
Yankee
ZU
lu
Mr Eaves Modern
www.emigre.com

EMIGRE

No.70

The Look Back Issue

SELECTIONS FROM EMIGRE MAGAZINE #1 ~ #69

1984 ~ 2009

CELEBRATING 25 YEARS

In Graphic Design

Cochin

GEORGES PEIGNOT · 1912

Inspired (albeit loosely) by French artist Nicolas Cochin's copper plate engravings, Cochin's elegant style made it a popular choice at the start of the twentieth century.

Georges Peignot of Paris foundry Deberny & Peignot in fact created two typefaces called Cochin, with the second designed later in 1914. Although being named after the mid-eighteenth-century engraver Charles Nicolas Cochin, they are in fact not at all representative of the artist's typographical work. To confuse matters, also known as Sonderdruck and described as a Transitional Serif, Cochin has an unusual appearance with heightened ascenders, widened lower-case figures and a squared-up aesthetic to many of its upper-case letters. Its serifs are sharp and pronounced but the upper-case 'Q' does possess an exquisite tail, separated and positioned below the rounded form. Its popularity when released created many adaptations by other type foundries in the 1920s.

In 1977, British type designer Matthew Carter (Bell Centennial, p. 148; Galliard, p. 72) was commissioned by Linotype to refine and expand the Cochin family.

CATEGORY: Serif

CLASSIFICATION: Transitional

COUNTRY OF ORIGIN: France

DISTINGUISHING MARKS: Squared capitals; long ascenders on lower-case characters; small x-height; sharp serifs; open loop on bowl of lower-case 'g'

FURTHER SIGHTINGS: Ideal for use where a classical, European sensitivity is required

NOT TO BE CONFUSED WITH: Baskerville (p. 32); Caslon (p. 50); Galliard (p. 72)

OPPOSITE: Cochin's elegant and intricate letterforms employed for signage above a French restaurant.

FIELD FACTS_

The Deberny & Peignot foundry was created in 1923 from the merger of the Peignot and Laurent & Deberny foundries. Their most widely acclaimed typeface was Sans Serif Univers (see p. 224), designed by Adrian Frutiger. Released in 1957, it dispensed with naming conventions for differing weights and letter variations, such as Extended and Compressed, employing an innovative numbering system.

FIELD FACTS_

Initially known as Messenger, the typeface was renamed Courier after a change of heart by its designer, **Howard Kettler**. He later said: 'A letter can be just an ordinary messenger, or it can be the courier, which radiates dignity, prestige, and stability.' *

Courier

HOWARD KETTLER · 1955

CATEGORY: Serif

CLASSIFICATION: Slab Serif

COUNTRY OF ORIGIN: USA

DISTINGUISHING MARKS: Unbracketed serifs; rounded terminals; monospaced setting; minimal stroke contrast

FURTHER SIGHTINGS: Ideal for when a lack of refinement and a typed appearance is required

NOT TO BE CONFUSED WITH: American Typewriter (p. 26); ITC Lubalin Graph (p. 84); Rockwell (p. 102)

* Goodbye to the Courier font? – Tom Vanderbilt, *Slate.com*, 20 February 2004.

A truly global typeface and one of the most widely employed, this monospaced Slab Serif was the original typewriter typeface.

Commissioned by IBM in 1955, the core characteristic required of Courier was that all letters had to be monospaced (all characters given the same amount of space irrespective of their width) as its use on a 'strike-on' typewriter did not allow for benefits such as the kerning of characters, which digital typesetting today permits. This style of spacing creates an uneven appearance when Courier is typeset as text. However, it does have an advantage when columns of numbers or letters need to be aligned; when digitized in the early 1990s, Courier became very popular due to its tabular appearance and its no-nonsense aesthetic for word processing and technical documents.

As IBM did not trademark its creation and thereby ensure it possessed exclusive rights, its use on their competitors' typewriters became increasingly widespread until it was the standard font employed on nearly all machines globally. Even today, there is uncertainty as to whether anyone holds the copyright to the design – a fact that has encouraged the creation of many versions along the way.

OPPOSITE: Courier's neutral and slightly awkward appearance has made it popular as a typeface choice when the message needs to possess a raw innocence and restraint in its presentation.

Didot

ADRIAN FRUTIGER · LINOTYPE · 1991

Drawn from a number of type designs by Parisian designer and punchcutter Firmin Didot, Adrian Frutiger's revival of Didot's late eighteenth- and early nineteenth-century letterforms convey the elegance and transformation in type design of the period.

As with Didot's peers, such as Italy's Giambattista Bodoni (p. 40) and fellow Frenchman Pierre Simon Fournier, Didot's designs heralded the arrival of the period of 'Transitional' type design, when, thanks to innovations and improvements in punchcutting, printing techniques and ink and paper production, type design evolved greatly. Much greater contrasts were introduced into stroke weights and levels of detail and refinements were incorporated into the designs that pushed the boundaries of technical achievement. These 'Modern/Didone' typefaces were often copied and are reflective of the trends of the time.

From this period of typographic enlightenment, Firmin Didot and his family are recognized as pioneers and innovators owning and running a much respected print and publishing house in Paris in the early 1800s.

Adrian Frutiger's **Didot**, drawn for **Linotype** in 1991, is reflective of the types created by Firmin Didot in the first decade of the nineteenth century. In part, Frutiger drew also from types cut by Didot in a printing from 1880, *La Henriade* by Voltaire.

CATEGORY: Serif

CLASSIFICATION: Modern/Didone

COUNTRY OF ORIGIN: France

DISTINGUISHING MARKS: Vertical stresses; unbracketed hairline serifs; extreme stroke contrast; short extenders; sharp serifs on upper-case 'S'

FURTHER SIGHTINGS: An ideal choice for beauty, fashion and music product messages

NOT TO BE CONFUSED WITH: Bodoni (p. 40); Century (p. 52)

OPPOSITE: Didot here seen in the London Underground on an advertisement promoting electronic dance music trio Swedish House Mafia. Its elegant appearance and clear features make it ideal for display applications, as well as corporate and branding identity programmes, and it is valued as the reference point for all other 'modern' designs.

SWEDISH
HOUSE MAFIA
UNTIL NOW, OUT NOW
#1 ALBUM FEATURING 22 TRACKS
THE YEAR'S BIGGEST ANTHEMS
PLUS ALL THE SWEDISH HOUSE MAFIA SINGLES
INCLUDING THE #1 SMASH HIT
DON'T YOU WORRY CHILD FT JOHN MARTIN
Virgin RECORDS
#UNTILNOW
hmv
hmv.com

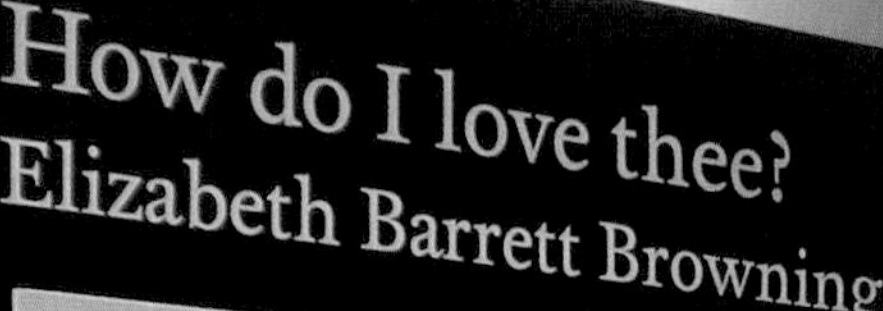

How do I love thee?
Elizabeth Barrett Browning 1806–61
Elizabeth Barrett Browning 1806–61
An early feminist, the first woman to be considered for the post of Poet Laureate, and a brilliant, incisive writer of progressive social and political ideas, Elizabeth Barrett Browning was a radical figure. Yet for many she remains the reclusive 'invalid of Wimpole Street' and the victim of a repressive Victorian father. This exhibition, drawing on manuscript and printed items, photographs and memorabilia from the British Library and the important collection of material relating to the Brownings and their circle at Eton College, celebrates the bicentenary of her birth on 6 March 1806.
It traces her life from her happy, precocious childhood amidst her large family in Herefordshire – where she studied Greek and published her first poems – to her London years of declining health and growing literary reputation, her burgeoning love for her fellow poet Robert Browning, their secret marriage and escape to a new and intensely fulfilling life in Italy.
The British Library would like to thank the Librarian, Michael Meredith, and the Provost and Fellows of Eton College for their generous loans to this exhibition, and the Browning Society for their help and support in its planning.

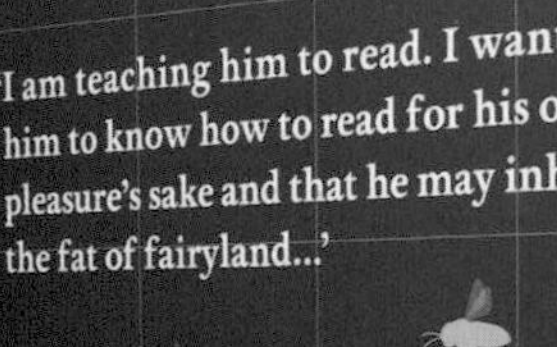

London Life 1835–44
While in Devon, Elizabeth suffered the departure of three of her brothers Edward ('Bro') to Jamaica, and Charles and George to Glasgow University On their return in 1835 Mr Barrett decided to move the family to London After three years in Gloucester Place they settled into 50 Wimpole Street in April 1838. Elizabeth's poetry collection The Seraphim was published in June; in August, ill again, she left London for Torquay. 1840 brought two heavy blows: on 17 February her brother Samuel died of fever in Jamaica and on 11 July Edward drowned in a sailing accident. Elizabeth later described this as a period of 'hopeless madness', but out of it came some of her finest work. Back in London, her fluctuating health kept her mostly confined to her room, dependent on her nightly dose of opium. She kept in touch with literature, politics and social affairs through magazines, visiting friends and a wide range of correspondents. Her next collection of poems appeared in 1844.
'I am teaching him to read. I want him to know how to read for his o pleasure's sake and that he may inh the fat of fairyland...'

FIELD FACTS_

Alexander Wilson was born in Scotland in 1714 but moved to London after completing his schooling in 1737. He created his own foundry in Glasgow with fellow Scot John Baine in the early 1740s, where they found great success supplying Scottish printers with type and in the process reducing their reliance on London and Dutch type suppliers. In later life Wilson went on to become the first professor of practical astronomy at Glasgow University, handing the management of the foundry to his descendants. The foundry sadly went bankrupt in 1845 under the management of his grandson, also called Alexander Wilson.

Foundry Wilson

DAVID QUAY, FREDA SACK · FOUNDRY TYPES · 1993

CATEGORY: Serif

CLASSIFICATION: Transitional

COUNTRY OF ORIGIN: UK

DISTINGUISHING MARKS: Incised serifs; large counters; double-storey 'g'; long flowing tail on upper-case 'Q'; strong vertical stroke; small contrast on stroke weights; ligatures on lower-case 'st' and 'ct'

FURTHER SIGHTINGS: KUNSTEN Museum of Modern Art Aalborg identity, Denmark

NOT TO BE CONFUSED WITH: Baskerville (p. 32)

An elegant revival of a mid-eighteenth-century design from renowned Scottish typefounder Alexander Wilson, this beautifully crafted and considered modern-day Serif possesses a character that is both charming and refined.

Based on a 1760 design by Scot Alexander Wilson, the design by British Foundry Types for Foundry Wilson also draws inspiration from the work of the eminent eighteenth-century designer John Baskerville. A 'lively and robust' face, the family consists of a range of weights along with a complementary set of floral ornaments redrawn from original designs of the time.

Quay's and Sack's methodical research, analysis and beautiful recreation of Wilson's earlier design came about through a commission for ITC. However, the end design was never released and together they continued to refine and expand the family to release it themselves through their own foundry and named it in Alexander Wilson's honour.

OPPOSITE: Foundry Wilson used for an exhibition at the British Library about Victorian poet Elizabeth Barrett Browning, providing context to her life story. Designed by Grade Design.

Friz Quadrata

ERNST FRIZ/VICTOR CARUSO/THIERRY PUYFOULHOUX · ITC/LINOTYPE · 1965

There is nothing like a team effort to produce results from a tough assignment. The development of Friz Quadrata is a case in point – to get the existing family of typefaces together has taken the combined talent of three type designers a great many years.

Friz Quadrata dates back to 1965 when it was created by Swiss designer Ernst Friz for VGC (Visual Graphic Corporation) as a single-weight typeface. In 1974, a Bold weight was added by Victor Caruso for ITC in conjunction with VGC. Two decades later, two italics were designed and added to the family by Thierry Puyfoulhoux.

Its stone-carved, chiselled aesthetic gives Friz Quadrata a classical appearance that lends itself to use mainly in display type projects. Because of this authoritative appearance and carved presence it has been adopted by a variety of organizations, from colleges and political organizations and even through to punk bands, who wish for a solid and serious presentation but one with a quirk. It has been used for text applications with varying degrees of success but its uneven stroke weights, unusually formed terminals and open lower-case bowls make for more difficult reading.

CATEGORY: Serif

CLASSIFICATION: Inscribed

COUNTRY OF ORIGIN: USA

DISTINGUISHING MARKS: Bold simple strokes with subtle, minimal flaring terminals; asymmetrical crossbar on 'E' and 'F'; descender on upper-case 'J'; open lower-case bowls; thorn-like serifs; curved stroke endings

FURTHER SIGHTINGS: *Scarface* titles, Black Flag and Bad Religion logotypes

NOT TO BE CONFUSED WITH: Albertus (p. 24); Optima (p. 220)

OPPOSITE: From punk bands to pharmacies (seen here in Berlin), Friz Quadrata has been employed in a myriad of applications.

KAISER-APOTHEKE
KAISER
APOTHEKE
KAISER
APOTHEK
KAISER APOTHEKE
seit 1888
WELEDA

FIELD FACTS_

Galliard was named after a style of Renaissance dance and music that was popular all over Europe at the time that Granjon lived. The galliard was an energetic and playful movement combining jumps, leaps and hops, and its liveliness is reflected in the forms of Carter's design.

Galliard

MATTHEW CARTER · **ITC** · 1978

CATEGORY: Serif

CLASSIFICATION: Old Style

COUNTRY OF ORIGIN: USA

DISTINGUISHING MARKS: Sharp, incisor-like serifs; elegant, calligraphic letter forms; distinctive italics and small capitals; vertical stress

FURTHER SIGHTINGS: Yale University; Southern Methodist University; Collin College, Texas; Regis College, Boston

NOT TO BE CONFUSED WITH: Cochin (p. 62); Garamond (p. 74); Granjon (p. 78)

OPPOSITE: Galliard's instant success when released contributed to it being inducted, with 22 other typefaces, into the Museum of Modern Art and shown in their Standard Deviations exhibition in 2011.

Inspired by the type created by the sixteenth-century master letter-cutter Robert Granjon, five centuries later Galliard serves as a fitting tribute to the Frenchman's work.

Robert Granjon's work as a type designer has been revered through the ages. His designs are noted for their legibility, grace and exceptional beauty. Although Matthew Carter did not base his Galliard on any one particular type that Granjon cut, he took the essence of his work and, employing contemporary technologies, created a more finessed revival. In his own words, Carter was aiming for 'a serviceable, contemporary, photocomposition typeface based on a strong historical design… not a literal copy of any one of Granjon's faces – more a reinterpretation of his style'.

The creation of Galliard was a long time coming. The seed of an idea was planted in 1957, not with Carter but with type student Mike Parker, who was seeing the types of Granjon at the Plantin-Moretus Museum in Antwerp. He was captivated by what he saw, and wanted to make these types available to a wider audience. It was only in later years when Parker was director of typographic development at Mergenthaler Linotype that he realized his ambition with the appointment to the company of Matthew Carter as a type designer in 1965. Years later, with interruptions to their progress occurring, they finally completed the design with Galliard being launched in 1978.

Garamond

CLAUDE GARAMOND · 1480–1561

Noted for its outstanding legibility and readability, the name 'Garamond' has been applied to so many variations and revivals that nowadays it's best to refer to Garamond as a style rather than as any one particular cut.

It is named after French punchcutter **Claude Garamond**'s designs of the sixteenth century. Research by English type historian Beatrice Warde led her to publish in *The Fleuron*, a British typography journal, in 1926 her discovery that many of what were believed to be Garamond's designs held at France's Imprimerie Nationale (the French Government Printing Office) were in fact the work of a later French type designer, Jean Jannon. Jannon's typefaces were seized by the French government and renamed, then became the house style for France's Royal Printing Office founded by Cardinal Richelieu in 1640.

Jannon's work was produced 80 years after Garamond's but, as time passed and history blurred, the assumption took hold that the many revivals created were based on the letterforms of Garamond rather than on those of Jannon. Confused? Well, it gets more confusing as we enter the twenty-first century. Nowadays, most major foundries offer a 'Garamond' typeface, which probably makes it the most redrawn and recut typeface in existence. So some cuts are based on Garamond's designs, a number are based on Jannon's, and with new designs based on both men's work coming from ITC and Apple Computers.

CATEGORY: Serif

CLASSIFICATION: Old Style

COUNTRY OF ORIGIN: France

DISTINGUISHING MARKS: Delicate bracketed serifs; small counters; large apertures; low x-height; long extenders; ascender capped with downward slope; small eye in lower-case 'e'; long tail on lower-case 'a'

FURTHER SIGHTINGS: Commonly seen in publishing and editorial design globally but also used widely for logos

NOT TO BE CONFUSED WITH: Galliard (p. 72); Granjon (p. 78); Sabon (p. 106)

OPPOSITE: A typographical mosaic made up from Garamond in the University subway station (*Tunnelbana*) in Stockholm, Sweden.

FIELD FACTS_

The italics for Garamond are based on italics designed by Robert Granjon, Claude Garamond's assistant. The typeface Granjon (p. 78) is also based on an early sample of Garamond but renamed to avoid confusion with the many other Garamond revivals. The typeface Sabon (p. 106), designed by Jan Tschichold, is also classified as a Garamond revival.

FIELD FACTS_

Frederic W. Goudy, one of America's all-time greatest type designers, was accredited with designing well over 100 typefaces. He was also a prolific writer and published close to 60 books.

Goudy

FREDERIC W. GOUDY · ATF (AMERICAN TYPE FOUNDERS) · 1915

CATEGORY: Serif

CLASSIFICATION: Old Style

COUNTRY OF ORIGIN: USA

DISTINGUISHING MARKS: Upward ear on lower-case 'g'; upward swelling on baseline strokes of 'E' and 'L'; rounded curves; small eye on lower-case 'e'; varying stroke weights; flared baseline terminals on upper-case 'E' and 'F'

FURTHER SIGHTINGS: Commonly seen in publishing design employed as a text face

NOT TO BE CONFUSED WITH: Bell (p. 36); Caslon (p. 50); Garamond (p. 74)

OPPOSITE: Goudy Handtooled, an in-line version of Goudy Bold.

Of all the work produced by the prolific American master of type design Frederic W. Goudy, the eponymous Goudy is the best known and has endured in popularity, being employed in various roles, from a text face to display and packaging uses.

Originally called Goudy Old Style when released in Roman form, this quirky Serif is an instant classic. It is said to be inspired by typefaces of the Renaissance but look more closely and you will see that it possesses a number of design quirks that emanate more from its designer than from historical reference points. It has a gentle quality to its appearance, with rounded curves and a softer style to its serifs when compared to its contemporaries. During the decade following its release, Goudy added to the portfolio of weights Italic (1918) with ATF type designer Morris Fuller Benton (designer of Century, p. 52), Bold (1916–19) and Extra Bold (1927). Goudy also designed Heavyface in 1925 for Lanston Monotype while art director there. Other variations were created but Goudy contributed only his name.

As with Garamond, Goudy is acclaimed for its legibility and readability in printed applications, while its Bold weight is valued by designers working in display formats. This has helped to maintain its popularity to the present day, and has prompted many imitations by rival foundries, who want to associate themselves with the Goudy name.

Granjon

GEORGE W. JONES · LINOTYPE · 1928

Despite its classical appearance, this recreation of Garamond (p. 74) was designed in the early twentieth century – approximately 400 years later. It is regarded as one of the finest revivals of a Garamond design and was named after Robert Granjon, a contemporary of Claude Garamond.

George W. Jones, who at the time was working for England's Linotype company, took as his source of inspiration a 'Garamond'-cut typeface that was printed in the book *Historia Ecclesiastica* by Parisian Jean Poupy in 1592. Thanks to the confusion caused by Garamond cuts being attributed to both Claude Garamond and Jean Jannon, the typeface was named Granjon to avoid confusion and to create a separation from the other Garamonds being marketed at the time.

Robert Granjon was an eminent printer, type designer and punchcutter of the mid- to late sixteenth century, who worked for the renowned scholar and printer Christopher Plantin in Antwerp, Belgium. Although he cut many Roman typefaces, he was notable for his elegant and beautiful italic Serif designs. These were often used in conjunction with a Garamond Roman cut as they paired so well in structure, balance and stroke weights. Granjon is an excellent book typeface and is still often used in publishing today.

CATEGORY: Serif

CLASSIFICATION: Old Style

COUNTRY OF ORIGIN: USA

DISTINGUISHING MARKS:
Delicate, incisor-like serifs; high stroke contrast; ascender capped with downward slope; small eye in lower-case 'e'; small bowl in lower-case 'a'; vertical stress

FURTHER SIGHTINGS:
Reader's Digest magazine

NOT TO BE CONFUSED WITH:
Bembo (p. 38); Galliard (p. 72); Minion (p. 86)

OPPOSITE: Robert Granjon's italic designs were noted for their elegant and refined construction and appearance.

All art is

but imitation

OF NATURE

SENECA

FIELD FACTS_

Christophe Plantin, who Granjon worked with for over a decade, was the founder in the 1560s of one of the greatest printing and publishing businesses whose longevity – it existed for over two centuries – was a testament to its success. Much of his printed works were written by scholars, linguists and theologians of the time and can still be seen today in the Plantin-Moretus Museum in Belgium which also houses two of the oldest surviving printing presses in the world.

Granjon vs Adobe Garamond

[p. 78] [p. 74]

The sixteenth-century types of Claude Garamond have been reinterpreted so many times, it's better to think of 'Garamond' as a genre rather than any specific typeface. Most contemporary font families are actually a combination of Garamond's roman designs with italics from another typefounder of the same era, Robert Granjon. That is the case with these two typefaces. <u>**Adobe Garamond**</u>, one of the more studied and commonly used renditions of this pairing, is a modern adaptation of an Old Style book text face, but it stays fairly true to its sources. <u>**Granjon**</u>, on the other hand, was designed in the 1920s specifically to fit the needs of the Linotype machine, which had various width requirements, including the restriction that each italic glyph must match its roman counterpart. The result is still remarkably lovely, but Granjon just can't match the elegance and readability of Adobe Garamond.

The small dots of Granjon's 'i' and 'j' sit quite high above the body.

Adobe Garamond's 'S' and 's' lean forward. Granjon's stand more upright.

Adobe Garamond's second and third strokes cross. Granjon's 'W' is a simpler design with only three upper terminals.

Adobe Garamond has slightly longer descenders than Granjon, whose 'g' is especially stunted.

Adobe Garamond's 'J' tail has a teardrop terminal. Granjon's 'J' ends with a taper.

Wigs JGor 234 Granjon

Wigs JGor 234 Adobe Garamond

Adobe Garamond has an angled stress, typical of a French Old Style. Granjon's stress is nearly vertical.

Adobe Garamond has a small spur extending beyond the vertical stroke of the 'G'.

Adobe Garamond's serifs are sturdier and slightly cupped (concave). Granjon's relatively light serifs sit flat on the baseline.

Adobe Garamond's lining figures descend and ascend. Granjon's are all at cap height.

FIELD FACTS_

The Guardian newspaper has long been heralded as an innovator in typography and layout design. In 1988, the newspaper was redesigned by David Hillman. Acclaimed for its innovative, yet controversial, masthead employing dual typefaces (Helvetica and Garamond Italic), its *G2* supplement by Hillman in 1992 helped pave the way for editorial design and formats to be challenged and experimented with.

Guardian Egyptian

PAUL BARNES, CHRISTIAN SCHWARTZ, BERTON HASEBE · COMMERCIAL TYPE · 2005

CATEGORY: Serif

CLASSIFICATION: Slab Serif/ Egyptian

COUNTRY OF ORIGIN: UK

DISTINGUISHING MARKS: Unbracketed serifs; wedge-shaped serifs; refined design over other slab serifs/ Egyptians; squarish arches

FURTHER SIGHTINGS: Guardian online

NOT TO BE CONFUSED WITH: PMN Caecilia (p. 44); Clarendon (p. 54); Rockwell (p. 102)

OPPOSITE: Influenced by Egyptian typefaces created in London foundries in the mid-nineteenth century and by contemporary Dutch type, the range of groundbreaking typefaces for *The Guardian* now allow for huge flexibility when presenting a diverse range of subject matter in the paper, from news to detailed financial listings.

In one of the most ambitious type programmes ever commissioned by a newspaper, a typeface family was created for British newspaper *The Guardian*'s redesign. Consisting of just over 130 styles, the lead family is a contemporary Slab Serif.

The Guardian newspaper in the UK underwent a reformatting in 2005, changing from its broadsheet format to a 'Berliner' format more commonly found in European papers such as *Le Monde* in France and *Die Tageszeitung* in Germany. The new smaller format meant the newspaper was easier to handle and its dimensions allowed for a greater flexibility in page layout.

Mark Porter, creative director at *The Guardian* who oversaw the redesign, recognized that the newspaper needed a suite of new typefaces to get the most from the new format and invigorate the paper's presentation and branding. The solution after many trials and much experimentation was a new Egyptian family for headlines created in eight differing weights (ranging from 'hairline' to 'black') with another family for text purposes only (in four weights). A complementary Sans Serif (Guardian Sans Headline) was also created in eight weights. This was produced by slicing off the serifs of the aforementioned Headline Slab Serif to maintain a relationship in their appearance. Several other variations were developed including a Condensed suite.

ITC Lubalin Graph

HERB LUBALIN · ITC · 1974

A Geometric Egyptian typeface based on renowned graphic designer Herb Lubalin's earlier typeface design of ITC Avant Garde Gothic (p. 132). Its big rectangular serifs and monoline appearance make it a stand-out choice for display and headline applications.

Lubalin was known for creating a diverse range of designs in the 1960s and 1970s, from poster and magazine work (including *Eros*, *Fact* and *Avant Garde*) to packaging and identity work. Some of his most notable creations are seen in the journal *U&lc* (*Upper and Lower Case*) which he edited and served as art director for the **ITC (International Typeface Corporation)** until his death in 1981. ITC was a US type manufacturer (the first non-hot-metal foundry), which Lubalin co-founded with Aaron Burns and Edward Rondthaler. His typographic experimentation, direction and editorial design in *U&lc* not only showcased the company's products but paved the way for a revolution in expressive typographic design, each issue becoming a must-have collector's item in the design and type communities.

The strong, no-nonsense quality of **ITC Lubalin Graph** projects an honesty and practicality, making it friendly and authoritative – ideal for communicating important messages in advertising and display projects.

CATEGORY: Serif

CLASSIFICATION: Geometric Slab

COUNTRY OF ORIGIN: USA

DISTINGUISHING MARKS: Geometric forms; circular bowls; open counter on upper-case 'R'; monoline stroke width; rectangular or square serifs; flowing tail on 'Q' cuts across bowl; large x-height; single-storey 'a'; unbracketed serifs; straight leg with serif on upper-case 'R'

FURTHER SIGHTINGS: IBM, *U&lc* magazine; Wahaca restaurant chain

NOT TO BE CONFUSED WITH: American Typewriter (p. 26); Calvert (p. 46), Courier (p. 64); Rockwell (p. 102)

OPPOSITE: ITC Lubalin Graph's earthy and no-nonsense appearance lends itself to messages where clarity and an honesty is integral to a brand's communications.

FIELD FACTS_

ITC Lubalin Graph was born from the seminal ITC Avant Garde typeface. This typeface was developed from the original logo created by Lubalin for the groundbreaking *Avant Garde* magazine, which he also designed. ITC Avant Garde, with its close letter spacing and rounded geometric forms, was so widely used during the 1970s that, to many, it has become emblematic of the entire decade.

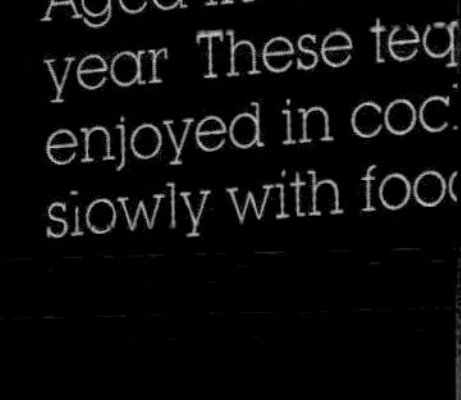

Tequila
Blanco (white)
Un-aged with a clean, strong flavour of agave. Great as an appetizer with sangrita or to enjoy with food
Reposado (res
Aged in oak bo
year These teq
enjoyed in coc
slowly with foo

NATIONAL
PARK
SERVICE
National Park Service
U.S. Department of the Interior
Gettysburg
National Military Park
Visitor Center

Minion

ROBERT SLIMBACH · ADOBE · 1990

CATEGORY: Serif

CLASSIFICATION: Old Style

COUNTRY OF ORIGIN: USA

DISTINGUISHING MARKS: Contrasting thick and thin stroke weights; economical letter width; rounded dots on the lower-case 'i' and 'j'; circular counters and bowls; long descenders and ascenders; squared characters; sharp and elegant serifs

FURTHER SIGHTINGS: Smithsonian Institution; Red Lobster restaurant chain; *1Q84* by Haruki Murakami; Brown University, USA; Universiteit Leiden Holland; *The Queen* film; Loyola

NOT TO BE CONFUSED WITH: Baskerville (p. 32), Caslon (p. 50), Foundry Wilson (p. 68)

OPPOSITE: Minion's elegance and authority lends itself well to display typography of national historical importance.

Inspired by the letterforms of the late Renaissance, Robert Slimbach's beautifully elegant typeface design was created as a book and text font for Adobe but its flexibility and large family has meant it's been employed on a far wider range than it was intended for.

Clear and balanced in its construction and incredibly legible and readable when set as reading text, even in very small sizes, **Minion** can be used for almost any application. It has a refinement and precision to its letterforms that makes it feel quite contemporary when employed, despite its ancestral inspiration being hundreds of years in the past. Late Renaissance types that are likely to have provided inspiration include the works of Baskerville and Caslon.

In 1991, while working for Adobe, Slimbach was awarded the highly prestigious Prix Charles Peignot from Association Typographique Internationale for excellence in type design. In 2000, he oversaw an OpenType update and refinement of Minion, which was released as the retitled Minion Pro. With 64 fonts in varying optical sizes and including a Condensed weight, Minion is not only one of the largest typeface families available but also one of the most elegant.

Mrs Eaves

ZUZANA LICKO · EMIGRE FONTS · 1996

Named after Sarah Eaves, John Baskerville's housekeeper who later became his wife, Zuzana Licko's beautiful revival of Baskerville is noted for its feminine elegance – suitable for use in fine book typography – and is one of the world's most popular contemporary Serif designs.

Mixing the traditional with a contemporary approach, **Mrs Eaves**'s design incorporates a number of modern typographic details that accommodate the advantages afforded by today's reproduction methods over its inspiration, Baskerville. Heavier in weight than other revivals, yet still retaining Baskerville's strong vertical stresses, it was Licko's wish that the typeface should reflect the softer, heavier impression of printing with lead type, with its resultant ink spread, rather than the crisp perfection of photoset/digital types of classic Serifs. It is this quality that adds an increased period feel to the typeface's aesthetic and accounts for much of its charm.

Another notable design feature of Mrs Eaves is its distinctive and elegant ligatures. A number of additional ligatures are included in the font in addition to 'fi', 'ffi' and 'fl'. Also included are 'ct', 'sp' and 'st', which, when set in long passages of text, create beautiful typographic details reminiscent of classic eighteenth-century typesetting.

CATEGORY: Serif

CLASSIFICATION: Contemporary Serif

COUNTRY OF ORIGIN: USA

DISTINGUISHING MARKS: Open tail on lower-case 'q'; 'ct', 'sp', 'st' ligatures; looser spacing over typefaces of similar appearance; small x-height; top and bottom serifs on upper-case 'C'; wider lower-case characters

FURTHER SIGHTINGS: Radiohead *Hail to the Thief*; Penguin Classics (Penguin Books)

NOT TO BE CONFUSED WITH: Baskerville (p. 32); Granjon (p. 78); Sabon (p. 106)

OPPOSITE: Advertising example for Mrs Eaves typeface family; detail showing outlined construction of the upper-case R; detail on the extraordinary and elegant ligatures that the typeface family contains. The near left example shows the XL family variant that possesses a larger x-height.

FABLE LIII. ***The* Trumpeter.**

— [SET IN MRS EAVES XL NARROW] —

A Trumpeter in a certain army happened to be taken prisoner.
HE WAS ORDERED *immediately* TO EXECUTION
but pleaded **excuse** for
HIMSELF,
that it was *unjust*
a person should suffer *death*, who, far from an intention of mischief, *did not even wear* an offensive weapon.
So much the rather,
replied one of the enemy
SHALT THOU DIE;
since without any design of *fighting thyself*,
THOU EXCITEST OTHERS TO THE
bloody business:
for he that is the *abettor* of a
BAD ACTION
IS AT LEAST EQUALLY WITH HIM THAT
***commit* it.**

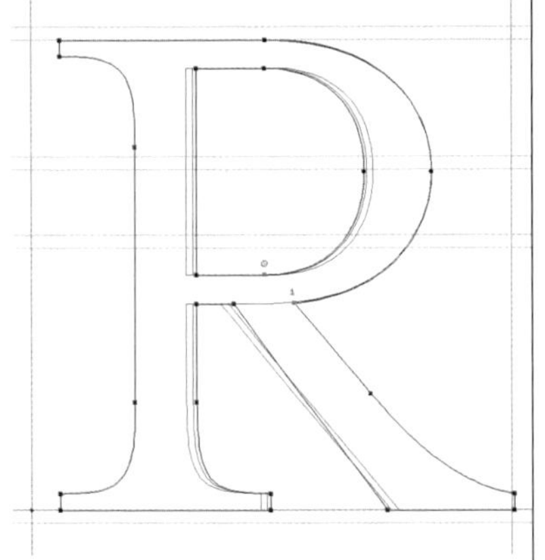

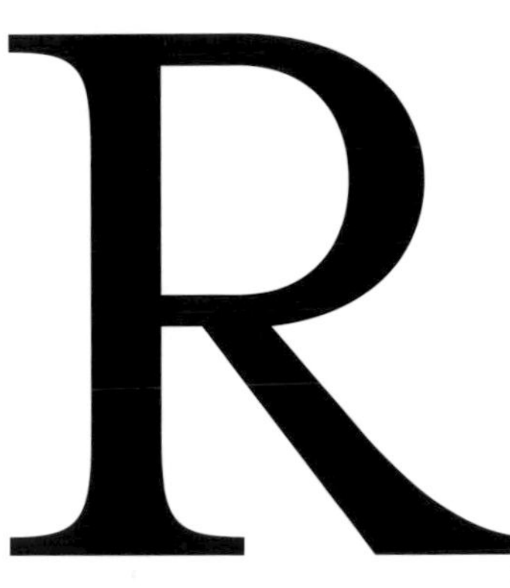

FIELD FACTS_

John Baskerville (p. 32) was no stranger to controversy, with his type designs and printing methods often criticized by his peers. Sarah Eaves, while John Baskerville's housekeeper, became his mistress after her husband Richard Eaves deserted her and her five children. Upon her husband's death, Baskerville and Mrs Eaves were able to be wed and she soon assisted with the typesetting and printing of his work. After Baskerville's death in 1775, Sarah continued his work, printing unfinished volumes.

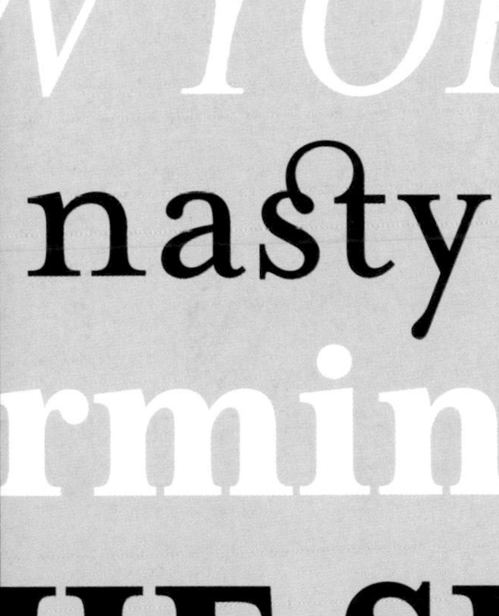

TO RETRA
BUSINESS
SCHOOL?
DN, 05/09
SACO
DE PAPEL
SUSPEITO
FECHA METRO DURANTE
DUAS HORAS
PUT
AFGHAN
WOMEN
ON THE
MAP
MAIS
VELHA
DO
MUNDO
MORREU
FELIZ
SÓ UMA
EMPO
M, 6/2009
OBAMA: IL FAUDRA
UN TEMPS CONS ÉRABLE
POUR SORTIR DE
LA CR E
IGREJA
RECOMENDA
SETE DIAS
DE SEXO
PICKS UP
SPEED

Neutraface Slab

CHRISTIAN SCHWARTZ · HOUSE INDUSTRIES · 2008

CATEGORY: Serif

CLASSIFICATION: Geometric Slab

COUNTRY OF ORIGIN: USA

DISTINGUISHING MARKS: Unbracketed serifs; minimal stroke contrast; low x-height; straight leg with slab serif on upper-case 'R'; asymmetrical baseline serifs on upper-case 'A'

FURTHER SIGHTINGS: Despite its strong display credentials, ideal for setting of long texts

NOT TO BE CONFUSED WITH: Calvert (p. 46); ITC Lubalin Graph (p. 84); Rockwell (p. 102)

OPPOSITE: Neutraface Slab was launched in 2008 with five display weights and four text weights with accompanying italics and special characters. Seen here used in the typographical installation, Dois Tempos (Two Times), in Lisbon by Portuguese designers Artur Rebelo and Lizá Ramalho of the design studio, R2.

Derived from Neutraface, House Industries' hugely successful Geometric Sans Serif, comes a Slab Serif version. Initially proposed as a joke by lead designer Christian Schwartz, the US foundry approved of the concept and the typeface soon took up form.

House Industries' Neutraface has been hugely popular since its release in 2002 and has been applied to everything from food chains to James Bond movie posters. Schwartz's aim when designing the original Sans Serif was to create 'the most typographically complete Geometric Sans Serif family ever', interpreted from Austrian American modernist architect Richard Neutra's principles on architecture and design.* It was a hugely ambitious project. Schwartz worked closely with Ken Barber and Andy Cruz of House Industries in creating the vast range of letterforms for the differing weights and styles that made up the OpenType release. The typeface, despite its strong geometric construction, has a warmth to its appearance. Design features such as the low crossbars on the upper-case 'A' allied with the low middle arm of the upper-case 'E' provide the typeface with a nostalgic and modernist air.

In 2005, and with tongue firmly in cheek, Schwartz proposed adding serifs to the Geometric Neutraface as an extension to the range; to his surprise, House Industries liked the idea. Taking Neutraface No.2 as the base, Schwartz worked with Kai Bernau and Susana Carvalho on the text and display designs.

* Schwartz, Christian. 'Neutraface'. www.christianschwartz.com

Jason Castle • CastleType

SAN RAFAEL, USA

Jason Castle, the founder of CastleType, has had a love of everything related to the alphabet ever since he could write. His delight in letterforms led him to study calligraphy and eventually digital type design.

His independent digital type foundry has been supplying designers with quality fonts since 1990 and with over 100 fonts in 50 font families, possesses a very diverse collection, including many Art Deco and classic revivals as well as CastleType originals. CastleType also has created custom type designs for clients such as Chevron, Shiseido and *Rolling Stone* magazine.

Q: When was it you became aware of letterforms and typography?
A: I've been interested in letterforms since at least third grade, when my teacher complained to my parents that my handwriting was 'ostentatious'. When I was 11, my father taught me copperplate script (which he learned in business school in the days when business letters were handwritten), because I think he noticed my love of letterforms. I've always loved books, magazines, anything printed. I still love calligraphy, especially Arabic calligraphy, but also graffiti as well as paintings and photography that include letterforms.

Q: Was it a conscious decision to become a type designer or something you had always felt you had an affinity with and evolved into?
A: The possibility of doing digital type design did not even exist when I was younger. So, I tried many careers during my twenties and thirties (music, computer programming, desktop publishing), trying to find something that not only inspired me, but also took advantage of my unique set of innate abilities. In my twenties, I went through a 'Medieval period' in which I not only performed Medieval music but also took up calligraphy again, with a focus on Medieval and Renaissance styles. So, many years later, when I read an article about Judith Sutcliffe doing digital typefaces based on Medieval and Renaissance models, I was inspired to try it myself. I bought a copy of *Fontographer*, started experimenting,

OPPOSITE: CastleType's original typeface design, Chinoise, is based on hand-lettering reminiscent of an ancient style of Chinese square-cut ideograms (sometimes cut into wood). Available in upper and lower case (which comes with alternate letterforms), its distinctive, Condensed style is softened by the slightly rounded corners.

ABCHINOISE

DEFGHIJKL

RIGHT: **Shàngó Regular**, a part of the Shàngó family (*see* Shàngó Gothic p. 108).

FAR RIGHT: Jason Castle, founder of CastleType.

BELOW: **Sculptura** is a revival of a 1957 typeface, originally designed by the Swiss designer, Walter J. Diethelm (1913–1986).

ABCDEFGHIJ
KLMNOPQRS
TUVWXYZ

SCULPTURA

then I wrote to Judith, who advised me not to quit my day job. But, I eventually did, and have never had any regrets. With my visual orientation and love of graphic arts (especially typography), knack for languages, analytical skills, and overall perfectionism, digital type design seems like a perfect fit for me.

Q: Your typeface collection reflects a wide spectrum of approaches and styles and a number of revivals. Where do you get your ideas for starting a new design or deciding on a typeface to revive?

A: My first two attempts at digital type design were Goudy Text and Goudy Lombardy, perhaps because of the Medieval influence. I'll never forget how excited I was when the first page of Latin text set densely in Goudy Text came out of my printer. I imagined I was Gutenberg with a laser printer. After those two fonts, I started work on Goudy's drawings from the Trajan capitals, just to see whether I could render all the fine details. (This was before Adobe released their Trajan.) At the time, I was just doing type design for fun. But, thanks to a friend who was a graphic designer, I was soon commissioned to digitize Radiant Bold Extra Condensed for a large department store. Soon after that, *Publish* magazine approached me to digitize several fonts (Agency Gothic, Trio, Eden, Metropolis, Standard, etc.). So, many of my earlier fonts were simply digitizations of designs that were not available in digital format at that time. As for getting ideas for designs, something will just catch my eye as I'm looking through old books or type catalogs, Russian constructivist posters, and so on. I used to be more impulsive about this, but now I stop to consider whether I really want to spend hundreds of hours working on a particular design. So, it must have some special quality about it (that I can't quite put my finger on) for me to make that sort of commitment. Of course, there are dozens of projects that I thought would be beautiful and fun, and then set them aside after a few hours. I'm not as imaginative as many type designers, so I feel more comfortable with revivals and extending existing designs.

Q: Is there a specific process you follow on each occasion? Or does each typeface demand a differing approach?

A: It depends on whether the typeface is commissioned or my own design. Commissioned work always involves working with artwork that is provided, and I try to stay fairly close to the model, unless I think the design needs improving and talk the client into making changes. Working with the creative director at Shiseido was unique in that he knew precisely what he wanted (more so than most clients). So, that involved a lot of drafts sent back and forth (with translation between English and Japanese!) over a period of several months. He was more perfectionistic than I was at the time, so it was challenging, but very rewarding to create such a polished product. It definitely raised the bar for me. For my own designs, I often work from sketches I do at the coffee house (yes, sometimes on a napkin), or directly on the computer, or a combination of both. Maybe I'll see a half dozen letters on an old poster and want to create a whole alphabet based on them. Many of my designs are based on Russian lettering from the 1920s and 1930s, so the challenge is to create Latin letters that do not exist in the Cyrillic alphabet. This process always fascinates me, as I continue to learn more about letterforms.

Q: A great many of your typeface designs feature complex letterforms with high levels of craftsmanship. How do you ensure consistency across the design and maintain the font's integrity?
A: Thousands of hours of hard work! Lots of printed drafts fastened to the wall, living with the fonts for a while, trying them out in different environments and projects, and occasionally asking for feedback from my colleagues. And, of course, experience helps. I've been playing with letterforms for a very long time, and after 20 years of doing type design I'm still developing my eye.

Q: With thousands of fonts available today to purchase and download for free, what qualities are essential for a typeface to distinguish itself from the competition?
A: I wish I knew the answer to that!

Q: How do you ensure your designs are protected?
A: I just hope for the best. Hopefully, there are still enough honest people in the world that type designers can continue to make a living.

Q: To the budding typeface designers out there, what advice would you give them in designing their own font?
A: The same advice that I was given when I started: 'Don't quit your day job!' Type design is not for everybody; it requires a good eye in combination with analytical skills and a willingness to spend hours doing detail work that would drive most 'normal' people crazy. There is so much more to type design than just making pretty letters (letter spacing and kerning, for example). So, I would encourage someone considering this path to make an honest appraisal of their skills and personality. I recently went out to lunch with a group of young type designers. They were a shy group, so to break the ice I asked them, 'Is type design something you would do even if you weren't getting paid?' Without hesitation, they all answered, 'Yes!' That's the right answer. If one is not passionate about this (and willing to work hard with no guarantee of making any money), then it's probably not the right choice.

OPPOSITE TOP: Zuboni Stencil is a bold, capital titling typeface based on a Russian design from around 1920 (original designer unknown).

OPPOSITE LEFT: Warrior is a robust 3D Egyptian-style revival, available in seven weights (Hairline, Extra Light, Light, Medium, Regular, Bold, Black) in addition to three decorative styles: Shaded (3-dimensional), Inline and Open.

OPPOSITE FAR RIGHT: Carisma, another CastleType original, a clean, elegant and understated humanist Sans Serif design.

ZUBONI

ABCDEFGHI
ДОКТОР ЖИВАГО
JKLMNOPQ
МАСТЕР И МАРГАРИТА
RSTUVWXYZ

ABCDEFG
HIJKLMN
WARRIOR
VWXY&Z

Ca
riSma

Perpetua

ERIC GILL · MONOTYPE · 1929

Eric Gill's most popular Serif typeface was inspired by classical engravings and remains a timeless design, with its clean lines containing many considered and intricate details.

Commissioned by **Monotype**'s Stanley Morison, the development of **Perpetua** took many years, with redesigns, criticisms by the Monotype management, distractions due to the creation of other typefaces (Gill Sans being one of them) and rejection of the first italic to accompany the Roman. However, seven years after Gill had been commissioned by Morison, the typeface was eventually launched. Morison's idea for the new typeface – as part of his programme to create revivals and new typefaces in the early twentieth century – was for a design of an epigraphic nature rather than a calligraphic one. This was the starting point for Perpetua's development and a number of serif details reflect this influence and Gill's knowledge and experience with stone carving and engraving.

CATEGORY: Serif

CLASSIFICATION: Transitional

COUNTRY OF ORIGIN: UK

DISTINGUISHING MARKS: Clean-cut chiselled lines; small diagonal serifs (lower-case 'r', 't', 'y'); bracketed serifs; high-stroke contrast; short, curved tail on upper-case 'Q'; descender on upper-case 'J'

FURTHER SIGHTINGS: Ideal for long passages of texts, often found in text books

NOT TO BE CONFUSED WITH: Baskerville (p. 32); Goudy (p. 76); Granjon (p. 78)

OPPOSITE: A rare sighting of Perpetua used in a display application.

FIELD FACTS_

Perpetua's first outing was in a limited edition book entitled *The Passion of Perpetua and Felicity* by Walter H. Shewring. Perpetua took its name from the title of the book; the idea was for its accompanying italic to be called Felicity. However, the first 'Felicity' design was rejected due to it being a sloped Roman rather than the cursive italic requested by the Monotype Board. When it was subsequently redesigned a year later, it was also renamed.

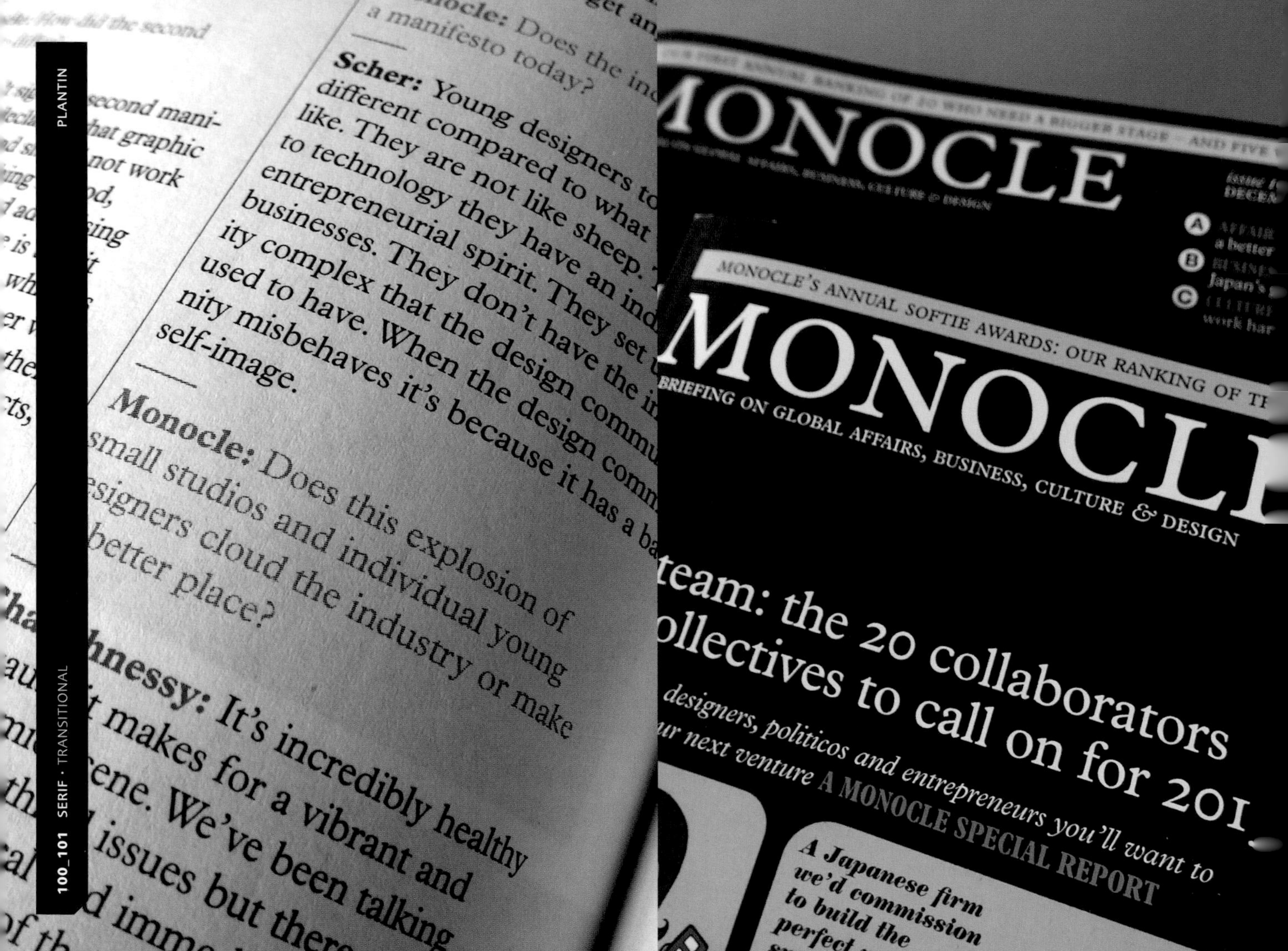
a manifesto today?
Scher: Young designers
different compared to what
like. They are not like sheep.
to technology they have an
entrepreneurial spirit. They set
businesses. They don't have the
ity complex that the design
used to have. When the design
nity misbehaves it's because it has a
self-image.
Monocle: Does this explosion of
small studios and individual young
designers cloud the industry or make
better place?
It's incredibly healthy
makes for a vibrant and
We've been talking
issues but there
second mani-
that graphic
not work
MONOCLE
MONOCLE'S ANNUAL SOFTIE AWARDS: OUR RANKING OF
MONOCLE
BRIEFING ON GLOBAL AFFAIRS, BUSINESS, CULTURE & DESIGN
team: the 20 collaborators
ollectives to call on for
designers, politicos and entrepreneurs you'll want to
next venture A MONOCLE SPECIAL REPORT
A Japanese firm
we'd commission
to build the
perfect retail
space

Plantin

MONOTYPE DESIGN STUDIO · MONOTYPE · 1913

CATEGORY: Serif

CLASSIFICATION: Transitional

COUNTRY OF ORIGIN: UK

DISTINGUISHING MARKS: Large x-height; large counters on lower-case 'a' and 'e'; reduced ascender height and descender depth; reduced contrast in stroke weights

FURTHER SIGHTINGS: *Monocle* magazine; *The Flavour Thesaurus*

NOT TO BE CONFUSED WITH: Baskerville (p. 32); Mrs Eaves (p. 88)

OPPOSITE: In recent years there has been a resurgence in Plantin's use due to its economical and effective impact on set type. The typeface's ability to hold ink well whatever the material, combined with its supreme legibility, thicker letterforms and a distinctive edge to its design make it ideal for editorial and publishing purposes – seen here in *Monocle* magazine.

The Plantin typeface was inspired and influenced directly by the wealth of type that the sixteenth-century printer Christophe Plantin collected over the years and in honour of his efforts and contribution was named after him.

Although no one person can be accredited with designing Plantin, Frank Hinman Pierpont, who oversaw its development, is recognized as one of its key founders. Working for the **Monotype Corporation** at the start of the twentieth century as foundry manager, he wanted to design a typeface that would print consistently well on a variety of coated and uncoated stocks, and that would retain a high degree of legibility. A visit to the Plantin-Moretus Museum in Antwerp provided plenty of inspiration – samples, photos and a wealth of reference material of Plantin's type collection, including a type cut by Robert Granjon (p. 78). With this, Pierpont had all the ingredients he would need to create Plantin.

The historical family tree doesn't end there, though. As the Plantin typeface was inspired by the work of Robert Granjon and others, who in turn were inspired by the designs of Claude Garamond, so Plantin in later years influenced the development of Times New Roman (p. 110) developed by Stanley Morison and Victor Lardent at Monotype.

Rockwell

FRANK HINMAN PIERPONT/MONOTYPE DESIGN STUDIO · MONOTYPE · 1934

Based on a typeface produced in 1910, this classic Slab Serif has proved popular ever since its creation. Although inspired by early wood-cut display faces, its development through the years has created a variety of weights, providing enough flexibility for it to be used with lighter weights as both a successful text face and a display and heading typeface in its bolder, heavier incarnations.

In 1910, the Inland Type Foundry launched Litho Antique, designed by William A. Schraubstadter. Its immediate success in the USA and Europe meant a decade later, in 1920, American Type Founders issued a revival, with esteemed American type designer Morris Fuller Benton (*see* p. 52) creating a number of additional weights soon after. This new release was entitled Rockwell Antique and was published in 1931. Benton went on to create another heavier weight of **Rockwell** the same year, naming it Stymie Bold. This titling variation has caused much confusion over the years, masking as it does the relationship between the two typefaces.

Three years later, **Frank Hinman Pierpont** (*see* p. 100), in conjunction with **Monotype**, issued their own Rockwell, with adjustments in letter weights, spacing and additional characters.

Because of its even stroke weight, clarity in presentation, and imposing aesthetic, Rockwell has been adopted and redefined for a number of logotypes globally, including *Playboy* and the Public Broadcasting Service.

CATEGORY: Serif

CLASSIFICATION: Geometric Slab

COUNTRY OF ORIGIN: USA

DISTINGUISHING MARKS: Unbracketed serifs; minimal stroke contrast; circular round shapes; moderate x-height; short extenders; moderate character widths; unbracketed serif on apex of upper-case 'A'

FURTHER SIGHTINGS: Docklands Light Railway, London; Washington State Lottery

NOT TO BE CONFUSED WITH: American Typewriter (p. 26); Calvert (p. 46); ITC Lubalin Graph (p. 84)

OPPOSITE: The industrial tone of Rockwell provides an imposing sign above these offices in London.

A. HOLT & SONS LTD.
EST. 1864
115

Rockwell vs ITC Lubalin Graph

[p. 102] [p. 84]

ITC Lubalin Graph and Rockwell both have a geometric structure, with circular round shapes and rectangular slab serifs, but ITC Lubalin Graph's geometry is more extreme. Rockwell has a few wonky shapes, some designed to accommodate readability, some simply relics of 1930s design. ITC Lubalin Graph, on the other hand, is graphically pristine, with strict circles, horizontal terminals, and tight spacing. Everything aligns the way you'd want it to in a poster, but the same uniform qualities would make a paragraph of ITC Lubalin Graph a painful read. In short, Rockwell can be used for short texts at relatively small sizes; ITC Lubalin Graph was made for the big stuff.

ITC Lubalin Graph has an unusual 't' with a straight tail connecting to the stem at a 90° angle.

ITC Lubalin Graph has a single-storey 'a'. Rockwell's is double-storeyed with an oval bowl.

Rockwell's upper serif is two-sided, extending to both sides of the 'A'.

Like Helvetica, all the terminals in ITC Lubalin Graph are either horizontal or vertical. The curved strokes in Rockwell end at an angle that is perpendicular to the direction of the stroke.

Ate aif GQR Rockwell

Ate aif GQR ITC Lubalin Graph

if GQR

Rockwell's 'f' has a hook. ITC Lubalin Graph's is trimmed vertically.

The tail crosses into the interior of the ITC Lubalin Graph 'Q'.

In the lighter weights of ITC Lubalin Graph, the large 'R' bowl is open – its leg never meets its stem. Rockwell's high-waisted 'R' has an unusually small bowl with a long leg.

ITC Lubalin Graph has a bearded 'G' with a long horizontal stroke. Rockwell's horizontal stroke is unusually short.

ITC Lubalin Graph's dots are rectangular. Rockwell's are circles.

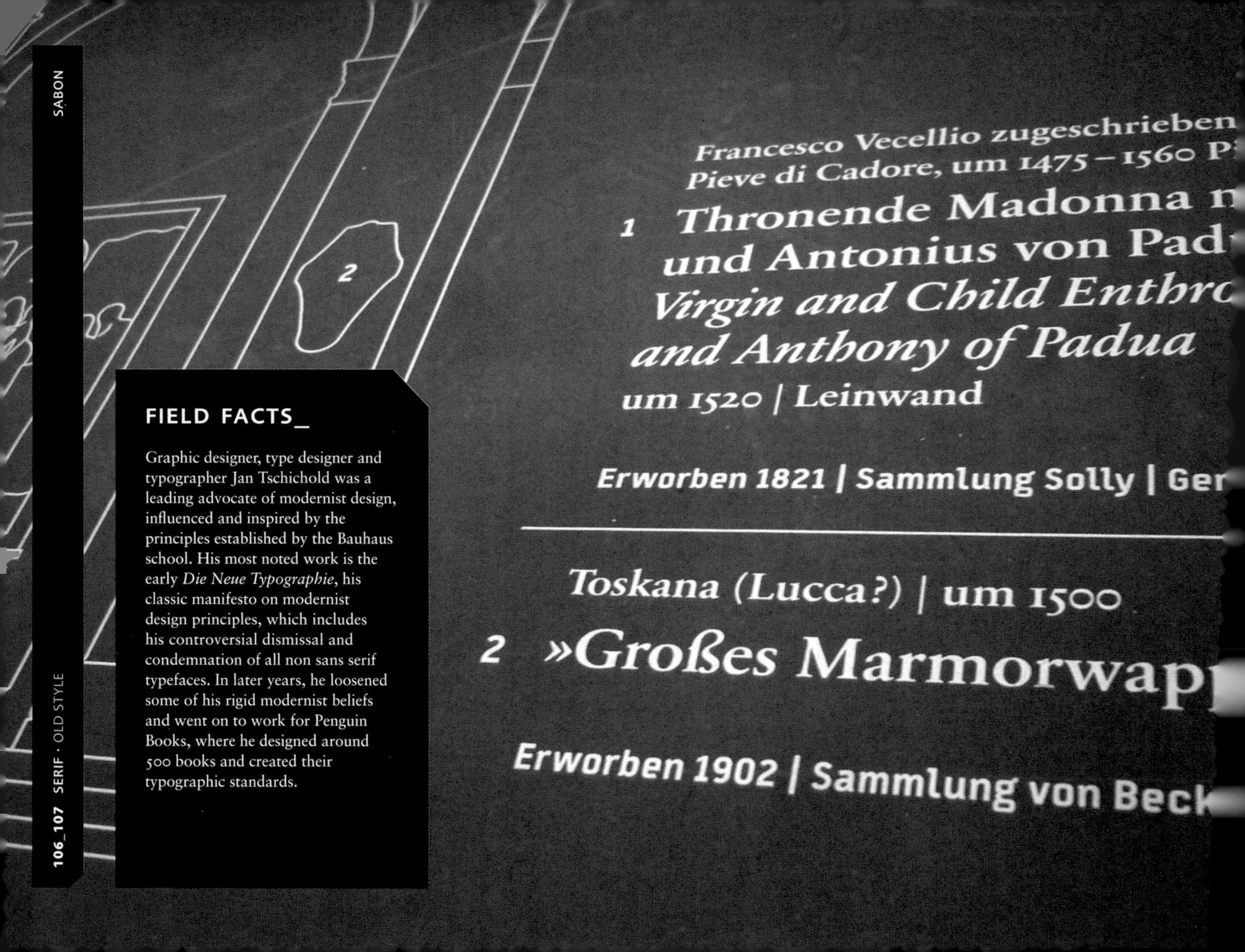

Francesco Vecellio zugeschrieben
Pieve di Cadore, um 1475–1560 P

1 Thronende Madonna m
und Antonius von Pad
*Virgin and Child Enthro
and Anthony of Padua*
um 1520 | Leinwand

Erworben 1821 | Sammlung Solly | Ger

Toskana (Lucca?) | um 1500
2 »Großes Marmorwapp

Erworben 1902 | Sammlung von Beck

2

FIELD FACTS_

Graphic designer, type designer and typographer Jan Tschichold was a leading advocate of modernist design, influenced and inspired by the principles established by the Bauhaus school. His most noted work is the early *Die Neue Typographie*, his classic manifesto on modernist design principles, which includes his controversial dismissal and condemnation of all non sans serif typefaces. In later years, he loosened some of his rigid modernist beliefs and went on to work for Penguin Books, where he designed around 500 books and created their typographic standards.

Sabon

JAN TSCHICHOLD · LINOTYPE/MONOTYPE/STEMPEL · 1967

CATEGORY: Serif

CLASSIFICATION: Old Style

COUNTRY OF ORIGIN: Germany

DISTINGUISHING MARKS: Open counter on upper-case 'P'; upper-case 'Q' tail centred under figure; upper-case 'J' possesses hook; lower-case double-storey 'a'

FURTHER SIGHTINGS: Stanford University

NOT TO BE CONFUSED WITH: Garamond (p. 74); Goudy (p. 76); Granjon (p 78)

OPPOSITE: Sabon's design possesses a great elegance and because of its legibility makes it ideal for printing at all sizes. Here it is used for identity and signage at Berlin's Museumsinsel (Museum Island) and paired with the Sans Serif FF Typestar.

Inspired by the design of Claude Garamond's Roman typefaces and Robert Granjon's italics, this 'modern' classic is regarded as one of the most beautiful Old Style revivals created and is certainly one of the most legible.

Commissioned by not one but three type foundries working together, Jan Tschichold was charged with the creation of a new typeface that would work across the existing metal type technologies of the time to create and provide a consistency in design and printing when used on both Monotype and Linotype machines.

Named after Jacques Sabon, who was a student of the great type designer Claude Garamond, Sabon's design was sourced in particular from a 14-point Garamond Roman specimen sheet printed in 1592 by Konrad Berner, a printer from Frankfurt who ran the Egenolff-Berner foundry. Tschichold's design possessed a number of innovative design traits, which increased its success over its peers. It was fractionally narrower than existing Garamond types, which allowed for more characters to be used when setting and thereby produced savings in ink and paper. Its serifs were also fractionally bolder and stronger, allowing for legibility to be maintained even when printed small. A further feature was that the differing weights for roman, italics and bold occupied the same width when typeset, thus reducing the mathematics needed to work out lengths of texts before setting.

Shàngó Gothic

JASON CASTLE · CASTLETYPE · 2007

Designed by US type designer Jason Castle, Shàngó is a revival design inspired by the classic titling typeface released in 1936 as 'Schneidler-Mediaeval mit Initialen', designed by German type designer, calligrapher, teacher and publisher Professor F. H. Ernst Schneidler.

Schneidler's work for the Bauer Type Foundry in the mid-1930s led to a number of elegant typefaces being created. **CastleType**'s Shàngó, a revival of his cut Schneidler Medieval, is an intricate and elegant display typeface that appears only in upper case and possesses a fine stroke weight across its letterforms, with a modern and masculine tone to its aesthetic. The typeface includes a full set of Cyrillic and Greek characters, which makes it ideal for dual language applications (as shown opposite).

CastleType has extended the Shàngó family over the years. It is currently available in four styles: **Shàngó Gothic** (shown opposite); Shàngó Classic (available in three weights: regular, medium and bold); Shàngó Chiseled (a design that exaggerates the impression of carved letterforms); and Shàngó Sans.

CATEGORY: Serif

CLASSIFICATION: Roman Inscribed

COUNTRY OF ORIGIN: USA

DISTINGUISHING MARKS: Thin monoline stroke weight; small, refined serifs; angled uprights on upper-case 'M'; extended tail on upper-case 'Q'

FURTHER SIGHTINGS: Ideal for communications and displays where a historical context is required

NOT TO BE CONFUSED WITH: Trajan (p. 112)

OPPOSITE: Shàngó Gothic employed by design studio togetherdesign.gr for Field House Garden Grave, a permanent exhibition in the gardens of the Archaeological Museum of Thessaloniki, Greece. The typographic approach is a hybrid of Roman and Greek inscriptional elements, which are combined successfully using just the one typeface.

ΕΠΙΓΡΑΦΕΣ ΧΑΡΑΓΜΕΝΕΣ
ΣΤΑ ΤΑΦΙΚΑ ΜΝΗΜΕΙΑ
INSCRIPTIONS CARVED
ON FUNERARY MONUMENTS
Το να ζεις είναι να αφήνεις ίχνη.
To live is to leave traces.
— M. Foucault

ΚΟΙΝΟΤΗΤΕΣ
ΤΗΣ ΘΕΣΣΑΛΟΝΙΚΗΣ
FOREIGN COMMUNITIES
IN THESSALONIKI
Οι ξένοι αποτελούσαν ένα μεγάλο τμήμα του πληθυσμού της Θεσσαλονίκης. Πολίτες άλλων πόλεων της Μακεδονίας ή άλλων επαρχιών της ρωμαϊκής αυτοκρατορίας, Εβραίοι, Ρωμαίοι, μετανάστες ιταλικής καταγωγής (οι λεγόμενοι negotiatores, δηλ. συμπραγματευόμενοι) που ασχολούνταν με το εμπόριο και τις επιχειρήσεις, συνέθεταν την πολυεθνική φυσιογνωμία της ρωμαϊκής Θεσσαλονίκης. Αν και δεν είχαν δικαίωμα συμμετοχής στην πολιτική ζωή της πόλης, ήταν οργανωμένοι σε συλλόγους επαγγελματικούς ή λατρευτικούς. Θάβονταν όλοι στα ίδια νεκροταφεία.
Foreigners made up a large segment of Thessaloniki's population. Citizens of other Macedonian cities or other provinces in the Roman Empire, Jews, Romans, immigrants of Italian extraction (the so-called negotiatores, i.e. businessmen) who were engaged in commerce and enterprise, comprised the multi-ethnic profile of Roman Thessaloniki. While they did not have the right to participate in the city's political life, they were organized into business or religious associations. They were all buried in the same cemeteries.

FIELD FACTS_

With Microsoft shipping **Times Modern**'s close relative **Times** as part of its Windows OS software since the early 1990s, Times has become one of the most widely used typefaces in history. The number of copies installed on PCs in the world surpasses 1 billion units with an expected 2 billion units operating by 2014.*

Times New Roman

STANLEY MORISON/VICTOR LARDENT · MONOTYPE · 1931

CATEGORY: Serif

CLASSIFICATION: Transitional

COUNTRY OF ORIGIN: England

DISTINGUISHING MARKS: Large x-height; short descenders; narrower character width than other serifs

FURTHER SIGHTINGS: One of the most popular Serifs in the world; used widely and available as a system font on most computer platforms

NOT TO BE CONFUSED WITH: Baskerville (p. 32); Perpetua (p. 98); Plantin (p. 100)

* Gartner, Inc. June 2008

OPPOSITE: Founded in 1785 by John Walter, a former coal dealer, *The Times* newspaper is one of the oldest and most influential newspapers in Britain today. The first issue was printed as the *Daily Universal Register*, being relaunched as *The Times* on 1 January 1788. A default font on PCs today, it's often the 'go to' Serif type for millions.

Despite its prevalence, Times can deceive the unwary fontspotter because it has had so many incarnations in its long history. With Times Modern, used exclusively by *The Times*, being the most recent version of this elder statesmen among Serif typefaces.

The original **Times New Roman** was created by **Monotype**'s **Stanley Morison** and **Victor Lardent**, a designer at *The Times* newspaper, back in 1931 (but first used by the paper in 1932). Since then *The Times* has employed numerous variations of the typeface. In 2006/2007 as *The Times* moved from a broadsheet to a smaller tabloid format the demands placed upon the existing typeface (the bespoke house font Times Classic created in 2001) meant that an improved version had to be developed.

To respond to the paper reducing in dimensions and the need to use text at a smaller size, the new Times Modern had to increase space usage and provide greater legibility when printed at smaller sizes. Despite its redesign, it still retained the core character features of the original Times, whilst communicating the heritage of such a world-renowned newspaper. The redesign was overseen by Ben Preston of *The Times* and Neville Brody and his consultancy Research Studios.

Trajan

CAROL TWOMBLY · ADOBE · 1989

Named after a Roman emperor and inspired by *capitalis monumentalis* type – the carved capital inscriptions on the memorial Trajan's Column in Rome – this is a contemporary classic of type from *c.* 113 AD.

The inscription at the base of Trajan's Column is regarded as one of the finest examples of the Roman alphabet. Carol Twombly's revival design for Adobe was not the first to take its inspiration from these ancient letterforms but is certainly the most popular and regarded as the most refined and complete typeface of its kind, thanks in part to her addition of modern punctuation, graphical and mathematical symbols and numerals.

Its beauty, elegance and authoritativeness have led to it being used constantly since its launch on everything from movie titles (movie posters employing Trajan include *The Mummy*, *Star Wars*, *Master and Commander*, *Northanger Abbey*, to name but just a select few) to book covers, and from political communications to corporate branding. In particular, because of its 'important' aesthetic it is often used on non-fiction book covers and movie posters to denote a title's 'serious' content while still presenting a classic and accessible appearance.

CATEGORY: Serif

CLASSIFICATION: Roman Inscribed

COUNTRY OF ORIGIN: USA

DISTINGUISHING MARKS: All upper case; thin stroke weight; moderate contrast; refined serifs; elongated tail on 'Q'

FURTHER SIGHTINGS: Trajan's dignity and authority means it can often be seen on books and in film titling

NOT TO BE CONFUSED WITH: Shàngó Gothic (p. 108)

OPPOSITE: It is believed that the fine serifs applied to Roman alphabet inscriptions were the result of the letterforms being painted upon the stone prior to carving, although others would argue that it was an aesthetic applied by the stonemasons. Whatever the truth, these historical letterforms have influenced type design for over 2,000 years, with their use still popular today. Some of the carvings have stood the test of time too – seen here in Rome, Italy.

SPQR

IMP·CAESARI

NERVAE·AVG·

WALBAUM-ANTIQUA

Perl 1120 — Min. ca. 2 kg à M. 15.70

gierende … s Johann Gensfleisch von … at sich … t jener Schnelligkeit Bahn … Bedeutu … dung bemessen. Erst im … ßburg … in Jahr später in Bamberg

Die Buchdruckerkunst war bereits im Jahre 1468 in Augsburg seßhaft, wo man mit ihr den Nürnbergern um zwei Jahre den Rang abgelaufen hatte, und 1482 tritt sie gleichzeitig in Erfurt, Passau und München auf, denen Leipzig nur um ein Jahr voraus ist, während die kleinen Reichsstädte Memmingen und Reutlingen mit den beiden

Nonpareille 1121 — Min. ca. 4 kg à M. 8.60

u End … ehnten und Anfang … ts in … nd, Frankreich und … die w … mit der Bezeichnung … n der … tenbergs einen ganz

Die Kriege des siebzehnten und achtzehnten Jahrhunderts haben zweifellos der Entwicklung der graphischen Künste bedeutenden Schaden verursacht. Doch was in dieser Zeit einerseits versäumt worden war, sollte zu einer anderen mit einem Schlage wieder

Petit 1122 — Min. ca. 5 kg à M. 7.10

arbei … wohl ein Papier, … end, … nt, mit ziemlich … druc … icht zu dick und … Auße … llte dieses Papier … eren … ngst vermoderten

Es ist wohl unerläßlich, für Liebhaberbände und Bücher mit Künstlerholzschnitten ein gutes, den Anforderungen der Ästhetik und Technik gerecht werdendes Papier zu verwenden. Handpapiere wären in diesem Falle den

Borgis 1123 — Min. ca. 5 kg à M. 6.50

wohl … gemeinen mehr … s kün … en Motiven ge- … lockt … t ihre Buntheit … afzul … n. Hauptzweck

Daß viele der neueren Briefmarken, in erster Linie jene der amerikanischen Republiken, dann die der englischen Kolonien, graphische Kleinkunstwerke von oft bewundernswerter Feinheit sind, braucht

Korpus 1124 — Min. ca. 6 kg à M. 6.20

in d … , die treibende … schä … . Schön klingt … as O … gstens nicht so … lirre … Goldstücke, die

Die Reklame ist eine Kunst, und zwar keine so leicht zu erlernende, wie viele schon zu ihrem eigenen Leidwesen erfahren haben. Sie erfordert eine liebevolle und aufmerksame Behandlung.

Cicero 1125 — Min. ca. 7 kg à M. 6.10

n L … phien kennt, … s zu … des vorigen … Deut … d hergestellt

Die Lithographie soll aber als selbständige Kunstgattung hervortreten und sich nicht durch Nachahmung schlechter Arbeiten in

Mittel 1127 — Min. ca. 7 kg à M. 6.—

ten … ugnisse ist das Japanpapier; es ist sehr weich

Tertia 1128 — Min. ca. 8 kg à M. 5.90

ar … anntlich seiner Zeit als Erfinder weit

Text 1129 — Min. ca. 10 kg à M. 5.60

M … k im neunzehnten Jahrhundert

Doppelmittel 1130 — Min. ca. 12 kg à M. 5.20

n … d Philosophie in China

Dreicicero 1131 — Min. ca. 14 kg à M. 5.—

ie … e Kaiser Meneliks

Viercicero 1132 — Min. ca. 16 kg à M. 5.—

chische Plastik

WALBAUM SCHRIFTEN

SCHRIFTGIESSEREI

F. A. BROCKHAUS / LEIPZIG

Walbaum

JUSTUS WALBAUM · 1800

CATEGORY: Serif

CLASSIFICATION: Modern/Didone

COUNTRY OF ORIGIN: Germany

DISTINGUISHING MARKS: Vertical stresses; squarish forms; reduced contrast in stroke weights against other 'moderns'; large x-height; lower-case 'b' no baseline serif; upper-case 'Q' tail 'stepped'

FURTHER SIGHTINGS: *Wired* magazine; *Berliner Zeitung* newspaper

NOT TO BE CONFUSED WITH: Bodoni (p. 40); Century (p. 52)

OPPOSITE: Around 1800, type designer Justus Walbaum designed the serif typeface Walbaum Antiqua and the corresponding italics (Walbaum Kursiv) as well as a Blackletter typeface (Walbaum Fraktur). Shown are details of a rare and beautiful Walbaum type specimen by F. A. Brockhaus, Leipzig.

Inspired by other Didone (or 'modern') typefaces of the time, such as Bodoni and Didot, Walbaum's elegant letterforms at the time contributed to a peak in typographic design and development in the late eighteenth to early nineteenth century and created the best example of a German modern face.

In contrast to Bodoni and other similarly constructed Serif designs that possess strong vertical stresses and an increased contrast between the thick and thin strokes of the letterform (with the thins being almost hairline), Walbaum's typeface exudes a friendlier and warmer tone. Recognized as more legible than its peers, these factors contribute to making Walbaum suitable for reading texts in addition to display and heading applications.

A self-taught typographer, **Justus Walbaum** became an engraver of musical scores after trying several other professions, including those of spice merchant and confectioner. It was during this period that he learned to cut punches for type, later opening his own type foundry in 1796 and then moving to Weimar in 1803. In 1836, he sold his company. More than 80 years later, in 1918, the esteemed German type foundry H. Berthold obtained the Walbaum foundry and duly discovered the original Walbaum matrices.

Wile

CYNTHIA HOLLANDSWORTH BATTY · MONOTYPE · 1998

What better gift is there, upon retirement from a long-standing career in the creative industry, than to not only have a new typeface named after you, but to have it created especially for you?

This is exactly what happened to Don Wile, a much-loved and respected executive at Agfa Compugraphic, to mark his retirement. Designed by US type designer Cynthia Hollandsworth Batty, this refined Serif design is an Old Style typeface possessing wedge-shaped serifs and open proportions, providing it with an elegant and slightly feminine quality. The upper case is inspired by inscriptional letterforms and this can be witnessed in their low-contrast stroke weights and terminals.

After Wile's retirement, Wile became readily available and has been employed with great success in text and display settings for publishing and editorial purposes. Other typefaces designed by Hollandsworth Batty include Hiroshige and ITC Tiepolo from her foundry Alpha Omega.

CATEGORY: Serif

CLASSIFICATION: Old Style

COUNTRY OF ORIGIN: USA

DISTINGUISHING MARKS: Wedge-shaped serifs; open proportions; diamonds over lower-case 'i' and 'j'

FURTHER SIGHTINGS: A rare spot, but Wile would be most commonly seen in publishing environments

NOT TO BE CONFUSED WITH: Garamond (p. 74); Perpetua (p. 98); Sabon (p. 106)

OPPOSITE: Coralie Bickford-Smith's designs for the Penguin English Library series of classic titles employs Wile in a minimal, understated, yet hugely effective manner on the range of books.

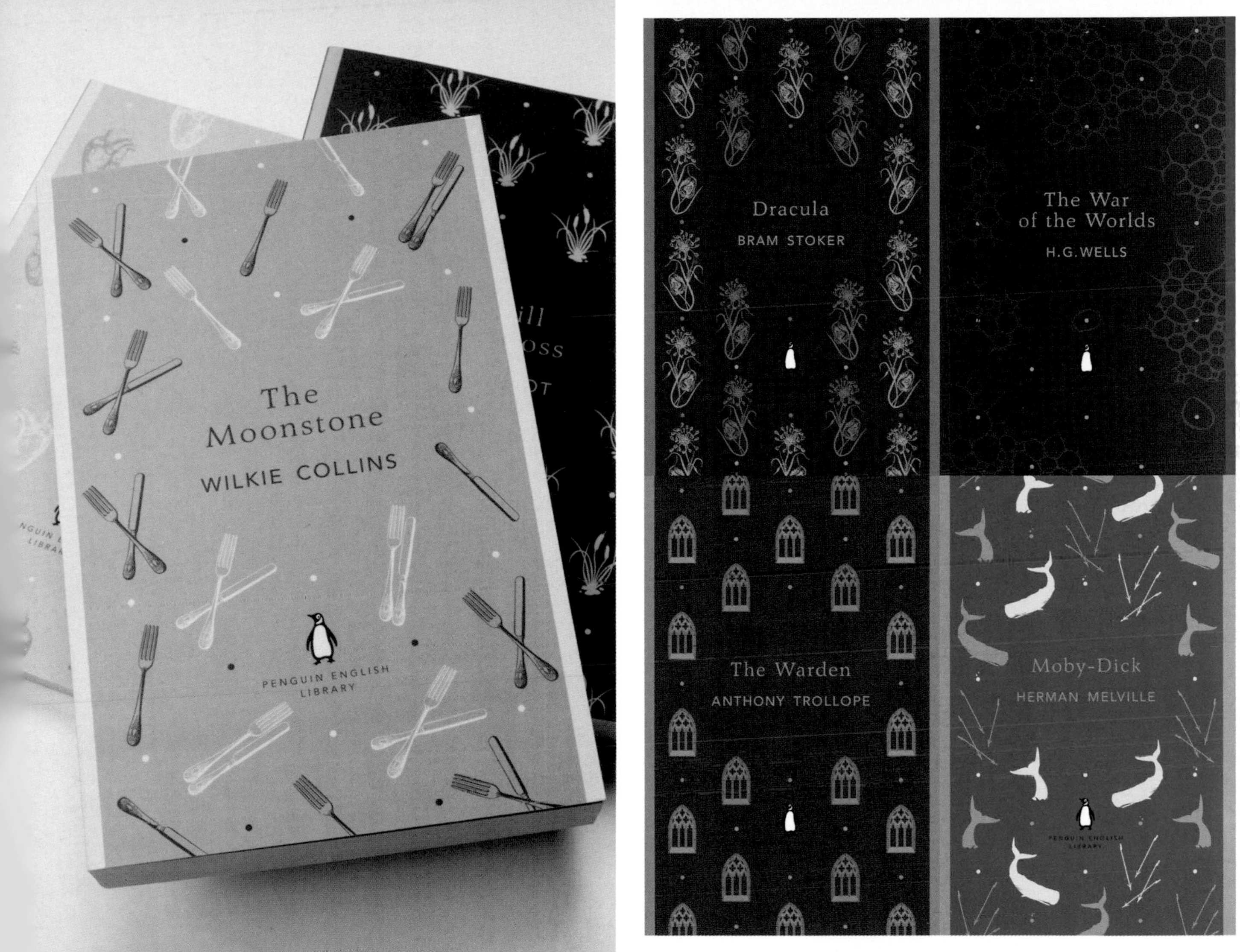

The Moonstone
WILKIE COLLINS
PENGUIN ENGLISH LIBRARY
Dracula
BRAM STOKER
The War of the Worlds
H.G.WELLS
The Warden
ANTHONY TROLLOPE
Moby-Dick
HERMAN MELVILLE

Sans Serif

OPPOSITE: Futura Bold in use as three-dimensional wayfinding in the Barbican Centre, London, UK (p. 180).

Aktiv Grotesk

RON CARPENTER, FABIO HAAG · DALTON MAAG · 2010

As a response to his long and intense hatred of Helvetica, Bruno Maag, managing and creative director of London foundry Dalton Maag, and his team set about creating an alternative to the widely used Helvetica by creating their own Grotesque typeface family.

Despite Helvetica being one of the most universally employed typefaces on the planet, Bruno Maag felt that an alternative could be created which would iron out the many issues they felt were wrong with the Helvetica design. Furthermore, the addition of a Grotesque to Dalton Maag's portfolio of typefaces was also needed. Originally from Switzerland, Maag claims to have never used Helvetica and when studying at Basel (the legendary Swiss design school) his and his peers' preference was always to use Adrian Frutiger's Univers typeface as a true expression of Swiss typography, with his opinion of the typeface having been 'better crafted with better proportions'.*

Aktiv Grotesk certainly has a degree more warmth than Univers, which some see as quite cold and harsh. However, the differences between Aktiv Grotesk and Helvetica are also subtle, and Maag's design sits somewhere between the two. Maag and his team have successfully created a typeface that removes Helvetica's quirks and yet is warmer than Univers. The new design when compared to other Grotesques is cleaner and more evenly coloured (the visual tone of blocks of text on a page when typeset), making it a successful alternative to Helvetica as a result of their efforts.

CATEGORY: Sans Serif

CLASSIFICATION: Grotesque

COUNTRY OF ORIGIN: UK

DISTINGUISHING MARKS: Moderate x-height; stroke endings cut 90°; moderate descender length; double-storey 'a'; closed apertures; rounded shapes near circular; square dot over letter 'i'

FURTHER SIGHTINGS: A recent release, so sightings rare but expect contemporary print and wayfinding applications to employ it as an alternative to Helvetica

NOT TO BE CONFUSED WITH: Akzidenz Grotesk (p. 122); Helvetica (p. 192)

**Creative Review* magazine, July 2010.

OPPOSITE: Wayfinding design by Nick Kapica/SV Associates for New Zealand's Massey University *Te Ara Hihiko* College of Creative Arts building, devised in English and Maori.

FIRE ACTION
FIRE
toy store
animation lab
mixing suite
north stair
toilet
wharepaku
shower

sasha waltz & guests
Dialoge 09
Neues Museum
Sasha Waltz
Museumsinsel Berlin
Bodestraße 1–3
18.–23. 27.–30. März 2009

Akzidenz Grotesk

GÜNTER GERHARD LANGE · H. BERTHOLD AG · 1896/1958

CATEGORY: Sans Serif

CLASSIFICATION: Grotesque

COUNTRY OF ORIGIN: Germany

DISTINGUISHING MARKS: More circular counters and bowls (over Helvetica and Univers); subtly varying stroke weight; double-storey lower-case 'a'; short offset tail on 'Q'; tail of 'R' forked from bowl

FURTHER SIGHTINGS: American Red Cross; *Objectified* film poster; Thalia Theater Halle posters

NOT TO BE CONFUSED WITH: Arial (p. 128); Helvetica (p. 192); Univers (p. 224)

OPPOSITE: Its extreme legibility, large range of weights and flexibility allows Akzidenz Grotesk to be used in a myriad of applications including text, display and wayfinding usages. Poster design by Nick Kapica/SV Associates for German dance company Sasha Waltz & Guests.

Often mistaken for Helvetica (p. 192) or Univers (p. 224), Akzidenz Grotesk was their ancestor and inspiration and is deemed the 'original' Sans Serif.

Although similar in appearance to its aforementioned relations, Akzidenz Grotesk possesses visual differences by comparison in its proportions and has subtly varying stroke weights, providing the letterform with more character and a softer, warmer edge over its rivals.

Its roots date back as far as 1880, when the design is believed to have been formed from Walbaum or Didot Serif fonts, whose proportions are similar when the serifs are removed. Up until the 1950s, Akzidenz Grotesk (Akzidenz meaning 'trade type' and Grotesk meaning 'Sans Serif') was a collection of differing Grotesque faces by a variety of designers. However, it was in this period that the renowned **Günter Gerhard Lange**, art director for the German type foundry **H. Berthold AG**, embarked on a process of enhancing and revising the typeface, providing it with increased flexibility and further consistency of design while keeping the core features of the nineteenth-century originals. Over the years, Berthold issued further releases with foreign language character sets and variations such as Book, Compressed, Old Face, Rounded and Stencil, making it one of the most widely used and successful typefaces of all time.

ARROZ
SIVARIS
REDONDO
BASMATI
CATEGORÍA EXTRA
VENERE
CARNAROLI
BOMBA

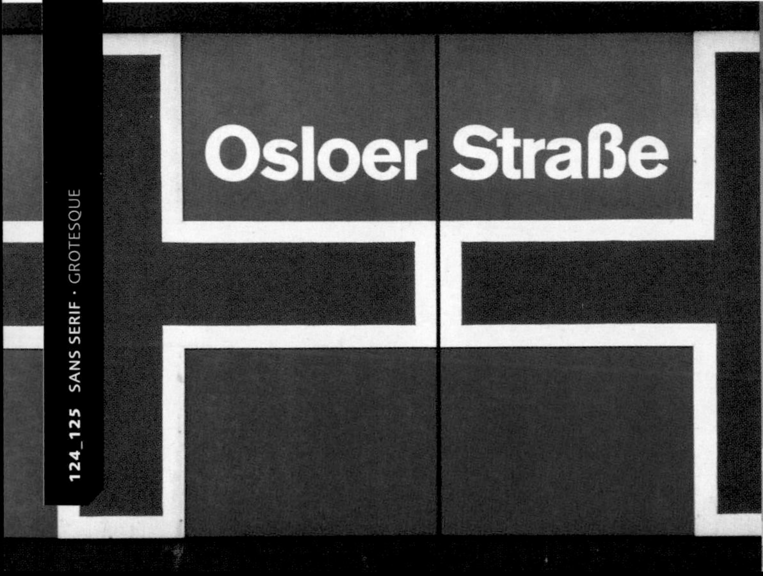

Osloer Straße

rejec
Tanya Marriott
Richard Henry
Toy Sculpture
Cloth and polymer clay

FIELD FACTS_

In 1957, Max Miedinger of the Haas Foundry in Switzerland used Akzidenz Grotesk as the basis to develop the Neue Haas Grotesk typeface, which was later renamed Helvetica (p. 192). In addition, Adrian Frutiger's Univers (p. 224) also released in 1957 takes inspiration from Akzidenz Grotesk.

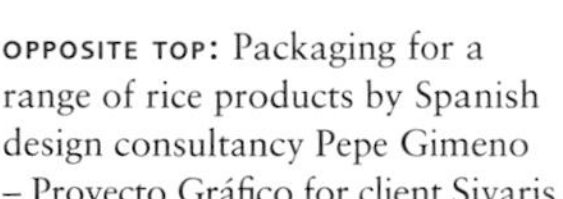

OPPOSITE TOP: Packaging for a range of rice products by Spanish design consultancy Pepe Gimeno – Proyecto Gráfico for client Sivaris.

OPPOSITE FAR LEFT: Signage at a U-Bahn station in Berlin.

OPPOSITE LEFT: Detail from Massey University's OLDSCHOOL NEWSCHOOL exhibition designed by Nick Kapica/SV Associates and Matthijs Siljee employing Akzidenz Grotesk for both display and captioning.

ABOVE AND RIGHT: Projection installation and detail showing Akzidenz Grotesk used for German dance company Sasha Waltz & Guests. Design by Nick Kapica/SV Associates.

7,000
Baby
Change
Accessible
Toilet
“As I walk into the stadium and look
at the ground it feels like I've come
home, my spiritual home.”
– Wolves Fan

FIELD FACTS_

FS Albert's design was inspired by Jason Smith's son Albert, who, as a young child, carried a few extra pounds. His baby's weight gain and rounded forms served as the basis for the **FS Albert Extra Bold** weight, which possesses a rounded aesthetic and warm personality.

FS Albert

JASON SMITH · FONTSMITH · 2002

CATEGORY: Sans Serif

CLASSIFICATION: Humanist

COUNTRY OF ORIGIN: UK

DISTINGUISHING MARKS: Rounded corners on terminals; slightly narrower character width; slab serif on upper-case 'I' and 'J'; minimal stroke contrast; angled cut at top of ascenders (noticeable more on bolder weights); large apertures; open counters

FURTHER SIGHTINGS: Virgin Mobile; The Shard skyscraper, London

NOT TO BE CONFUSED WITH: Bliss (p. 150); Fedra Sans (p. 164); Foundry Sterling (p. 170)

OPPOSITE: Raw Design Studio's bold and emotive wayfinding and display typography for Wolverhampton Wanderers (Wolves) Football Club employs FS Albert in all public areas of the club's stadium.

Created out of the need for a typeface that would work well within a corporate environment and would provide blue-chip organizations with a warm and friendly presentation, Jason Smith's FS Albert typeface design has resulted in a modern-day classic.

In an age when many corporate communications can appear dry and cold, it was Smith's intention to create a typeface that would negate this insincerity and instead serve up a more approachable, flexible and friendlier appearance. Created as an independent release, FS Albert soon took off and has been adopted by organizations and graphic designers globally. Its rounded edges, clean and simple letterforms, minimal stroke contrast and a range of weights from Thin to Extra Bold have provided the designer using FS Albert with a highly versatile Sans Serif font.

Jason Smith founded **Fontsmith** in 1999 and is dedicated to designing and developing typefaces for both independent release as well as bespoke fonts for international clients. In addition, they are highly regarded for designing unique typefaces for many television broadcasting companies in Europe (*see* Designer Profile p. 290).

Arial

ROBIN NICHOLAS, PATRICIA SAUNDERS · MONOTYPE · 1982

Being packaged with nearly all versions of Microsoft's Windows operating system, and in recent years with Apple's OS X, has made Arial probably the most widely available typeface on the planet. However, availability rarely equates to popularity, and its comparison with Helvetica still causes much caustic debate among typographers and designers.

Often confused with Helvetica (p. 192), Arial lacks some of the smoother characteristics, the finesse and the range of its stablemate, serving a purpose as a generic Sans Serif.

Created initially as a typeface to work on IBM bitmap laser printers (with the name Sonoran Sans Serif) and based on the typeface Monotype Grotesque, Arial was designed to provide increased readability at varying resolutions, compensating for the deficiencies of non-litho printing methods and on-screen display. To this end, Arial features softer and fuller curves and more open counters. Although a 'simpler' design than Helvetica, it matches Helvetica very closely (many would say too closely) in proportion, weight and width.

In 1990, following further development of Arial with IBM, it was then licensed to Microsoft, who announced it as an 'alternative to Helvetica', causing quite a stir among the type and design communities.

CATEGORY: Sans Serif

CLASSIFICATION: Grotesque

COUNTRY OF ORIGIN: USA

DISTINGUISHING MARKS: More rounded curves and counters; no tail on lower-case 'a'; near-straight tail on upper-case 'R'; no spur on upper-case 'G'; end of terminals on upper-case 'C', 'G' and 'S' cut at an angle; top of lower-case 't' cut at an angle

FURTHER SIGHTINGS: Commonly found on PCs across the world

NOT TO BE CONFUSED WITH: Helvetica (p. 192); Univers (p. 224)

OPPOSITE: A controversial choice? Many saw Microsoft's adoption of Arial as an excuse for them to avoid paying Linotype's licence fee for Helvetica (Apple had done so). As such, Arial has been held in disregard among the majority of professional typographers and graphic designers. This hasn't prevented it from popping up on the odd wonky sign, however.

THE LADY FLORENCE HALL
21 DEPTFORD BROADWAY

Arial vs Helvetica

[p. 128] [p. 192]

Arial is famous for existing only as a replica, employed by a company who wanted to avoid licensing the real deal: Helvetica. So it's no wonder these two are similar. Arial even matches all Helvetica's character widths and spacing – which accounts for some of its awkward, forced shapes. Still, despite all its mimicry, Arial does have a different pedigree. It is mostly based on older English Grotesques, rather than the Swiss/German tradition of Helvetica. This results in letterforms that are slightly more open, less cold and calculated. But these minor differences are nearly imperceptible to the untrained eye. An easier way to tell these two apart is by knowing their natural habitat. Helvetica is used (sometimes even worshipped) by professional designers. Arial is a computer default, invoked without a second thought by Microsoft Office users. So you're much more likely to see Helvetica in the logo of an international brand, and Arial in an office memo.

Gas

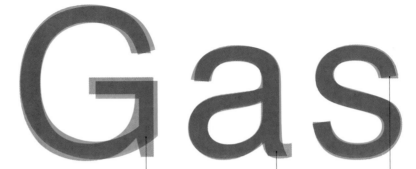

In light to regular weights, Helvetica's 'a' has a tail that faces laterally. Arial's tail is stunted and sits flat on the baseline.

All of Helvetica's strokes end flatly, either parallel or perpendicular to the baseline. Arial's curved strokes have a slightly angled terminal.

Helvetica has a bearded 'G'. Arial lacks that spur.

Gas QRrt 3 Arial
Gas QRrt 3 Helvetica

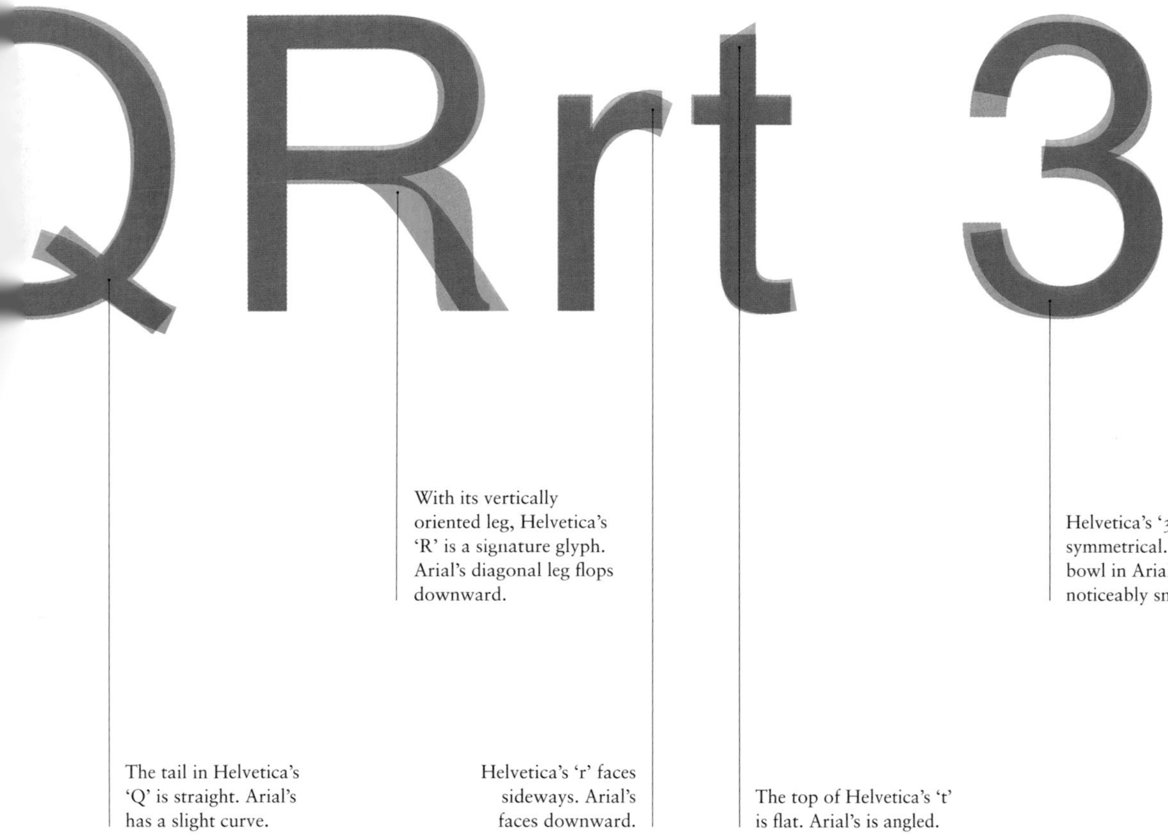

QRrt 3

With its vertically oriented leg, Helvetica's 'R' is a signature glyph. Arial's diagonal leg flops downward.

Helvetica's '3' is nearly symmetrical. The upper bowl in Arial's '3' is noticeably smaller.

The tail in Helvetica's 'Q' is straight. Arial's has a slight curve.

Helvetica's 'r' faces sideways. Arial's faces downward.

The top of Helvetica's 't' is flat. Arial's is angled.

FIELD FACTS_

Herb Lubalin created a Serif version of ITC Avant Garde Gothic in which he added large rectangular serifs to the existing Sans Serif design. Titled ITC Lubalin Graph (p. 84), it was used in conjunction with ITC Avant Garde Gothic in a number of Lubalin's designs.

ITC Avant Garde Gothic

HERB LUBALIN, TOM CARNASE · **ITC** · 1970

CATEGORY: Sans Serif

CLASSIFICATION: Geometric

COUNTRY OF ORIGIN: USA

DISTINGUISHING MARKS: Monoline; large, rounded open counters and curves; very narrow 'S'; open counter on upper-case 'R'; horizontal cut on terminals; geometric appearance; large x-height; all-cap ligatures; circular rounded forms

FURTHER SIGHTINGS: *glee* TV series; hedkandi records; Macy's; adidas; Rite Aid; Media Markt; Kroger

NOT TO BE CONFUSED WITH: Avenir (p. 136); Chalet (p. 154); Futura (p. 180)

OPPOSITE: New York's famous Macy's department store employs the elegant ITC Avant Garde Gothic as a reflection of the retailer's high fashion offering.

Based on Herb Lubalin's logo design for US *Avant Garde* magazine, this innovative, elegant and modern-looking Sans Serif is still popular with typographers and designers today, being employed in a range of contexts, from corporate identities and music packaging graphics to book covers and television station branding graphics.

Lubalin's original logotype for *Avant Garde* magazine was an innovative arrangement of geometric monoweight upper-case letters with backslanted capital 'A's and overlapping characters. Handcrafted with a compass and a T-square, the resulting design has a highly constructed appearance, consisting of straight lines and circles, evoking the 1920s German Bauhaus movement. Lubalin worked with **Carnase**, a partner in his design company, to turn the upper-case logotype into a mixed-case typeface consisting of many unique alternative characters and ligatures. In later years, additional weights were added to the family, with a Condensed typeface being drawn up by Ed Benguiat, a friend of Lubalin, in 1974.

Because of the geometric nature of its letterforms, **ITC Avant Garde Gothic** works extremely well as a display face and for short lengths of text but is not ideal as a reading face for long texts.

MILTON GATE

60 CHISWELL STREET

OPPOSITE: Even when reduced to a near hairline stroke, ITC Avant Garde Gothic's distinctive forms are still clearly identifiable when set in **Extra Light**.

THIS PAGE: ITC Avant Garde Gothic's geometric forms have long been the basis and inspiration for many of the world's most successful logotypes and brands, including organizations such as sports clothing manufacturer adidas. Its clean lines and pure shapes convey sophistication and friendliness.

Avenir

ADRIAN FRUTIGER · LINOTYPE · 1988

Meaning 'future' in French and inspired by early, highly structured, Geometric typefaces such as Futura (p. 180) and Erbar, Swiss typeface designer Adrian Frutiger's Avenir has a warmer, more Humanist appearance, reminiscent of his earlier eponymous typeface.

Frutiger's aim was to create a linear Sans Serif but to make use of the aesthetic qualities and trends that had pervaded type development in the twentieth century, combining heritage with modern-day preferences and needs. By no means a pure geometrical design, it possesses subtly varying stroke weights, with the verticals being thicker than the horizontals and an imperfectly circular form in the 'o'.

Its feel is that of a very modern typeface: clean, clear and refined, with a Humanist quality; a design that is flexible and refined enough to use for reading texts as well as display and headline work. In 2004, Frutiger, with Linotype type director Akira Kobayashi, revisited the design of Avenir to create Avenir Next, which was an improvement on the existing design and contained additional true italics, a range of Condensed weights and small caps. The new design allowed for increased on-screen legibility and readability at smaller point sizes.

CATEGORY: Sans Serif

CLASSIFICATION: Geometric

COUNTRY OF ORIGIN: Germany

DISTINGUISHING MARKS: Strong geometric appearance; minimal contrast; arms intersect at stem on 'k'; circular forms are rounded; slight angled terminals; large counters; moderate x-height, extenders and character widths; double-storey 'a'; flat apexes

FURTHER SIGHTINGS: Hong Kong International Airport; Apple Maps app; *Dwell* magazine; BBC Two television station; Starbucks branding; Costco

NOT TO BE CONFUSED WITH: ITC Avant Garde Gothic (p. 132); ITC Bauhaus (p. 140); Futura (p. 180)

OPPOSITE: Avenir employed in the logotype for the Dutch city of Amsterdam's tourism branding.

400? moi?
PHILIPS
ING
I amsterdam

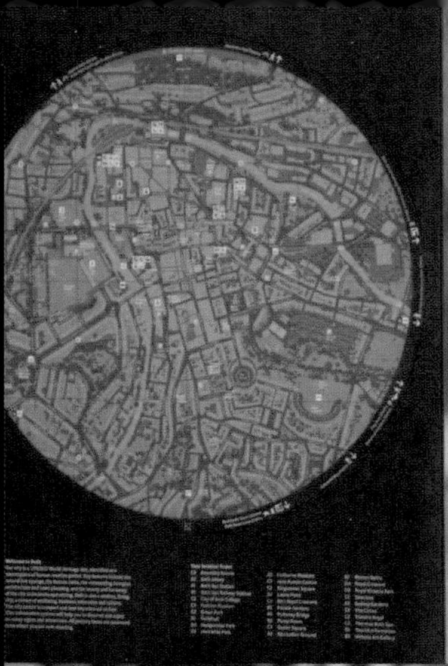

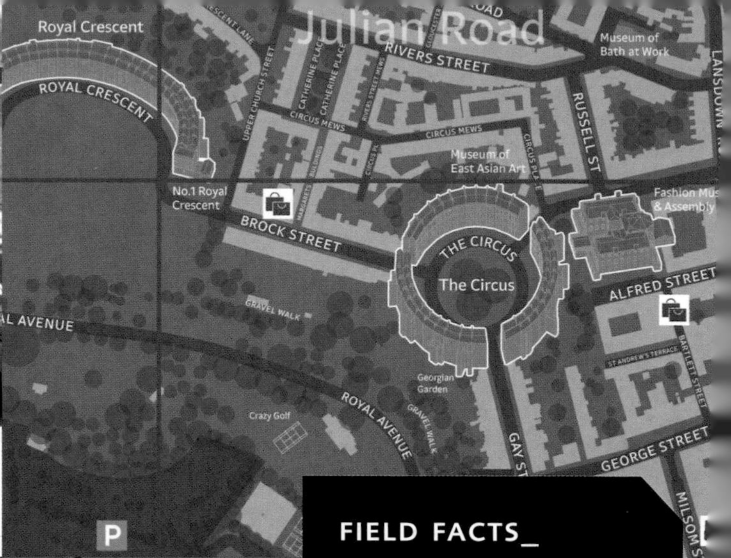

FIELD FACTS_

The UK's David Quay is one of the leading designers in type design and lettering. Now based in the Netherlands, he established The Foundry (*see* p. 198) with Freda Sack in 1990, which specialized in designing exclusive typefaces. He now works on a variety of global commissions and also lectures internationally. Ramiro Espinoza from Argentina founded ReType in 2007 to market his own typefaces. He has been a contributor to *Tipográfica* and *Tiypo* design magazines and has worked freelance for FontShop International on typeface designs.

Bath City

DAVID QUAY, RAMIRO ESPINOZA · 2010

CATEGORY: Sans Serif

CLASSIFICATION: Humanist

COUNTRY OF ORIGIN: UK

DISTINGUISHING MARKS: Vertical stress; moderate contrast; large apertures; open counters; angled terminals; straight leg on upper-case 'R'; tapered ascender above crossbar on lower-case 't'; large x-height; round dot above 'i'

FURTHER SIGHTINGS: City of Bath

NOT TO BE CONFUSED WITH: FS Albert (p. 126); Bliss (p. 150); Fedra Sans (p. 164)

OPPOSITE: The Bath City typefaces, seen here in use in wayfinding system and displays, although unique, are deemed to 'pay tribute' to alphabets described as 'English vernacular' by historian James Mosley and reflect the values and forward-looking nature of the beautiful city of Bath.

Creating a custom typeface to reflect the historic British city of Bath was the challenge set to the designers, who were briefed to produce a family that not only reflected the city's values and history but would also work in a contemporary signage and orientation system.

In 2009, London-based studio FWDesign won the tender to design and create a graphic identity for the city of Bath. A key part of the brief was that a new typeface should be created to work in a multitude of contexts, including information displays and signage systems to aid locals and visitors alike. FWDesign commissioned David Quay and Ramiro Espinoza to create the new typeface to partner their innovative directional and location signage, which employed a circular motif to reflect Bath's history when it was a Roman walled city.

The new typeface was also required to work in a range of sizes and to complement a fresh graphic identity for Bath, which included new maps of the city, that was being developed at the same time. Experimenting with both Sans and Serif designs, a Sans Serif was favoured. As the project progressed, however, a complementary Serif design was also created to help organize into hierarchies a complex array of information.

ITC Bauhaus

ED BENGUIAT, VICTOR CARUSO · ITC · 1975

Although not created at the time of the Bauhaus School, this homage to the principles of the Bauhaus and the aesthetic of the time is drawn from the school's professor, Herbert Bayer, who designed the experimental typeface Universal.

In 1925, German architect and founder of the Bauhaus School Walter Gropius commissioned Austrian artist Herbert Bayer, who had recently been appointed to oversee the Druck und Reklame (printing and advertising) workshop, to design a typeface to be used on all Bauhaus printing. The resulting prototype typeface Universal was a simple, unadorned Geometric typeface with a strong circular motif and only appearing in lower case. Developed from a straight edge and a compass, this acted as the basis for Ed Benguiat and Victor Caruso's revival in 1975.

The US designers' typeface does shy away from its ancestral starting point; for example, Benguiat and Caruso elected to have open-ended strokes rather than the closed counters of Universal. In addition, an upper case was created where before there was none and five weights were added. Suitable only for display and headline work, similar typefaces in shape and form (and inspired by Bayer's designs) are Linotype's Blippo, Pump (p. 310) and Herb Lubalin's ITC Ronda.

CATEGORY: Sans Serif

CLASSIFICATION: Geometric

COUNTRY OF ORIGIN: Germany/USA

DISTINGUISHING MARKS: Circular and geometric construction; motif and rounded aesthetic; inverted semicircles form 'x'; open counters on numerous letters; monoline stroke; very small counters on upper case; bold weight only; vertical tail on upper-case 'Q'

FURTHER SIGHTINGS: The Killers album sleeves; www.newsgator.com

NOT TO BE CONFUSED WITH: ITC Avant Garde Gothic (p. 132); Chalet (p. 154); Futura (p. 180)

OPPOSITE: The key features in ITC Bauhaus's construction can be seen in this example with its rounded corners, open counters, circular 'O' and minimal contrast.

FIELD FACTS_

The Bauhaus School, although having only a short existence from 1919 to 1933, had a profound impact and influence on twentieth-century art and design. Founded on the principles of the Arts and Crafts philosophy, an international design movement that was created as a response to the growing industrialization of the time, its influence on all aspects of visual communications, product design and architecture is still greatly felt today.

Wayne Thompson • ATF (Australian Type Foundry)

MEREWETHER, AUSTRALIA

ATF (Australian Type Foundry) began in 2001 as a commercial outlet for the fonts of designer Wayne Thompson. Prior to setting up ATF, Wayne worked for 17 years as art director in several advertising agencies, and now works full-time as a type designer.

Today, ATF retails almost 100 original typefaces through online outlets around the world, and continues to design and market new type designs, also producing custom designs and typeface modifications for a large range of advertising clients.

Q: How was it you became a type designer?

A: Looking back, I think I always had a natural attraction to type, even as a child. For instance, at the age of about ten my dad gave me a battered second-hand Letraset catalogue. I adored that book, and copied letters from it on to old bits of wood with a paintbrush. I wasn't thinking about a career at the time, I was just enjoying myself. When I finished high school my dad wanted me to be an engineer, but I wanted to be a photo-journalist and ended up (after some argument) studying communications. I did three hours a week of graphic design.

Our college had a Compugraphic photo-typesetter with a choice of maybe ten fonts including Hobo and Souvenir. By graduation, I'd decided on graphic design as my profession, but still didn't have a consciousness of typography. I worked my way up to art director in an agency, and during this time the digital revolution happened. Macs and the internet opened my eyes to typography (with some help from my Neville Brody books) and I began to explore type design in my home time. In 1996 I designed Dallas, audaciously sent it to Robert Slimbach and – to my surprise – he replied with suggestions. So, between 1996 and 2002 I designed as many Display typefaces as I could manage, mostly in my spare time outside my agency jobs (but also sometimes at work), with a view to selling them on the Web. Ten years after designing my first face, I decided to go full-time with my own type foundry.

OPPOSITE TOP LEFT, RIGHT: From early development sketches through to tests and the final design Arum Sans, a Humanist Sans Serif typeface. Available as an OpenType family of ten complementary weights, the fonts are versatile enough to be used for high-end text setting as well as for display purposes. Design by Wayne Thompson.

OPPOSITE BOTTOM MIDDLE, FAR RIGHT: Acumen, a new Sans Serif for both text and display purposes in ten weights.

OPPOSITE BOTTOM LEFT: Wayne Thompson, type designer and founder of ATF.

jewelle
STAR of AFR
fanciful notions of wea
DIAMOND
The largest uncut gem ever seen
CARAT
asured f
d from the ca
&
acumen
312
&
cosmopolitan
Acumen is a new sans serif family in 10 weights from Australian Type Foundry. Ultra modern and minimal Acumen is intended to be a workhorse typeface for both text and display use.
23 1Q

Q: How does your experience as a graphic designer inform your work today?

A: I'm a fussy sod, and I became a type designer primarily because I could never find a font to do quite the job I required. It's different now, of course, there are so many more choices. But you have to remember that, back then in Australia, we had a font menu that comprised Helvetica, Goudy, Garamond, Gill Sans and a bunch of wacky Display faces. There wasn't much else, and even when new fonts became available agencies were suspicious of online purchasing in the early days of the internet. It sounds absurd now, but it was easier to just design my own headline in vectors, and expand them into a font later on.

I don't think I could be a full-time type designer without my earlier experience as a graphic designer. When designing type, I have to retain some perspective on how it's likely to be employed by the end user. The experience of being a graphic designer – and needing fonts for particular purposes – has heavily informed my choices and direction today.

Q: Your typeface collections reflect a wide spectrum of approaches and styles. Where do you get your inspiration for starting a new design?

A: Inspiration comes from all over the place. It might be a chalkboard menu in a cafe, or a piece of rusty signage. Sometimes I see a piece of design for which the type choices are not quite right, and think about how to improve them. Occasionally, simply encountering type in everyday life (as we all do) is enough for me to identify a style or genre which has room for more members. But mostly my inspiration comes from seeing the inspiring work of other type designers and wanting to make fonts as good as theirs. I surround myself with type, and notice vernacular type constantly in newspapers, shop windows, products in the supermarket. I have a messy office full of sketchbooks, books, magazines and drawers full of paper scraps containing half-formed ideas. I can't help it, I swim in a sea of type, and bit by bit it seeps in through my skin and comes back out imbued with a touch of my own personality.

So I don't have to worry about ideas. I have too many, and not enough time to explore them all.

Q: Your typefaces Dallas and ITC Django are based on the handwriting of family and friends. What are the challenges of designing Script typefaces versus Roman and more traditional styles?

A: There are huge challenges in designing any typeface, but text typefaces are much more difficult than Display typefaces. I started with Display faces and stayed there for many years because I was scared of text faces (with good reason). I'd produced 30 or 40 Display faces before I tackled my first text family (Halvorsen, 2006). The primary reason is spacing. A Display face can tolerate haphazard spacing, and sometimes – such as in grunge designs – it can even enhance the effectiveness. And stroke thickness and rhythm can all be variable in a Display face. But text faces are intended for continuous reading, with good rhythm and spacing paramount to avoid distraction to the eye. This makes production of text faces far more time-intensive, and very sensitive to inconsistencies. On top of that there is an even bigger challenge: how to make your text design unique without adding unnecessary detail. I am fascinated by this pursuit, and the release of dozens of high-quality Sans Serif families every year proves it is possible. My most recent Sans Serif family, Acumen, is an addition (I hope) to the pool of commercially viable Sans Serif text families out there.

ABOVE AND RIGHT: Details of a range of script and hand-lettered designs from Wayne Thompson's sketchbooks. As he describes: 'I have a messy office full of sketchbooks, books, magazines and drawers full of paper scraps containing half-formed ideas. I can't help it, I swim in a sea of type.'

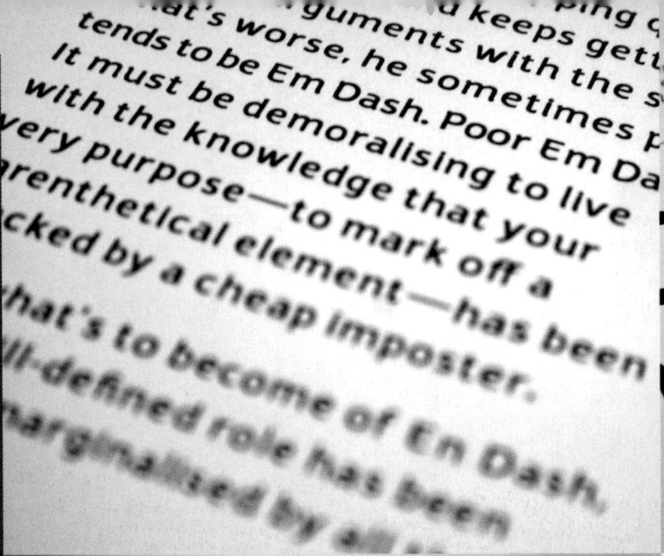
ery purpose—to mark off a
renthetical element—has been
cked by a cheap imposter.

abcdefg
ABCDEFGHIJK
cruise
nantucket
rocky coastline
afternoon bree
is a signature of the ves

sailin
lateaf

cruise
nantucket
sailing
BOLD ITALIC
south
late afternoon

Q: Having established ATF in 2002, what changes have you seen in typeface development in terms of design and technological advances and how has this affected the way you work?

A: The main thing that has changed in the past ten years is the explosion of typefaces that use advanced OpenType features, especially in the script and handwriting genres. Those styles are not really part of my oeuvre, I'm more of a Sans Serif guy, so I haven't had the pressing need to explore those technical capabilities in depth.

I'm not as strong as I could be when it comes to the technical end of font-making. I have included some OpenType features in more recent fonts (starting with Halvorsen, 2006) and I can do it on a basic level, but it's something I need to learn more about.

Q: What's the most unusual application that you have seen one of your typefaces used in?

A: I used to have a free font that I gave away called Jungle Bones. It was very quirky and childish, but quite popular as a free download. Never in my wildest dreams did I think anyone would find a sensible use for it. But in 2009, I was contacted by a Californian electronic games manufacturer who wanted to license the font for use in character names on-screen. Also, I was recently contacted about my typeface Spud by a customer who wanted to reproduce it on metal stamps.

Q: What advice would you give to anyone thinking of designing their own typeface for the first time?

A: I would say, 'The wand chooses the wizard, Harry', perhaps in a Yoda voice, because I tend to mix up my fantasy genres. What I mean is, don't do it because it's trendy or glamorous, but because you can't do anything else. You have to be obsessed by type and have some natural talent upon which to build. Even though it's really difficult, I certainly wouldn't discourage anybody from designing their own font. I would suggest that – unlike me – you start with a text face NOT a Display face. Display faces are easier, yes, but why not jump in at the deep end? Why not learn as much as you can? The difficulties of rhythm, spacing and balance in a text face are crucial to the understanding of legibility and all typography. It makes sense to start at the core, I think. Do Display faces later on, when you need a less challenging project with a higher fun component to keep up the interest.

I think students only see the glamorous bit, the sketching and creative part, without understanding that it's 80% technical and can be tedious at times. Most graphic designers only do one typeface. So if you want to be a type designer, you need to be persistent enough to push through the difficult times.

OPPOSITE: Halvorsen is one of the first releases of an international quality OpenType family from ATF. A modern Sans Serif with a large x-height, making it ideal for text applications.

Bell Centennial

MATTHEW CARTER · LINOTYPE · 1978

Matthew Carter's task of designing a new typeface to meet specific technical challenges for AT&T's hundredth-anniversary phonebook resulted in the innovative and highly regarded typeface Bell Centennial.

Commissioned by AT&T to design a replacement for their existing phonebook typeface, Bell Gothic, the brief required a typeface that would provide increased legibility and a saving in the amount of paper used. Carter's solution was to create a condensed Sans Serif that would work at very small sizes (6 point), thus allowing for more characters to be placed on a single line. This not only stopped the running of addresses on two lines but also negated the need to abbreviate the majority of them, thereby reducing the page extent of the new phonebooks. The smaller extent helped the company save millions of dollars.

With printing a typeface on lightweight and porous newsprint stock at small sizes comes the problem of ink spreading and filling in, and a subsequent drop in character legibility. Carter's solution was to introduce oversized ink traps into the letterforms, which would fill in and negate the ink spread when printed. At larger sizes, these character traits are very pronounced but when small they are hardly visible.

CATEGORY: Sans Serif

CLASSIFICATION: Gothic

COUNTRY OF ORIGIN: USA

DISTINGUISHING MARKS: Condensed form; exaggerated ink traps; reduced contrast between strokes; sturdy appearance; square dot over letters 'i' and 'j'; double-storey 'a'; lowered horizontal bar on 'A'; square cut letters on terminals; increased letter spacing

FURTHER SIGHTINGS: Mazda UK; *Yellow Pages*

NOT TO BE CONFUSED WITH: Fedra Sans (p. 164)

OPPOSITE: Bell Centennial. Four weights were created, each with a specific task to perform within the directories: Bell Centennial Address, Bold Listing, Name and Number and Sub-Caption.

RDMAN Chris Fort Barry Sau 415 332-8533
rent Fort Barry Sau 415 339-9291
rent Marie Fort Barry Sau 415 332-8533
RDSAW William 415 924-3722
William 415 924-5113
rdware & Supplies Waterstreet Co
8 Caledonia Sau 415 332-4318
RDWIDGE N 415 259-0667
rdwood Flooring Vince Triscell Novato 415 892-3993
RDY D & S 415 258-0258
Erich 16 Janes M Vly 415 383-9642
Essie 14 Braun Ct M C 415 332-1061
Jos 16 Janes M Vly 415 383-3047
Rima 415 472-3412
Walter 415 388-7556
ARE Alberta 56 Rosemont Av S Ansimo 415 456-4885
Gary Ann 415 459-8880
William 415 888-8963
ARELIK Harry 1441 Casa Buena Dr C M 415 927-1332
ARFORD Jennifer 44 Sequoia Rd Frfx 415 485-4935
Sandy 401 The Alameda S Ansimo 415 578-2857
ARGARTEN Tim 415 455-9124
ARGER Gilda 536 Shasta M Vly 415 888-8407
ARGES Chris & Elizabeth B 28 Baywood Ct Frfx 415 259-0402
Janet 415 578-2554
ARGRAVE Alex & Catherine 415 927-2017
David 450 Strawberry M Vly 415 389-5484
David 450 Strawberry M Vly 415 389-5488
argrave Fiduciary Advisors LLC
3030 Bridgeway Sau 415 729-9283
ARGREAVES David 276 Devon Dr S R 415 448-5180
David & Becky 276 Devon Dr S R 415 479-3016
Gordon 965 Magnolia Av Lrkspr 415 924-2582
S 415 464-0822
William 415 388-3439
William 415 388-4705
ARIRI Farhad & Mojgan 415 332-0287
Farnoosh 187 Cazneau Ave Sau 415 332-7533
ARKAVY Kamila 415 454-3136
Kamila 415 454-3416
ARKER Howard 30 Ralston Av M Vly 415 383-9458
ARKEY Teall 296 Union St S R 415 456-4818
ARKIN John 20 Minor Ct S R 415 472-2452
ARKINS Edward 206 Evergreen Dr Kntfld 415 461-4116
ARLAN Carol R 415 669-7850
David 415 888-2112
ARLAND C 415 663-9283
ARLE Jonathan Gabrielle 415 889-5334
Jonathan Gabrielle 6 Mateo Dr Tibrn 415 889-5381
Nancy 88 Ross S Ansimo 415 456-4008
Suzanne 415 383-0484
ARLEM Robert 415 888-2295
Robert 415 888-2298
ARLESS Linda 415 383-2693
Linda 415 389-1446
S 415 331-9985
ARLEY B L 415 883-4113
arley-Davidson Michael's –
No Charge To Calling Party 800 400-2011
ARLIB L & R 415 456-6661
ARLING Cal 415 479-4066
Cal C 415 479-2166
ARLOCK Michael 533 Redwood Ave C M 415 924-2318

Nancy 121 Redwood Dr Wdacr 415 488-1218
S 112 Filbert Av Sau 415 332-1857
Thomas R 15 Eliseo Dr Grnbre 415 461-1758
HARRINGTON David 415 382-8374
Diane 415 444-0957
Dominique 415 888-8304
Don 52 Corte Morada Kntfld 415 461-1310
Don 52 Corte Morada Kntfld 415 461-1343
Don 52 Corte Morada Kntfld 415 925-9045
Frank 28 Partridge Dr S R 415 457-2141
Frieda R 439 Calle De La Mesa Ign 415 883-4344
Gary 415 457-3030
Jane 415 888-2201
Jeff 140 Lagunitas Rd Lagntas 415 488-1271
K 415 485-1771
Karen 9 Somerset Ln M Vly 415 388-3847
Kenneth 49 Wimbledon Wy S R 415 456-8996
Laurel 731 Bay Rd M Vly 415 388-9988
Laurie 415 461-3421
Margaret Ms. 415 924-9349
Mark 415 419-5528
Mary 422 Redwood Ave C M 415 891-8557
Robert 415 381-6417
Scott 415 887-9362
Scott 271 Sycamore Av M Vly 415 388-5950
Stephen C & Leslie 415 499-8362
T 9 Somerset Ln M Vly 415 383-2512
Timothy 415 924-7858
Uta 415 925-1338
Harrington's Moving & Storage
4415 Paradise Dr Tibrn 415 435-3900
HARRIS Adam 106 Baltimore Ave C M 415 891-3446
Alan & Christine 415 388-1986
Andrew & Mary 8 Via Capistrano Tibrn 415 435-2502
Anne 102 Ryan Av M Vly 415 383-3931
Anne 102 Ryan Av M Vly 415 888-2345
Anne 102 Ryan Av M Vly 415 888-2346
Arlene L 415 479-8438
B 415 472-1924
Harris Bail bonds 775 E Blithedale AV M Vly 415 322-5002
HARRIS Barbara 415 331-0148
Barbra 415 482-9928
Barry 415 868-9621
Bernard & Bette 415 479-9613
Bernice 415 729-9039
Bourke 415 663-8682
Brent & Nanette 50 La Cuesta Lagntas 415 488-9068
C 415 453-5012
C 415 883-3880
C 415 888-8404
C & B 3 Penny Ln Frfx 415 455-0455
Carol Joy 415 883-2824
Charles 415 454-3460
Charles 415 492-1455
Charles 33 Santa Barbara Ave S Ansimo 415 306-7145
Christine 415 459-2518
Cynthia 415 332-6879
D 415 461-5159
D & G 415 381-3719
Damas Dawn 20 Calle Del Pinos Stnsn Bch 415 868-1919
Daniel 415 457-7515
David 26 Maybeck Nov 415 883-9059

Harris Victor Law Offices Of 1050 No
HARRIS Wyman C 306 Bella Vista Av Bel
Yvonne
Zoe
HARRIS-KUNZ Gillian
1115 Sir Francis Drake Bl Kntfld
HARRISON A
Anna
Anne 135 Barbaree Wy Tibrn
Antohny Sr 855 C S R
Harrison & Bonini 1122 Harrison San Fr
HARRISON C 150 Seminary Dr M Vly
C W 162 Knight Dr S R
Cory 2 Crescent Rd C M
David
David
David
David
Harrison Holding LLC 28 Liberty Ship W
HARRISON J S
James
James
James 402 Jewell S R
Jeremiah
Jj 105 Birch Av C M
Julie
Kathryn P 254 Mountain View Av S R
Kenneth
Harrison & Koellner LLC 238 Reed Bl
HARRISON L 41 Seminary Cove Dr M Vly
Lawrence M
Lewis 65 Montego Ky Nov
Louise
Louise
Lynn 173 Baypoint S R
M J
Marilyn 104 Sandpiper C M
Marsh
Michael 2 Round Hill Ter Belv Tibrn
Nina 240 Elvia S R
P
Ralph C 916 Via Casitas Lrkspr
Randy
Ray
Robert
Harrison Robert L atty 1000 4th S R
HARRISON Samuel 1053 Cresta Wy S R
Saml J 938 Bel Marin Keys Bl Bel Marin
Scott L
Scott L 118 Allyn S Ansimo
Stanley & Regina 450 Vista Del Mar S
Stephen 20 Lunada Ct S R
Steve
Teresa
Thora
Tom 2 Falmouth Cove S R
Tom L 49 Calypso Shores Ign
Vicki 140 Cintura Lagntas
William 100 Old Rancheria Rd Nicsio
HARROCH D
HARROD Patricia
Robert 811 Las Colindas S R
Susie

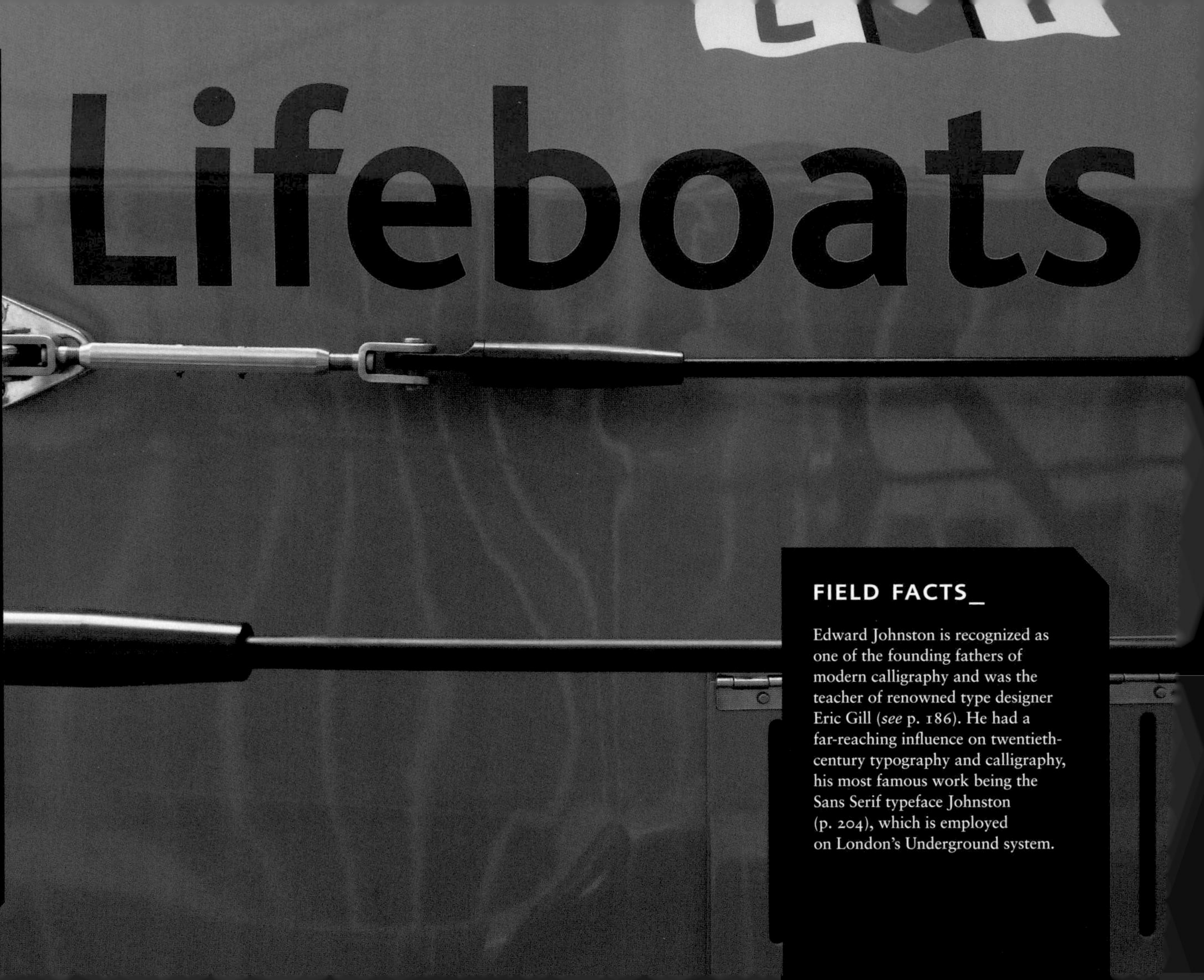

Lifeboats

FIELD FACTS_

Edward Johnston is recognized as one of the founding fathers of modern calligraphy and was the teacher of renowned type designer Eric Gill (*see* p. 186). He had a far-reaching influence on twentieth-century typography and calligraphy, his most famous work being the Sans Serif typeface Johnston (p. 204), which is employed on London's Underground system.

CATEGORY: Sans Serif

CLASSIFICATION: Humanist

COUNTRY OF ORIGIN: UK

DISTINGUISHING MARKS: Minimal stroke contrast; angled cut on extenders at top of 'E' and 'F'; large apertures; open counters; descender on upper-case 'J'; asymmetric terminals on lower-case 'f'; double-storey 'g'; large dot over 'i'; stem on lower-case 'b' and 'd' forms into bowl above baseline; short tail on stem of 'l'; long tail on 't'

FURTHER SIGHTINGS: Amazon Kindle; ABTA Travel Association; University of Idaho; RNLI

NOT TO BE CONFUSED WITH: FS Albert (p. 126); Gill Sans (p. 186); Frutiger (p. 176)

OPPOSITE: Bliss as used by the RNLI (Royal National Lifeboat Institution) in the UK.

Bliss

JEREMY TANKARD · JEREMY TANKARD TYPOGRAPHY · 1996

Designed by one of the UK's most respected type designers, Jeremy Tankard's Bliss is an elegant and practical typeface that was inspired by the ideas put forward by Edward Johnston in his book *Writing & Illuminating & Lettering* from 1906.

In Johnston's seminal work, he describes the concept of employing the proportions of a Roman square capital letter to a Sans Serif form to create a more balanced and acceptable design. This was the starting point for the development of Tankard's Bliss.

While studying at the UK's Royal College of Art, Tankard explored typeface design for his thesis and in his studies the first stages of Bliss's design were put to paper. It was some years later, following employment at corporate design consultancies, that Bliss was completed when Tankard set up his own studio and foundry.

The secret of Bliss's success lies in part in Tankard's detailed research and experimentation with other Humanist types, such as Johnston's Underground (p. 204), Gill Sans (p. 186), Transport, Syntax and Frutiger (p. 176). Bliss's design possesses softer forms and Humanist proportions, which contribute to a clearer definition of the letterforms, both in isolation and when set as texts, allowing the reader's gaze to flow along the line.

Bliss vs Frutiger

[p. 150] [p. 176]

Designed in the mid-twentieth century for wayfinding signage, **Frutiger** was the first typeface of its kind, based on the traditional structure of pen-based letters, but pared-down to its basic essence for the sake of clarity. **Bliss** follows a similar course, but isn't quite so minimalist, resulting in a warmer, more Humanist feel. Bliss also echoes some of the more characteristic shapes in Gill Sans (p. 186, particularly 'M', 'g', 'p'), revealing its British heritage, as opposed to the Swiss nature of Frutiger.

Frutiger's terminals on curved strokes are vertically sheared. Bliss's are angled.

The stems in Bliss's 'b', 'd', 'p' and 'q' do not extend beyond their bowls. Frutiger's do.

The diagonal strokes in Bliss's 'M' meet high above the baseline, similar to Gill Sans.

Bliss has a double-storey 'g' and its descenders are slightly longer than Frutiger's.

Meg boil GW Bliss

Meg boil GW Frutiger

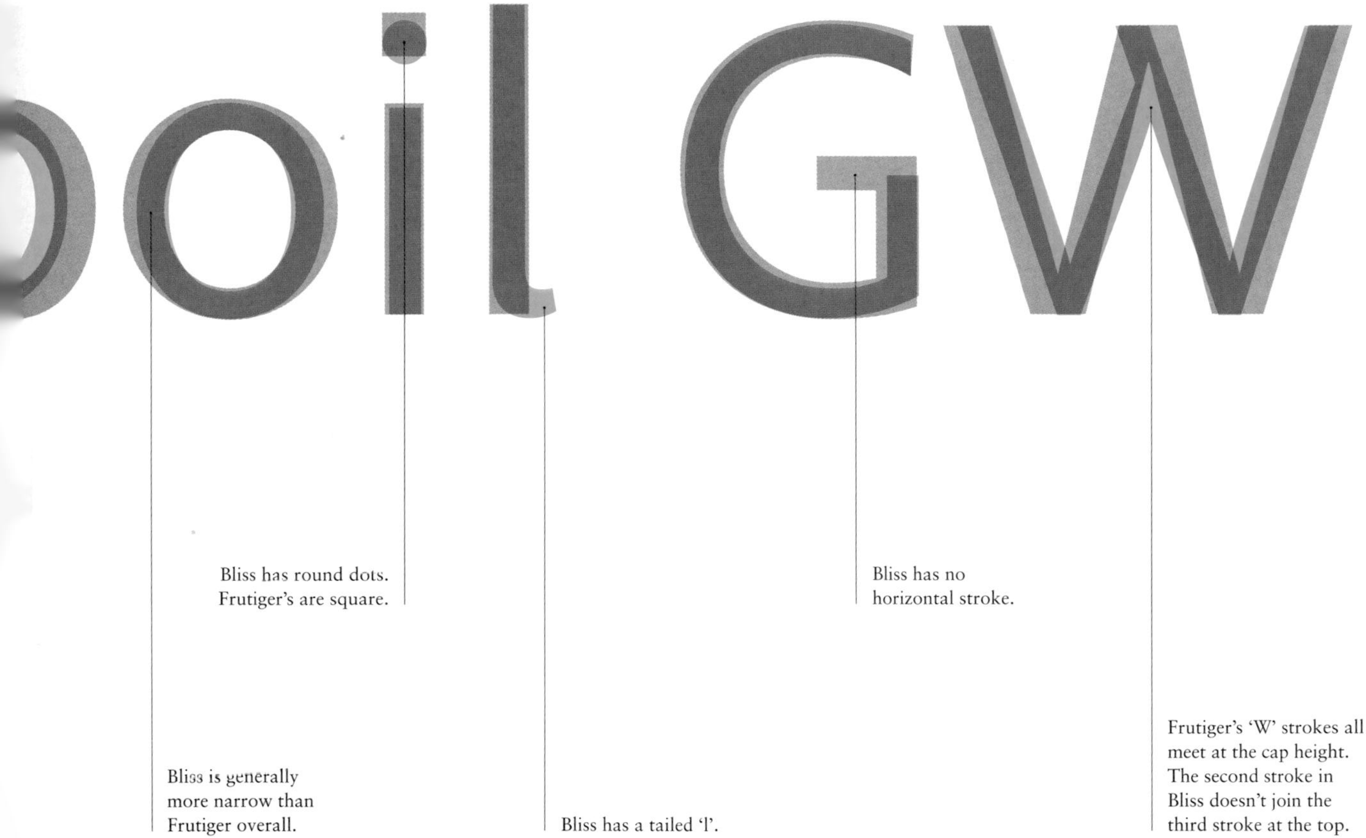

oil GW

Bliss has round dots. Frutiger's are square.

Bliss has no horizontal stroke.

Frutiger's 'W' strokes all meet at the cap height. The second stroke in Bliss doesn't join the third stroke at the top.

Bliss is generally more narrow than Frutiger overall.

Bliss has a tailed 'l'.

Chalet

'RENÉ ALBERT CHALET', KEN BARBER · HOUSE INDUSTRIES · 2000

From highly respected US foundry House Industries, this fun, clever and versatile typeface family has a 'global' and 'timeless' naming convention for its weights and styles along with a mischievous concept from its designer.

An elegant, monoline Geometric Sans Serif, reminiscent of both ITC Bauhaus and Futura, Chalet possesses a range of dynamic letterforms with each set of weights named after cities of the world: Paris (Light), London (Regular) and New York (Bold). Each weight is then offered in a range of three styles, with a period of time describing them. The more traditional Roman character set is the 1960s option with a varying character set for the 1970s and again for the 1980s. There is even a Tokyo option, which is a bold monoline with open counters, cut stems and exaggerated bars. A set of italics is also available but only for the Light cut and the collection even includes 100 silhouette images.

House Industries have built a reputation for not only their fun display typefaces but also for coming up with innovative ways to market their typefaces. For Chalet, House Industries created a fictional character in order to raise awareness of most designers' lack of knowledge when it came to the history of type and type design. Their false creation, René Albert Chalet, a supposedly acclaimed clothing designer from the 1940s, was much touted in the design press as the brains behind Chalet. He is still often credited, but never checked, by some parts of the design media.

CATEGORY: Sans Serif

CLASSIFICATION: Geometric

COUNTRY OF ORIGIN: USA

DISTINGUISHING MARKS: Monoline; rounded large counters and curves; angled, stylized 's' and 'S'; variations have open counters; diagonal crossbar on lower-case 'e'; horizontal cut on terminals; geometric appearance; large x-height

FURTHER SIGHTINGS: LEGO advertising

NOT TO BE CONFUSED WITH: ITC Avant Garde Gothic (p. 132); Avenir (p. 136); ITC Bauhaus (p. 140); Futura (p. 180)

OPPOSITE: Chalet, even at 1,000 feet up, can be clearly identified thanks to its circular forms and distinctive diagonal crossbar on the lower-case 'e'.

FIELD FACTS_

House Industries' sense of irreverence came to the fore when they were planning their Swiss revival. Initially, they aimed to create a stylized version of Helvetica, entitled Swiss Haus, but eventually came up with the concept of an imaginary Swiss modernist designer called Chalet, although the idea was too clever for many and the hoax went undiscovered for some time. However, the typeface was a global success and turned the foundry's fortunes around. Later they released a subfamily called Chalet Book closer to the Helvetica model, designed by Christian Schwartz.

FIELD FACTS_

To complement the display version of the Channel 4 typeface, a text version was created that had the quirky elements removed so as to aid legibility and readability. A Condensed version was also developed for the news that helped maximize captioning and a special cut of the main Headline face was done which possessed shortened ascenders to allow for tighter leading on pull-down menus.

Friday 10.00p
Grand Designs
channel4.com

Channel 4

JASON SMITH · FONTSMITH · 2005

CATEGORY: Sans Serif

CLASSIFICATION: Humanist

COUNTRY OF ORIGIN: UK

DISTINGUISHING MARKS: Minimal contrast; open bowl on lower-case 'g'; squared geometric presentation; rounded corners; curved lower stem of upper-case 'E'; slab serif on base of '1' and 'I'; slab serif at top of stem on lower-case 'i'

FURTHER SIGHTINGS: Channel 4, www.channel4.com

NOT TO BE CONFUSED WITH: DIN 1451 (p. 158); Eurostile (p. 160)

OPPOSITE: Fontsmith's bespoke typeface for the UK's Channel 4 TV station employed on screen idents and forthcoming schedule information.

A contemporary display typeface for a groundbreaking television channel, Fontsmith's revolutionary custom-built Sans Serif helped change the way TV channels presented themselves.

As part of a complete rebranding exercise by Channel 4 in 2004, Jason Smith worked closely with Matthew Rudd and Brett Foraker to create the British station's 'edgy' new logo and branding. Channel 4's programming remit had always been to push the boundaries and provide creative and forward-thinking television to its audience. In light of this, Jason Smith had to create a corporate typeface that not only complemented the new logo and the channel's ethos but also worked across a variety of media, from on-screen TV idents to Channel 4's printed material and advertising.

Visually unique, Smith's typeface contains a number of abstract quirks that make it readily identifiable as the Channel 4 brand even when the main logo is not accompanying it. Details like the lower case 'g', with its open geometric bowl, the rounded corners and its discretionary slab serifs make for a truly distinctive typeface and one that is at home on-air and off-air.

The channel's new identity was launched on New Year's Eve in 2004 and was a 'game changer' from the outset, resulting in Fontsmith designing bespoke typefaces for many other stations, including BBC One, ITV, Film4, Sky News, and Sweden's Kanal 5.

DIN 1451 / FF DIN

LINOTYPE, FONTFONT · 1931

Published as the German governmental typeface by their standards committee in 1936, DIN 1451 was originally used for their signage, such as motorway signboards, and for road signs, administrative and business purposes.

The Deutsches Institut für Normung (German Institute for Industrial Standards), otherwise known as DIN, selected Sans Serif DIN 1451 thanks to its legibility, clean lines and the ease with which it could be reproduced. Despite its somewhat prosaic beginnings, DIN has proved popular with the graphic design community the world over and has been employed for a myriad of applications, from editorial work to identity and branding projects, and by countless designers.

DIN's industrial structure and clean lines provide a contemporary, minimal aesthetic to printed work that has proved popular – both **Linotype** and **FontFont** offer their own variations of the typeface. Linotype's version retains the original titling and range of weights of DIN 1451 MittelSchrift ('medium type') for the roman and the EngSchrift ('condensed type'). FontFont's FF DIN, drawn up by Dutch typeface designer Albert-Jan Pool and released in 1995, uses more standard naming conventions: Light, Regular, Medium, Bold and Black. A greater number of weights, italics and a Condensed family (and even a rounded cut) allow for greater choice and flexibility for the designer.

CATEGORY: Sans Serif

CLASSIFICATION: Geometric

COUNTRY OF ORIGIN: Germany

DISTINGUISHING MARKS: Minimal contrast; large x-height; moderate extenders; large bowl on lower-case 'a'; rounded characters are oval; wide 's'; small tail on lower-case 'l'; rectangular dots above characters; diagonal strokes on upper-case 'M' meet above the baseline

FURTHER SIGHTINGS: Centre Georges Pompidou, Paris; New York City Ballet; London Design Festival; Salford identity, UK; www.scion.com; jetBlue airlines

NOT TO BE CONFUSED WITH: Letter Gothic (p. 208); FF Meta (p. 210)

OPPOSITE: DIN 1451 employed on the German autobahns makes for legible and precise reading, especially when travelling at speed.

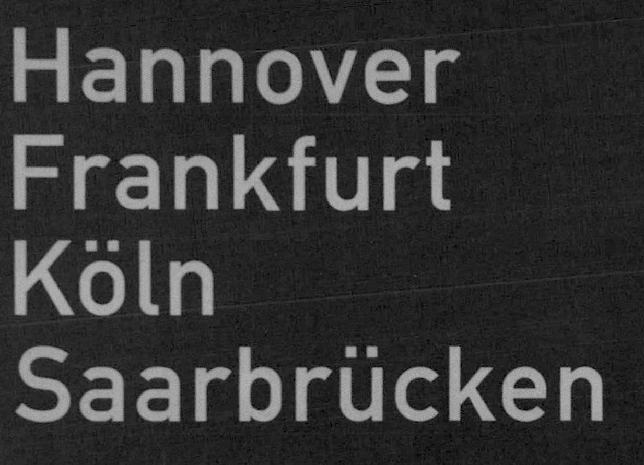

FIELD FACTS_

The creation of FontFont's FF DIN was in large part down to renowned type designer Erik Spiekermann. In San Francisco in 1994, Albert-Jan Pool and Erik Spiekermann attended the ATypI conference and shared a taxi from there to the airport. It was here Spiekermann discussed with Pool (with Pool's employer having gone bankrupt), that to earn some money he should look at OCR and DIN. Spiekermann had correctly identified that both typefaces had limited range and therefore a gap in the market existed to expand on this. One year later, FF OCR-F was launched, with FF DIN following soon after. The latter is still one of their biggest sellers today.

FIELD FACTS_

Eurostile is a popular choice for titling graphics, interior signage and displays for the science-fiction genre. So much so it is now *the* default typeface to be used when designing your own spaceship. Its roll-call in movies and on television includes (and I name just a few): *Aliens*, *Space 1999*, *Moon*, *Dr Who*, *Captain Scarlet*, *UFO*, *Star Trek* (titles and the original NCC-1701 *Enterprise* spaceship), *Battlestar Galactica* and *Dark Star*.

Eurostile

ALDO NOVARESE · LINOTYPE · 1962

CATEGORY: Sans Serif

CLASSIFICATION: Geometric

COUNTRY OF ORIGIN: Italy

DISTINGUISHING MARKS: Square-shaped with rounded corners; slight extension to letterforms; minimal contrast; closed apertures; large counters; near horizontal spine on 'S' and '2'

FURTHER SIGHTINGS: Casio identity; Diadora identity; Roland identity; Toshiba identity; *Star Trek: Enterprise*; Metropolitan Police, London; Eurovision Song Contest; *Final Fantasy XIII*

NOT TO BE CONFUSED WITH: DIN 1451 (p. 158); Gotham (p. 188); Helvetica (p. 192)

OPPOSITE: Not quite as 'future' focussed as when used elsewhere (*see* Field Facts) but Eurostile's appearance makes for an immediate and easy read.

Reflecting the aesthetic of the 1950s and 1960s, Eurostile's clean lines, squarish form and rounded corners lend it a technological quality that reflected the 'futuristic' design being created at that time. However, its popular usage several decades ago has led it to feeling somewhat dated when referring to the future, especially when compared to more recently created Sans Serif designs.

Italian **Aldo Novarese** was one of the best-known and prolific type designers of the 1950s and 1960s. His Eurostile was derived from the 1952 design Microgramma, an all upper-case version (created in collaboration with Alessandro Butti) of an existing design for the Nebiolo foundry. Having created this display face, it wasn't until a decade later that Novarese chose to complete the family by creating a complementary lower case. This new, complete range was titled Eurostile.

Although not wholly ideal as a text face, it can be employed for short lengths of text but is best used for display and headline work. Over the years, a range of Extended and Condensed weights has become available. Still widely used today, from video game interfaces and music industry graphics to science-fiction movies and blue-chip identities, its modern, clean presentation continues to project an image of the future and technology, despite its age.

FF Fago

OLE SCHÄFER · FONTFONT · 2000

A highly flexible typeface, FF Fago can be employed from food packaging to corporate branding and everything in-between. Its clean looks and large family make it suitable for use in a variety of 'tones' within graphic communications.

Designed by eminent German type designer Ole Schäfer, who, having worked at MetaDesign for a number of years and as a freelance type designer and typographer for clients such as Audi, VW and BVG, brought his experience of designing typefaces for a corporate environment to bear on this wide-ranging family. FF Fago is available in five weights, and each weight comes in three widths: Condensed, Regular and Extended. The differing widths were designed so that they could be combined together to create visually exciting letterform combinations while still using the one family.

Because of its open appearance and large counters it works well at very small sizes, making it ideal for detailed typographic work such as information graphics. Its professional and precise appearance also makes FF Fago ideal in an office environment.

CATEGORY: Sans Serif

CLASSIFICATION: Humanist

COUNTRY OF ORIGIN: Germany

DISTINGUISHING MARKS: Large x-height; variable width; open counters; flared lower-case 'x' strokes; double-storey 'g'; angled terminal at top of lower-case stem

FURTHER SIGHTINGS: *Frankfurter Rundschau*; Berlin Wall Timeline Exhibition; Arbeiterwohlfahrt (Workers' Welfare Association, Germany); Lekker Energie, RegModHarz Germany

NOT TO BE CONFUSED WITH: Fedra Sans (p. 164); FF Meta (p. 210)

OPPOSITE: FF Fago employed prominently as a part of a gallery display at the Berlin Wall.

Zweite Berlin-Krise

Bau der Berliner Maue

Second Berlin Crisis

Construction of the Wall

Abflug
departure

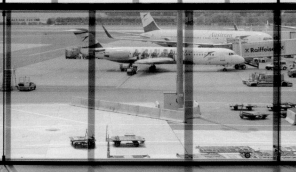

Fedra Sans

PETER BILAK · **TYPOTHEQUE** · 2001

CATEGORY: Sans Serif

CLASSIFICATION: Humanist

COUNTRY OF ORIGIN: Netherlands

DISTINGUISHING MARKS: Large x-height; short extenders; moderate width; minimal contrast; lower-case 'f' has descender; diamond dot above lower-case 'i' and 'j'; alternate font available with closed bowls on certain letters

FURTHER SIGHTINGS: Ideal for both text and wayfinding applications

NOT TO BE CONFUSED WITH: FS Albert (p. 126); Bliss (p. 150); Foundry Sterling (p. 170)

OPPOSITE: Wayfinding of Vienna Airport, Austria, created by Intégral Ruedi Baur Paris & Zürich and employing Fedra Sans throughout the entire site. Note the fun addition of movement to the letters for the departure gates.

Initially commissioned for a German insurance company, this elegant humanist typeface was intended to 'de-protestantize' Univers, the typeface the organization had been using since the 1970s.

After deciding that a more human presentation style was required for their corporate communications, insurance company Bayerische Rück turned to Intégral Ruedi Baur to oversee the process. The Paris-based agency worked with Dutch typeface designer **Peter Bilak** to create a replacement for Univers, which had been employed as part of the company's original corporate identity. Sadly, the project never came to fruition (it was shelved after Bayerische Rück was taken over) but Bilak continued to develop and refine the typeface, eventually making it available as a general release.

Bilak's elegant solution was **Fedra Sans**, a typeface that lends warmth, accessibility and flexibility to messages and, crucially, is equally at home on the printed page and on a computer screen, in either text or display applications. Its simple, informal appearance provides a softer tone to serious subject matter and, with five weights and a comprehensive range of character sets and symbols from many different languages, it is ideally suited for use by international organizations.

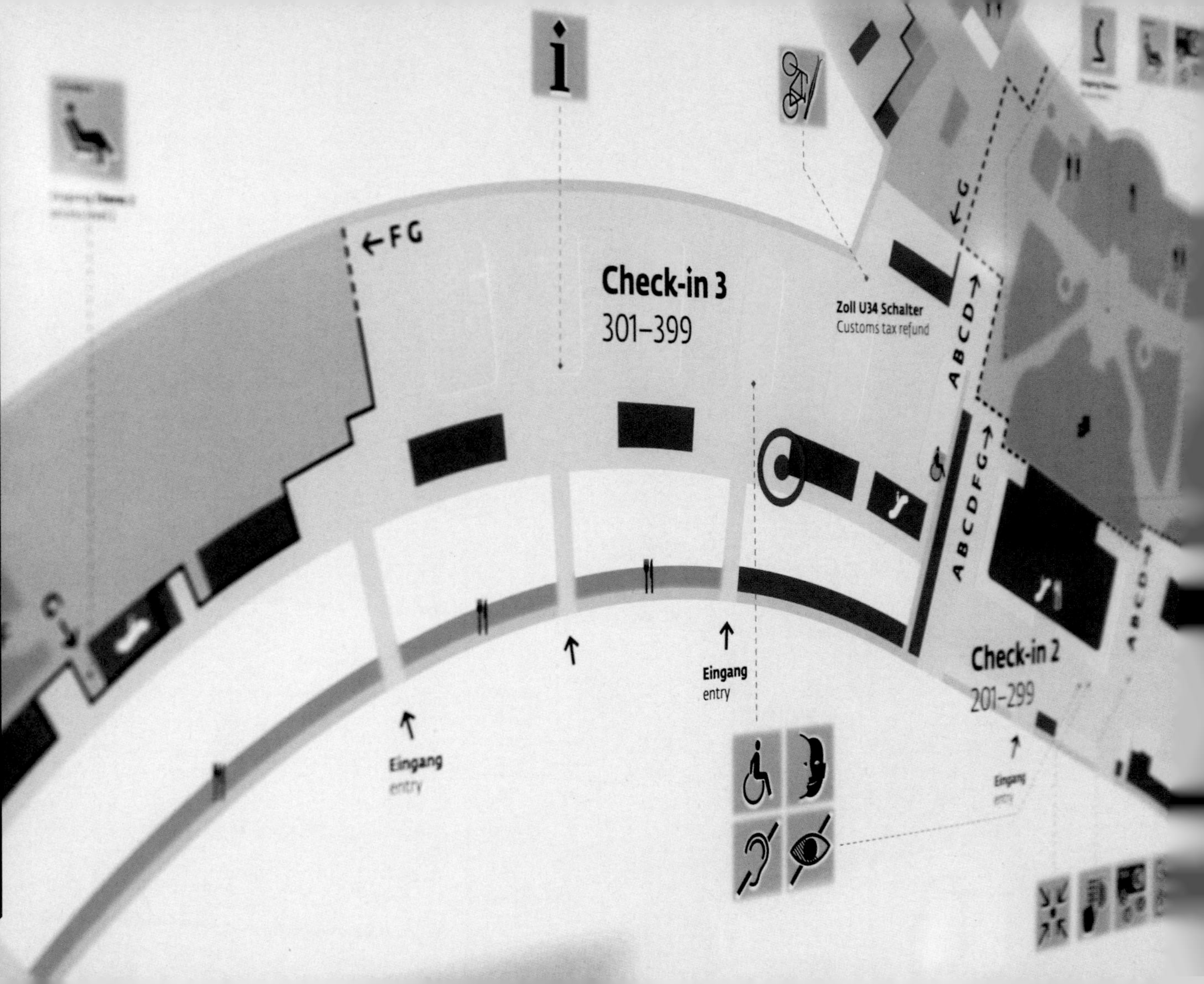

← F G

Check-in 3
301–399

Zoll U34 Schalter
Customs tax refund

← G

A B C D →

A B C D F G →

A B C D F G

Eingang
entry

Eingang
entry

Check-in 2
201–299

Eingang
entry

OPPOSITE, ABOVE, RIGHT: The design of the wayfinding system in Vienna Airport allowed design studio Intégral Ruedi Baur Paris & Zürich to utilize the many weights of Fedra Sans to their full advantage for a vast range of differing applications within the transport hub – from detailed typography for visitor maps, providing hierarchies of definition for differing areas, to more light-hearted decorative typography for welcome displays. A secondary dot matrix typeface was created to complement Fedra Sans by the consultancy with David Esser for illuminated displays.

modern construction
flowing lines
curves bending around form
shapes twisting and turning
different rhythms
Fenland a 14 font typeface
An extraordinary place with a strange, open beauty you won't find anywhere else. It has a unique landscape with its own history, its own culture, its own way of working—and its own way of talking.
miles
kilometers
volumes
centimetres
measurements
distances
capacities
dates
times
currencies

Fenland

JEREMY TANKARD · JEREMY TANKARD TYPOGRAPHY · 2012

CATEGORY: Sans Serif

CLASSIFICATION: Humanist

COUNTRY OF ORIGIN: UK

DISTINGUISHING MARKS: Modulating stroke weight; distinctive 'f' created from three strokes not two; tapering stems; near horizontal spine on 'S'; curved, flared leg on 'k'; large x-height; short ascenders and descenders; long extenders

FURTHER SIGHTINGS: A very new introduction but its distinctive features enable it to stand out and be recognized

NOT TO BE CONFUSED WITH: Frutiger (p. 176)

OPPOSITE: Promotional designs by Jeremy Tankard of his innovative and 'crimped' typeface, Fenland, whose letter shapes differ greatly from traditional Sans Serif forms.

Renowned British type designer Jeremy Tankard's design for Fenland approached the letter shapes in a very different manner, examining how, by altering the structure of the character shape, the inherent rhythm of a letterform could then be changed.

Tankard studied a number of typographic forms that had suffered from erosion, such as gravestones and their inscriptions, with the concept of how the weathering affected the letter shapes with the thinning and breaking of the character's strokes. This natural process of transformation he explored further as well as thinking about how it could be achieved 'mechanically'.

After much exploration, the principal idea that lies at the core of Fenland's varying and modulating strokes is the way a metal tube collapses in on itself when bent. The variation in the thickness of the tube formed the basis of the stroke modulation seen across all 14 weights of the Fenland typeface. An interesting, distinctive and innovative feature of the design is the lower-case letter 'f'. Where nearly all 'f's are drawn in two strokes, with the stem and curve forming one stroke and the crossbar the second, Fenland's 'f' is created from three strokes. The stem and curve are created from two separate strokes (shown opposite).

Foundry Sterling

DAVID QUAY, FREDA SACK · THE FOUNDRY · 2001

A modern Sans Serif design with a quintessentially English flavour, this highly adaptable and elegant typeface has a wide range of applications, from identity to signage systems.

Released in 2001, this modern classic by the renowned The Foundry was created with special attention to classical proportions and minimal form. Foundry Sterling's clean, functional and highly versatile family contains seven weights – Light, Book, Book Italic, Medium, Demi, Bold and Extra Bold – and is available in OpenType format for Mac and PC.

Foundry Sterling is a functional and eloquent typeface family that has its origins in the desire to create a modern sans design. The letterforms have been designed with particular attention to purity of form for information design use, resulting in the creation of a functional yet graceful typeface. The concept for Foundry Sterling evolved from a body of commissioned work for transport systems. Freda Sack was assisted in the development of the resulting typeface family by Foundry Types' senior type designer Stuart de Rozario, who was instrumental in the range of languages created.

CATEGORY: Sans Serif

CLASSIFICATION: Humanist

COUNTRY OF ORIGIN: UK

DISTINGUISHING MARKS: Elegant clean forms; no tail on lower-case 'b' and 'g'; angled terminal on 'g'; minimal contrast in stroke weight; angled stems on upper-case 'M'; large apertures; open counters; large x-height; moderate ascenders and descenders

FURTHER SIGHTINGS: University of Oxford

NOT TO BE CONFUSED WITH: Bliss (p. 150); Fedra Sans (p. 164); Gill Sans (p. 186)

OPPOSITE: Andrew Lawrence's and Nick Kapica/SV Associates' wayfinding design utilizes the clean and precise forms of Foundry Sterling in and around Airport SXF (formerly Berlin Schönefeld Airport).

restaurant
restaurant
besucherterrasse
visitor terrace
abflug
departures
ankunft
arrivals
B
departures
ankunft
arrivals
information

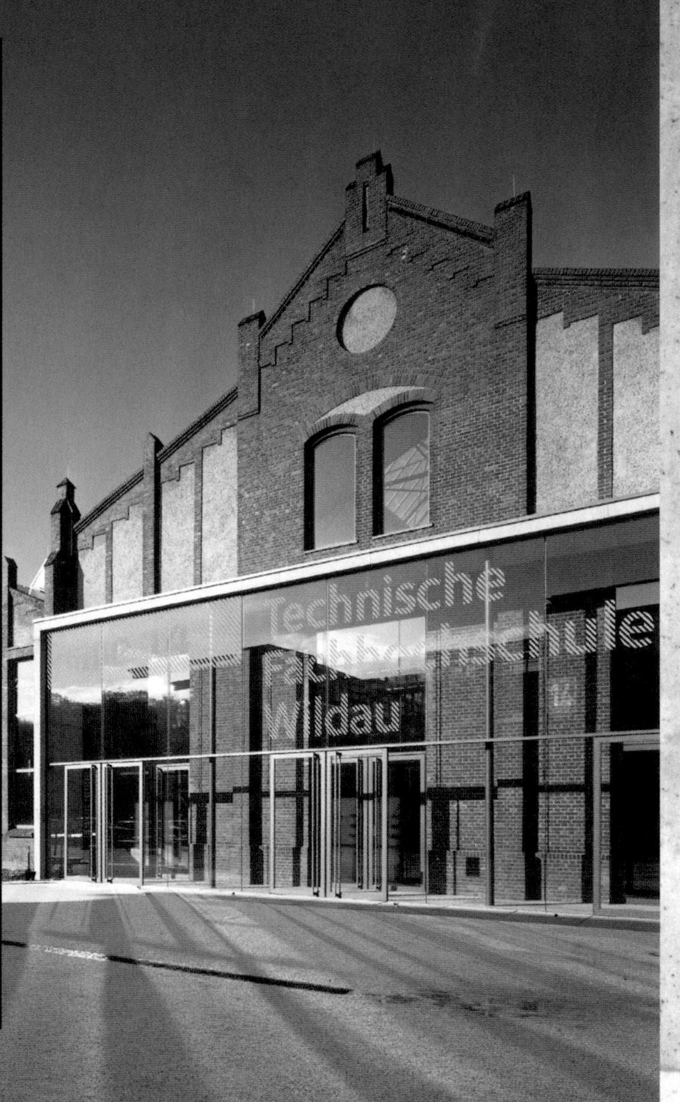
Technische
Wildau
Foyer
Hörsaal
Seminar
Labor
Besprechung
Büro
Aufzug
WC
A001–
A234
B001–
B107
Foyer
Seminar
Labor
B001
B002
B008

OPPOSITE, ABOVE AND RIGHT: For the University of Applied Sciences Wildau in Germany, designers Nick Kapica/SV Associates employed Foundry Sterling throughout the site for the wayfinding typography and identification of zones. A bright yellow colour palette combined with a distinctive chevron motif for the larger display types contrasted with the simplicity of Foundry Sterling's forms when it was used for detailed navigational typography.

MoMA
The Museum of Modern Art
Benvenuti!

Franklin Gothic

MORRIS FULLER BENTON · 1902

A true classic, influenced by German types of the early 1900s, and over a century old, this robust and distinct heavyweight Sans Serif still packs a punch today.

Designed by Morris Fuller Benton for the ATF (American Type Founders) company, the influence of German 'grotesks', as nineteenth-century Sans were referred to then (the term 'Gothic' was used in the USA), can be seen in Franklin Gothic's forms. European types such as Akzidenz Grotesk (p. 122) by the Berthold foundry in Berlin were also an influence.

The ATF foundry was formed in 1892 from a number of separate type foundries, resulting in ATF possessing an array of Gothic types, with weights ranging from Extra Condensed to Extra Extended. This type of Sans Serif had achieved great popularity in Europe in the nineteenth century and the same was true in the USA. In order to rationalize and consolidate the wealth of Sans typefaces ATF possessed, Benton proceeded to design the Franklin Gothic series in 1902, with ATF finally launching it in 1905.

Supposedly named after Benjamin Franklin, the typeface was at first employed primarily in display and headline settings for posters and flyers. Over time Benton created Condensed (1905), Wide (1906) and later a Book version, expanding Franklin Gothic's range and enabling it to be used for setting texts as well. Benton went on to create further weights and the News Gothic typeface.

CATEGORY: Sans Serif

CLASSIFICATION: Gothic

COUNTRY OF ORIGIN: USA

DISTINGUISHING MARKS: Double-storey 'a' and 'g'; moderate stroke contrast; bold appearance; vertical stress; closed apertures; small counters; angled terminals on 'C'; short extenders; square dot over 'i' and 'j'; varying stem width; short ascenders and descenders

FURTHER SIGHTINGS: Museum of Modern Art, New York; *Rocky* movie title; Type Directors Club; AXA Group (UK)

NOT TO BE CONFUSED WITH: Futura (p. 180); Gotham (p. 188); Helvetica (p. 192)

OPPOSITE: The Museum of Modern Art in New York employs Franklin Gothic for its abbreviated logotype 'MoMA' and for its navigational and promotional typography.

Frutiger

ADRIAN FRUTIGER · LINOTYPE · 1976

Asked to design a sign and directional system for Charles de Gaulle Airport in Paris, eminent type designer Adrian Frutiger went ahead and created a new typeface as well.

Frutiger's intention was to create a new typeface that not only complemented the new airport's modern architectural forms but also met the specific challenges of display typography within such an environment. Easy recognition at distances, at speed, from an angle and in low light were the criteria that had to be met.

Taking seven years to create, and originally called Roissy, **Frutiger** possesses great warmth in its appearance and its even and balanced letterform construction enables fast recognition of characters, making it easy to read and highly legible. Frutiger married the geometric forms of his Univers with that of more humanistic Sans Serif types. Despite being designed as a display and headline face, the classic Frutiger works extremely well as a text face and is much favoured and widely used in publishing, corporate identity and branding, and advertising applications.

CATEGORY: Sans Serif

CLASSIFICATION: Humanist

COUNTRY OF ORIGIN: Switzerland

DISTINGUISHING MARKS: Square dot over 'i' and 'j'; minimal stroke contrast; large x-height; upper-case 'R' possesses straight and curved tails; wide apertures; prominent ascenders and descenders

FURTHER SIGHTINGS: Amtrak; Telefonica O2; Charles de Gaulle Airport; DHL; Canadian Imperial Bank of Commerce (CIBC); Deutsche Bundespost; Scotiabank; National Health Service (UK); Flickr; Finnish Defence Forces

NOT TO BE CONFUSED WITH: Bliss (p. 150); Foundry Sterling (p.170); Gill Sans (p. 186)

OPPOSITE: Frutiger doing what it was first designed for. Here seen used for wayfinding typography at Schiphol Airport, Amsterdam.

Baggage hall

Arrivals hall

Gates F G H

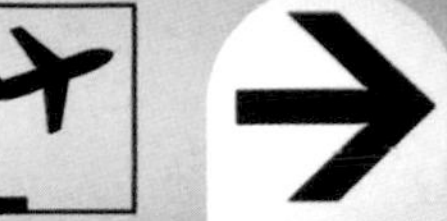

Transfer T8-9

LEFT, BELOW AND OPPOSITE: A truly international typeface, and loved by airports around the world it would seem. Frutiger here used on signage at Heathrow Airport, London; on a weathered gallery plaque; around the Lazio football stadium in Rome; and again for airport wayfinding in Singapore.

Customs
关税局
Kastam
சுங்கவரி
Sea-Air Transfer
海空转乘
Pindah Laut-Uda
கடல்-வான இடமாற்

Roma Termini
UN LUOGO DA VIVERE
SHOPPING
Roma Termini
Biglietteria
Shopping/Metro
Binari 1 e 2 Est
ai Treni
Nuova Classe A.
Il presente
che cambia il futuro.
Mercedes-Benz
Ha cambiato profilo. E ti permette di aggiornare il tuo.
Nuova Classe A. Il presente che cambia il futuro.
Mercedes-Benz

Futura

PAUL RENNER · **BAUER TYPE FOUNDRY** · 1927

CATEGORY: Sans Serif

CLASSIFICATION: Geometric

COUNTRY OF ORIGIN: Germany

DISTINGUISHING MARKS: Constant stroke weight; geometric appearance of circles, triangles and squares; diagonal intersecting tail on upper-case 'Q'; circular counters and ovals; strong vertical shading; asymmetrical lower-case 't'; rounded dot over 'i' and 'j'; long ascenders and descenders

FURTHER SIGHTINGS: Hewlett-Packard; Apollo 11 lunar module 'Eagle' plaque; McAfee; Louis Vuitton; Union Pacific; Costco; *2001: A Space Odyssey*; Absolut Vodka

NOT TO BE CONFUSED WITH: Avenir (p. 136); Chalet (p. 154); Gill Sans (p. 186)

OPPOSITE: When in Rome… big and bold at Rome's Stazione Termini rail station.

With its strong, clean, geometric appearance, influenced by the minimalist aesthetic of the Bauhaus, Futura is seen by many, despite not having any direct links with the Bauhaus School, as representative of the principles behind the movement's teachings.

Paul Renner's Futura was commissioned by the **Bauer Type Foundry** in Germany and released in 1927. The typeface is a combination of Renner's principled constructivist belief – that a modern typeface's form should be based on the circle, triangle and square – and the foundry's wish to impart a practicality and usability on his ideas and sketches. Working together to iron out Renner's more experimental forms with the design, the Bauer design studio soon developed a solid, practical and hardworking typeface family.

The success of the design is evident in the influence it has had on other Geometric typefaces, although its undoubted purity and simplicity, and its crisp near-perfection, have always kept it ahead of the pack. Futura is highly adaptable and works across a range of media. Used on countless corporate identities, products, films and advertising, its no-frills appearance, symmetrical forms and extensive range of weights and styles have made it highly popular with graphic designers and art directors alike.

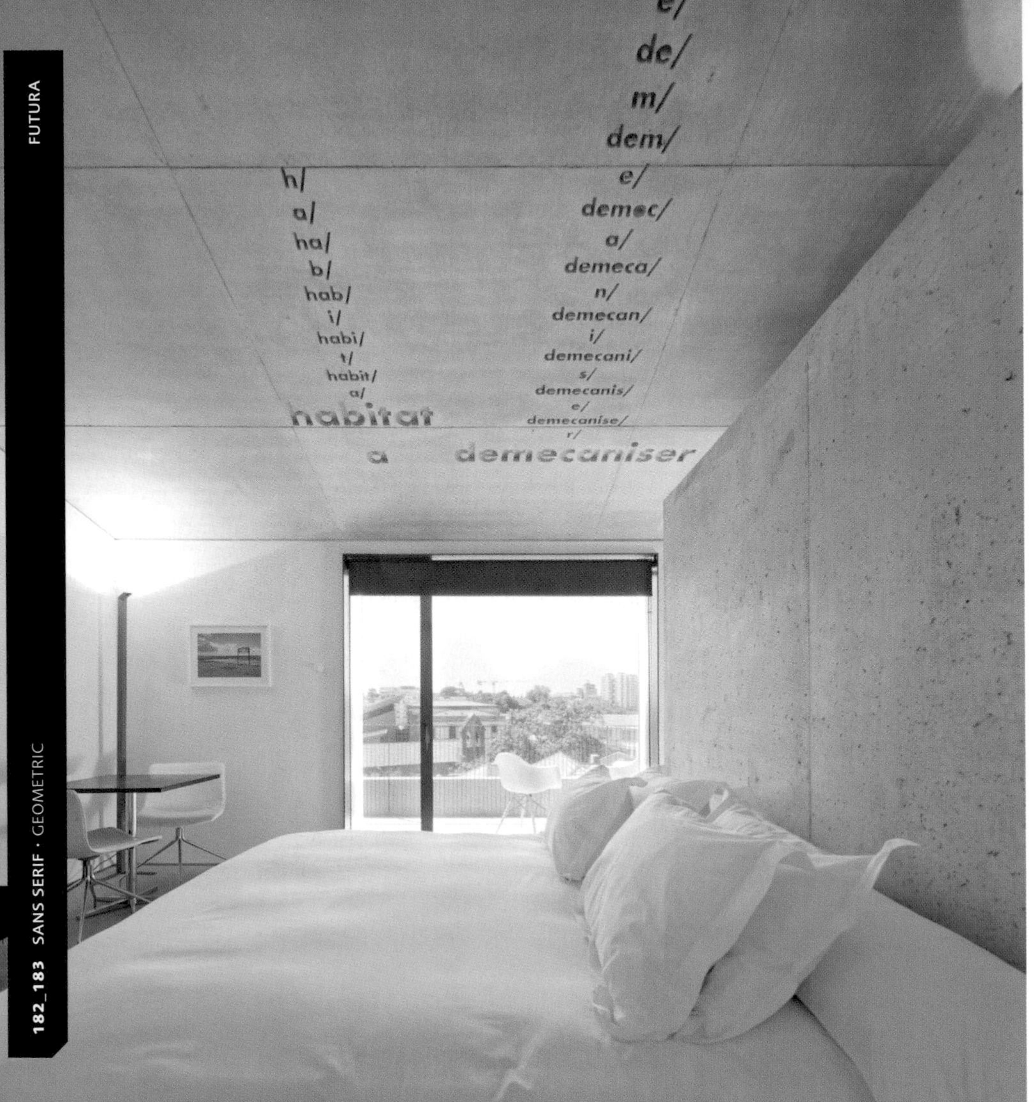

LEFT: Design studio R2's dramatic design for Portuguese guesthouse Casa do Conto (House of Tales) in Porto employs Futura and other types debossed into concrete ceilings and walls throughout all the rooms and guest areas. The phrases were set into concrete panels using Styrofoam letters placed in a formwork.

OPPOSITE: The Barbican Centre in London employs Futura throughout its site, from three-dimensional and backlit wayfinding to printed and online communications.

Cinemas
2 & 3
barbican
4 
frobisher
auditorium 1 & 2
frobisher rooms
art gallery
library
restaurants
hall
curve
tickets
theatre
cinema 1
pit
barbican

Futura vs Gill Sans

[p. 180] [p. 186]

Futura is the prototypical Geometric typeface. It is one of the first of its kind and unlike many followers it adheres fairly rigidly to its circular building blocks. **Gill Sans** isn't necessarily a Geometric, but is often dropped in that bin due to its circular 'o', low stroke contrast, and generally minimalistic letterforms. These typefaces also share classical Roman proportions in their caps (wide round shapes, narrow 'E', 'P', 'S', etc.) but this is where their similarities end. In most cuts, Futura is a much colder, more clinical face than Gill Sans, which has a warmth and wonkiness that make it more common wherever a little more personality is desired.

In most cuts, Futura's 'M' legs are splayed, with a middle vertex dipping below the baseline. Gill Sans has vertical legs and an atypically high middle vertex. In light to regular weights, Futura has pointed vertexes. Gill Sans has these sharp points only on its 'Vv', 'Ww' and middle of the 'M'.

Futura has a single-storey 'a'. Gill Sans's is double storey, with visible stroke contrast. While most of Gill Sans has a consistent stroke weight, there are glyphs, like this one, that show some modulation. Futura, on the other hand, is consistently monolinear – at least in the light to regular weights.

Like its 'j', Futura's minimal 't' has no curved tail.

Many of Futura's glyphs are vertically sheared, but some terminals, like those on the 'e' and 's', are cut at an angle perpendicular to the stroke. All Gill Sans's curved strokes terminate at a vertical angle.

Mats bjg GR Futura
Mats bjg GR Gill Sans

bjg GR

Futura's 'G' is essentially an open circle with a horizontal stroke. Gill Sans's terminates with a vertical sheer and includes both a vertical and horizontal.

Futura's 'j' descends in a perfectly straight line. Gill Sans's has a curved tail.

The leg of Futura's 'R' is straight, extending from the stem or near it. Gill Sans's bowed leg joins at the bowl and extends way beyond the body, making it a signature of the typeface.

Futura has a monocular 'g'. Gill Sans's binocular 'g' is a peculiar form that its designer jokingly compared to a pair of spectacles.

Most cuts of Futura have a fairly short x-height and long ascenders.

Gill Sans

ERIC GILL · **MONOTYPE** · 1928

Described as the 'Helvetica of England', Gill's typeface was originally produced as the standard typeface for use on the LNER (London & North Eastern Railway) but its first outing was as a hand-painted sign above a bookshop.

Eric Gill's masterpiece was borne from humble beginnings. Its starting point came in 1926 when Gill hand-painted a shop sign for a bookshop in Bristol. It is no secret that Gill took as his starting point, and inspiration, Edward Johnston's typeface for the London Underground (p. 204) as he had studied under and served as an apprentice to Johnston.

It was, however, in the late 1920s that **Monotype**'s Stanley Morison commissioned Eric Gill to develop his concepts for **Gill Sans** further into a full family. In part, this was to combat and counter the success German foundries were enjoying with typefaces such as Futura. Gill Sans was begun in 1926 and released by Monotype in 1928. Gill felt he could improve on Johnston's typeface, ironing out its 'faults' to create a perfect Sans Serif text face. Gill Sans's success was established after its selection for the LNER railway system; seen by the public on posters, timetables and even trains, the typeface took on a life of its own and came to be viewed by many as a national typeface for the UK. Its flexibility as both a display and text face added greatly to its success. Its clean lines, authoritative yet accessible tone and modern aesthetic reflected a nation embracing change.

CATEGORY: Sans Serif

CLASSIFICATION: Humanist

COUNTRY OF ORIGIN: UK

DISTINGUISHING MARKS: Flat-bottomed lower-case 'b' and 'd'; flat-topped 'p' and 'q'; varying upper-case character widths; even stroke weight; rounded dot over 'i' and 'j'; triangular-topped lower-case 't'; circular 'O'; double-storey 'g'; geometric elements

FURTHER SIGHTINGS: BBC; Benetton; Bentley Motors; Church of England; Farrow & Ball; John Lewis Partnership; Monotype Imaging; Penguin Books; Saab car company; Spanish government; Tommy Hilfiger

NOT TO BE CONFUSED WITH: Bliss (p. 150); New Johnston (p. 204)

OPPOSITE: Gill Sans utilized in contemporary steel signage.

FIELD FACTS_

Eric Gill (1882–1940) was a renowned British sculptor, artist, calligrapher and typeface designer. His other notable typefaces included Perpetua and Joanna. A deeply religious man, he was also a highly controversial figure thanks to his strident views and bizarre sexual activities.

FIELD FACTS_

In 2004, Gotham was employed as the typeface carved into the cornerstone for the Freedom Tower at the World Trade Center site in New York. The New York Port Authority, which owns the site, also owned the bus terminal on Eighth Avenue, which was a key inspiration for Frere-Jones when creating Gotham.

Gotham

TOBIAS FRERE-JONES · **HOEFLER & FRERE-JONES** · 2000

CATEGORY: Sans Serif

CLASSIFICATION: Gothic

COUNTRY OF ORIGIN: USA

DISTINGUISHING MARKS: Geometric appearance; wider character width; angled terminals on lower-case 'c'

FURTHER SIGHTINGS: New York University; *Inception*, *Moon* and *The Dark Knight* movie posters; Barack Obama 2008 campaign; *The Sartorialist* book; Chicago Olympics 2016 bid; Tom Ford; Fisher & Paykel; Discovery Channel logo; Coca-Cola; Tribeca Film Festival; Shepard Fairey's 'HOPE' poster

NOT TO BE CONFUSED WITH: Avenir (p. 136); Gill Sans (p. 186); New Johnston (p. 204)

OPPOSITE: President Obama on the campaign trail ably assisted by Hoefler & Frere-Jones's Gotham typeface.

Inspired by the many and varied traditional lettering forms of the American vernacular, particularly those used in New York's urban street signage and store front displays, this recent Sans Serif has achieved notable success, thanks in part to its clear and no-nonsense sensibility.

New York type foundry HF&J (**Hoefler & Frere-Jones**) were commissioned by men's magazine *GQ* to design a custom Sans Serif for use in its publication. HF&J's Principal and Type Director **Tobias Frere-Jones** used this project as an opportunity to explore and research the many forms of mid-twentieth-century display lettering that appeared in New York City. These ubiquitous letterforms, created by engineers and draughtsmen rather than type designers, provided **Gotham**'s design with a more functional and earthy starting point. A variety of signage, from metal shop signage to hand-painted trucks, all played a part in Gotham's creation.

In 2002, when *GQ*'s exclusive licence ended, HF&J marketed Gotham as a commercial typeface. Its nostalgic yet contemporary and functional aesthetic meant that it was soon adopted for use in print, identities, newspapers and packaging, to name just a few of its many applications. Nominated as the 'font of the decade' by *USA Today*, it gained wider success when used in Barack Obama's 2008 presidential campaign ('Change') and again in his 2012 'Forward' re-election campaign.

Avenir vs Gotham

[p. 136] [p. 188]

These are two studies in straightforward clarity. **Avenir** is Adrian Frutiger's attempt to tame some of the strict geometry of Futura. As such, the typeface is kinder to blocks of text and more approachable overall. Still, it's a modernist, geometric design. **Gotham**, on the other hand, achieves a plainness and simplicity from an entirely different approach. Its upper case was inspired by the sturdy, no-nonsense lettering of early twentieth-century architects and journeyman sign makers. For the lower case, Tobias Frere-Jones followed a model closer to Avenir, but it's much larger on the body than the predecessor.

The upper- and lower-case 'K' from Avenir have diagonals that meet at the stem. Gotham's leg extends from its arm.

One of the few letters in Gotham that could be considered particularly distinctive, the vertex of the 'M' comes to a point above the baseline.

MQKRjgf39 Gotham
MQKRjgf39 Avenir

Rjgf39

While they share very similar lower-case letterforms, Avenir has more moderate proportions compared to Gotham's very large x-height and short descenders.

Avenir's caps are patterned on classical Roman proportions with varying widths (letters with a stem are narrow, while round characters are wide). This results in a relatively high-waisted 'P' and 'R'. Gotham has an upper case with very uniform widths (the 'R' is nearly as wide as the 'O').

Avenir has round dots. Gotham has square dots.

Following the proportions of a traditional book face, Avenir's ascenders reach above the cap height. Gotham's compact ascenders are only as high as its caps, and because the x-height is so large it results in squat letterforms like the 'f'.

In the numerals, Avenir is closer to its Futura model: relatively narrow, with circular rounds and straight strokes on the '6' and '9'. Gotham's figures are wider, following the even proportions of the caps, resulting in oval rounds. Gotham also has a flat-topped '3'.

Helvetica

MAX MIEDINGER, EDUARD HOFFMANN · HAAS TYPE FOUNDRY · 1957

Helvetica is possibly the most widely used (and certainly the most famous) typeface in the world, adored and loathed in equal measures by designers and typographers everywhere. The neutral appearance, distinctive clean lines and clear legibility of Helvetica make it an easy spot to even the most relaxed font-spotter.

A true 'global' typeface, Helvetica was developed in 1957 by Swiss type designer **Max Miedinger** and **Eduard Hoffmann** of the **Haas Type Foundry** with the intention to create a new Sans Serif typeface to compete with the established Akzidenz Grotesk (p. 122). When launched, the typeface was originally called Neue Haas Grotesk, but when Linotype later adopted the typeface, they not only revised the design to work on their system but renamed it Helvetica (a derivation of 'Swiss') so as to appeal to a wider international market. In 1983, the original cut was redesigned and relaunched by Linotype as Neue Helvetica, a much larger, self-contained and structured font family (51 fonts in 9 weights) which adopted the numbering system employed by Univers (p. 224) to designate width, weight and stroke thickness.

Helvetica has been employed by many international organizations, including American Airlines, Apple, BMW, Lufthansa, Microsoft, the New York Subway and Panasonic to name but a tiny fraction.

CATEGORY: Sans Serif

CLASSIFICATION: Grotesque

COUNTRY OF ORIGIN: Switzerland

DISTINGUISHING MARKS: Moderate x-height; horizontal or vertically cut terminals at 90° angles; double-storey 'a'; square dot over letter 'i'; monocular 'g'; near circular rounded shapes; mildly curving leg on 'R'; low stroke contrast

FURTHER SIGHTINGS: A truly universal typeface, easily spotted in most environments

NOT TO BE CONFUSED WITH: Akzidenz Grotesk (p. 122); Arial (p. 128); Univers (p. 224)

OPPOSITE, CLOCKWISE FROM TOP LEFT: From big business to transport, clothing to luxury brands, Helvetica is everywhere. New York Subway signage system; US homeware store Crate & Barrel's delivery truck; American Apparel clothing store; airport wayfinding in Asia.

Subway
MTA New Yo
PERLA EXPRESS INC.
07093
USDOT 810938
Crate&Barrel
登机口 Gates E20 
登机口 Gates E51-E55
登机口 Gates E57-E62
American Apparel

FIELD FACTS_

In 2007, Helvetica became the only typeface to become a movie star. The self-titled film, directed by Gary Hustwit and released to international acclaim, celebrated Helvetica's 50th anniversary with commentary by leading graphic designers from all over the world about the phenomenon that also led to Helvetica being voted number one in FontShop Germany's 'Best Fonts of All Time'.

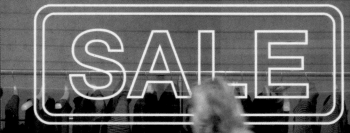

Goodman's
Royal
Green
Guildhall School
Superdry.
Lufthansa
Boeing 737-300
Seeheim-Jugenheim

INTERSTATE
10
WEST
Santa Monica
INTERSTATE
405
NORTH
Sacramento
ONLY
SOUTH
405
L A Airport
Long Beach
ONLY

Interstate

TOBIAS FRERE-JONES · FONT BUREAU · 1993–1994

CATEGORY: Sans Serif

CLASSIFICATION: Grotesque

COUNTRY OF ORIGIN: USA

DISTINGUISHING MARKS: Clipped terminals ('g', 'p', 'q'); oblique terminals on ascenders and descenders; larger x-heights; open counters; 90° angle to curved stroke terminals; slightly condensed

FURTHER SIGHTINGS: AIGA; Invesco Perpetual; Lamborghini; *Los Angeles Times*; Sainsbury's supermarkets; www.salomon.com; www.saucony.com; Smokey Bones; Staten Island Ferry Whitehall Terminal

NOT TO BE CONFUSED WITH: Chalet (p. 154); DIN 1451 (p. 158)

OPPOSITE: The US Federal Highway Administration's signage typeface (FHWA Series font) was behind Tobias Frere-Jones's inspiration for the Interstate collection.

Based around the US federal highway system's signage alphabets (FHWA Series font), Interstate's legibility and immediacy has led to its use in many other applications when fast and clear communication is a necessity.

A key aspect of any successful transport system's typography is to provide a driver with clear information, especially if one is hurtling past in a car at top speed. Frere-Jones took as his starting point the letterforms employed on the US Federal Highway Administration's signage, developing it into a more refined and flexible typeface that works well not only in display and headline scenarios but also in text and screen-based applications.

Working with Cyrus Highsmith, senior designer at the Font Bureau foundry, Frere-Jones has increased the typeface family into an extensive range of 40 styles that includes Compressed and Condensed, and with weights ranging from hairline to ultra black. Its versatility and the striking details it possesses, such as the terminals being cut at angles, have led to its adoption by a number of large corporations for communications and branding purposes.

Freda Sack • The Foundry/Foundry Types

LONDON, UK

The Foundry is one of the original independent type foundries, started in 1989–90 by David Quay and Freda Sack. Both partners of The Foundry continue to develop new typeface designs to expand the font collection. The Foundry has since become the trademark of this successful, reputable typeface library – now managed and run by Foundry Types Ltd.

The Foundry designers bring a combination of traditional and modern approaches to font design and implementation, having worked in every technological stage of type design since hot metal, particularly with digital font technology. Their pre-digital experience and skills lend integrity and quality to their type design.

Q: When was it you became aware of type and typography and how was it you became a type designer?

A: I have been an avid reader since an early age, and always interested in language and literature. I took calligraphy during art classes at school – nothing particularly creative or innovative, just straightforward hands (italic, etc.) and how to lay out poems and texts, sometimes with supporting illustration. I trained at Maidstone College of Art, in the School of Printing, on a graphic communication course, which was in effect pure typography. It included learning all the printing techniques and machine technology, with practical tasks – almost everything we designed was carried through to print by 'hot metal' setting and various methods of printing. This produced an intuitive understanding of form and function in typography and a tactile relationship with type and all its idiosyncrasies.

I didn't really set out to become a type designer – when I left college I 'fell' into type design when I was offered a job at Letraset, which was at the time a local company in Kent. The 'job' entailed using my 'artistic' skills as a photographic retoucher [one of the technical stages in the creation of dry transfer lettering, then the industry standard for creating artwork]. This entitled me to a 'union card' allowing me to work in the industry. The intention was that I would progress to the type design studio, which I did after a short period of time. That was the start, though I haven't stopped learning since with the many technological advances and changes of methodology over the years.

OPPOSITE TOP LEFT, BOTTOM MIDDLE, TOP RIGHT: The Brunel typeface developed for Britain's Network Rail organization.

OPPOSITE BOTTOM LEFT: Freda Sack, type designer and co-founder of The Foundry and her company Foundry Types.

OPPOSITE BOTTOM FAR RIGHT: Corporate typeface design for the World Wildlife Fund.

Paddir

Isambard

Kingdom

Brunel

WORLD WILDLIFE FUND

Climate change	CLIMATE CHANGE
Earth Hour	EARTH HOUR
Living Planet	LIVING PLANET
Global forest & trade	GLOBAL FOREST & TRADE

Q: How has your earlier pre-digital experience in typeface development benefitted your Foundry Types output?

A: The number of technological innovations have been numerous, from dry transfer to phototypesetting, through to the digital era, in which I was involved with helping to make the first type design applications more user-friendly. Printing and production methods, and the materials used, have also influenced how type is produced and employed. Having worked in 'hot metal', the reasoning behind all type measurement, spacing, kerning, leading, setting and so on was second nature to me. Starting typeface ideas in a sketchbook, developing them through to finished drawings on a drawing board, and then creating the actual artwork has given me a relationship with form that I believe would not have developed otherwise. With these skills it is possible to create 'perfect curves', and make adjustments as fine as a human hair, which may sound like it wouldn't make a great deal of difference to a shape, but believe me it does. Having had to accommodate many changes in technology, application and materials means that I always take these very important practical issues into consideration in the creation of a typeface design. Therefore I think that my pre-digital experience lends integrity, quality, and 'a human aspect' to the type designs we create.

RIGHT: Detailed workings for The Foundry's Foundry Wilson Serif typeface.

Q: Over the years, The Foundry/Foundry Types has earned itself a well-deserved reputation for creating innovative, functional, high-quality fonts. How did it come about and could you describe its design activities?

A: The Foundry is one of the original independent type foundries and was started as a partnership in 1989/90 by myself and David Quay. The Foundry is now the trademark of our successful, reputable typeface library, which is managed and run by my company Foundry Types Ltd. We both continue to develop new font designs to add to The Foundry collection.

David Quay and I met when I was working in Letraset's London studio. David had been asked to submit some letterforms created for book jackets to be developed into typefaces. He wasn't a typeface designer – he was an extremely good lettering artist, which is different – and it was my job in the Letraset studio to finesse his drawings and artwork them into whole typefaces. This process clearly fascinated him. When I left Letraset to freelance I collaborated on a few projects with David and eventually we worked together as partners. By the late 1990s David had become more involved in teaching, especially abroad, and the nature of our partnership had evolved. While we own The Foundry typeface library between us, to which we both add more typefaces as and when, David has his own design practice in Amsterdam, David Quay Design, where he specializes in fine typography and type design, and I run my company Foundry Types Ltd, developing and managing The Foundry library, and continuing to work on typeface commissions.

Q: Having designed typefaces over a number of years, what changes have you seen to typeface development in its design and technological advances?

A: In a career spanning 40 years (it doesn't seem that long) there have been many changes in technology in the creation of typefaces – from hot metal setting and designing typefaces for Letraset rub-down instant lettering to phototypesetting and the creation of massive character sets for OpenType format, including non-Latins.

I trained on, and was experienced in, the first digital applications for creating fonts, the IKARUS system – a digital tool to mechanically render artwork for reproduction. I initially designed and drew typefaces as usual, and used this new software to 'translate' the design into a digital carrier – a process, when mastered, that reduced the development time of a typeface. The design process soon became entirely digital (though still following through from hand-drawn designs).

I personally worked with the developers at URW in Hamburg to make the alphanumeric system, as far as possible, more visually intuitive and user-friendly for type designers. This system was the basis for the various type development applications used today. The new technology that was the downfall of many of the established, traditional type manufacturers has allowed small type foundries, and even individuals, to produce fonts. This, together with huge changes in communication through the World Wide Web, has enabled a new generation of type enthusiasts to make type design a career.

Q: Your typeface collections reflect a wide spectrum of approaches and styles with a number of revivals. Where do you get your ideas for starting a new design or in choosing a typeface to revive?

A: Typeface ideas often choose themselves! When we have a design in mind we try to get the initial concept (ethos or essence) sketched down on paper. Sometimes ideas are triggered by working in a particular genre while in the process of concept development for commissions. This was the case with Foundry Sterling, which came about through a number of signage-specific typefaces.

Time dictates when and if an idea is developed to become one of The Foundry typefaces. We have a drawer full of typefaces at various stages! Then there may be something 'in the wind' that reminds us we have just the concept sitting in there, it's the right time and we make an intense effort to develop it.

The Architype Collections came about only because it was suggested that we create some headline typefaces – we were reluctant at first because we had each designed many for Letraset. We became persuaded, after hitting on a theme that we both shared a passion for: the early years of the European avant-garde including De Stijl and the Bauhaus, and art movements more generally from the 1920s to 1940s. References were chosen from original sources and drawn and developed as near to the original as possible, and certain characters were drawn and added to make a workable character set. The original faces were seen to have been very groundbreaking, and we thought we could revive a few and credit the sources, making it an educational exercise at the same time.

Q: A number of your typefaces are digital versions created from legendary Dutch graphic and type designer Wim Crouwel's experimental alphabets of the 1950s and 1960s. How did this collaboration come about and what were the challenges involved in digitizing these letterforms?

A: Our relationship with Crouwel came about in 1996, when David travelled to Amsterdam and managed to have a meeting with him, initially to invite him to give a lecture in London to our society, ISTD (the International Society of Typographic Designers). Crouwel readily agreed. David then talked to him about the typefaces he had designed while a partner in Total Design, and was amazed to learn that none of his work was available digitally. We thought that Crouwel's typeface work was of major importance, especially his New Alphabet which had great significance at the time, when the new computer technology was in its early stages.

David suggested that The Foundry could digitize and license them, and Crouwel agreed to this as well. Along with the New Alphabet, in three weights, there was the Fodor alphabet which Crouwel designed for the Fodor Museum (part of the Stedelijk Museum in Amsterdam), Stedelijk (designed for the Vormgevers exhibition at the Stedelijk Museum) and Gridnik, which was originally designed for Olivetti. We released all six alphabets as Architype 3 – part of our Architype Collections series. Gridnik was quickly picked up by a few designers and we were asked if there were any more weights. This led us to further develop Gridnik into a separate family of four weights with Crouwel's blessing and collaboration. Foundry Gridnik has since proved to be a remarkably successful font.

The Foundry digitized Gridnik from the original pen and ink drawings that Crouwel's father had artworked with amazing precision – all the tiny rounded corners were perfect. Crouwel had developed the original idea for Olivetti as a typewriter font, using a basic grid of seven units. Employing multiples of seven, he arrived at a stem width of 56. From his system it was relatively easy to calculate the new weights that would be entirely in keeping with Crouwel's thinking, and also to design extra characters to complete character sets. Throughout our collaboration with Crouwel, we worked to his strict instructions on how the typefaces should appear, and of course we credit him, and he receives royalties from us.

BELOW TOP LEFT: Wim Crouwel, designer, artist, professor and museum director. Regarded as one of the most important designers in Dutch graphic design history, he is noted for his work for the Stedelijk Museum in Amsterdam from 1956 until 1982.

BELOW TOP MIDDLE: Stamp for PostNL (Dutch Mail), designed by Robin Uleman employing **Foundry Gridnik**.

BOTTOM LEFT, FAR RIGHT: London's Science Museum rebrand by design studio Johnson Banks with unique typeface design **SM Grid**, developed together with Foundry Types.

NOC✱NSF 100 JAAR
NEDERLAND 2012
1
✱SEOEL 1988
NICO RIENKS NAM VIJF MAAL DEEL AAN DE OLYMPISCHE SPELEN. HIJ WON TWEE KEER GOUD. ÉÉN MAAL IN SEOEL 1988 EN ÉÉN MAAL IN ATLANTA 1996. HIJ HEEFT DE BESTE ERELIJST VAN HET NEDERLANDSE ROEIEN.

SCIENCE MUSEUM
ABCDEFGHIJKLMN
OPQRSTUVWXYZÆŒ
abcdefghijklmn
opqrstuvwxyz

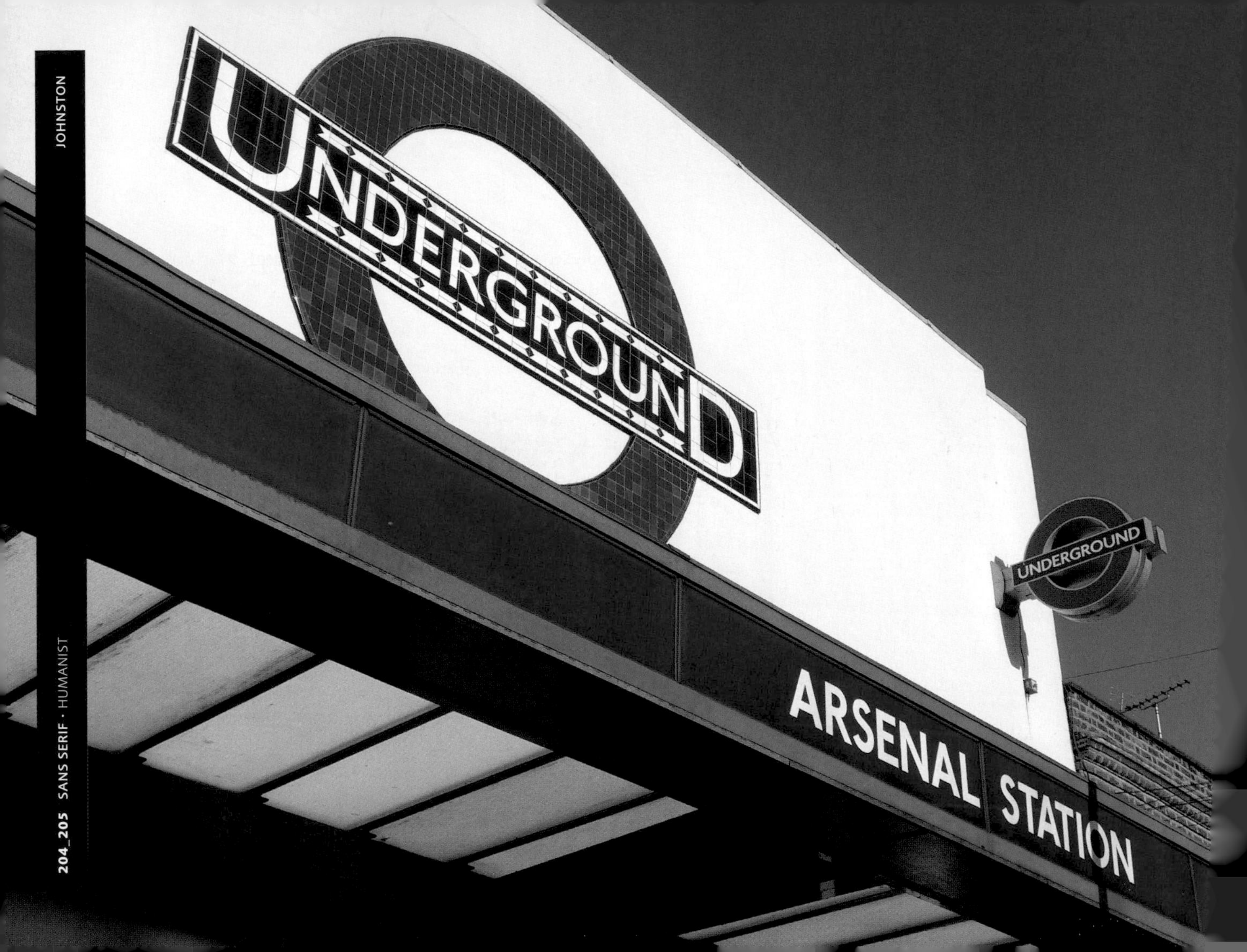
UNDERGROUND
UNDERGROUND
ARSENAL STATION

Johnston

EDWARD JOHNSTON · 1916

CATEGORY: Sans Serif

CLASSIFICATION: Humanist

COUNTRY OF ORIGIN: UK

DISTINGUISHING MARKS: Geometric; circular appearance; upper-case 'J' sits on baseline (Gill sits below); angled tail on 'Q' cuts into counter; straight leg on 'R'; crossbar at top of '3'; diamond-shaped dot at top of 'i' and 'j'; curl at bottom of lower-case 'l'

FURTHER SIGHTINGS: Just visit London and catch a bus, train or the Tube

NOT TO BE CONFUSED WITH: Gill Sans (p. 186)

OPPOSITE: New Johnston with the original Johnston, now available today as Johnston Underground by the P22 Type Foundry, a new revival of the earlier typeface being licensed to the foundry for release by the London Transport Museum.

Designed by Eric Gill's teacher, the eponymous Johnston is recognized for being the corporate typeface of the London Underground transport system. Gill contributed to the design of this highly recognizable face, which later had a direct bearing on his own work with Gill Sans.

Commissioned in 1913, with the typeface introduced in 1916, Johnston's brief was to create a corporate typeface for the then titled Underground Electric Railways Company of London. He was asked that the design not only be modern in appearance but that it also distinguish itself from the typography of advertising posters and hoardings at the time.

Originally called Underground, Edward Johnston's Humanist Sans Serif design was later renamed Johnston and came in just two weights: Ordinary and Heavy. The typeface that is used today is a variant called New Johnston, whose design was undertaken by Japanese type designer Eiichi Kono at design consultancy Banks & Miles in 1979. The new family, which carries the weights Bold, Medium and Light and replaced entirely the earlier typeface, is used across all public transport in London.

Despite New Johnston being an exclusive typeface, there are a number of 'versions' of Johnston commercially available. ITC Johnston is a variant created by UK type designers Richard Dawson and Dave Farey that carries the same weights and italics.

Kabel

RUDOLF KOCH · 1927

Influenced by the simple stone-carved letterforms of ancient Rome, Kabel's design is formed from their geometric shapes and also incorporates design elements from the Art Deco period, which help to stand it apart from other modernist types of the period.

Rudolf Koch's precisely crafted design of the Kabel typeface was first released by the German foundry Klingspor in 1927. Competition was strong then among the European type foundries as they worked in earnest to create new and unique Sans Serif type designs to capture the attention of the market. Kabel's Art Deco influences – the distinctive slanted crossbar on the lower-case 'e' and unusually styled lower-case 'g' with an open counter on the loop – contrast with similar modernist types of that period, such as Futura.

Two distinctive features of its design are the smaller x-height, which exaggerates the upper case (although in the later ITC release the x-height is increased for American advertising tastes) and the angular stroke endings. This last element gives it a quirky, fun dynamic, creating movement in the appearance of the characters when set. As such, with its clean lines and bouncing personality, Kabel is often used as the basis for commercial logos, advertising headlines and on-screen titling.

CATEGORY: Sans Serif

CLASSIFICATION: Geometric

COUNTRY OF ORIGIN: Germany

DISTINGUISHING MARKS: Monoweight geometric appearance; slanted terminals; slanted crossbar on lower-case 'e'; crossed central stems on upper-case 'W'; distinctive lower-case 'g' with open counter on loop; curved ear on lower-case 'g'; circular bowls

FURTHER SIGHTINGS: Monopoly; Toronto Maple Leafs hockey team; *Yellow Submarine* and *Lost in Translation* movies; NBC logotype; L'eggs pantyhose; UHU adhesives

NOT TO BE CONFUSED WITH: Chalet (p. 154); Futura (p. 180); Gill Sans (p. 186)

OPPOSITE: Kabel employed in the Piggly Wiggly logotype, an American self-service grocery store with sites across the States.

piggly wiggly

FIELD FACTS_

The IBM Selectric typewriter was a groundbreaking piece of technology; one could almost say it partly contributed to bridging the gap between the traditional typewriter and modern DTP (desktop publishing). Instead of traditional type bars, the Selectric employed a 'golf ball' with the characters applied to its outer casing. This was extremely sophisticated – whereas before the typewriter came with a fixed type style and size, the golf ball could be replaced with differing font sizes and typefaces, giving users a choice over the appearance of their documents.

Letter Gothic

ROGER ROBERSON · **MONOTYPE** · 1956–1962

CATEGORY: Sans Serif

CLASSIFICATION: Gothic

COUNTRY OF ORIGIN: USA

DISTINGUISHING MARKS: Curved serif on 'p', 'q' and 'r'; condensed appearance; thin stroke weight; extended horizontal bar on 'i' and 'j'

FURTHER SIGHTINGS: Seen when a raw and no-nonsense type approach is required

NOT TO BE CONFUSED WITH: American Typewriter (p. 26); Courier (p. 64); DIN 1451 (p. 158)

OPPOSITE: Letter Gothic possesses an unrefined and raw aesthetic but obviously that was far from the case concerning its design background and original intended application.

Developed for use on IBM typewriters, this monospaced typeface reflects the restrictions of its original usage with even letter spacing and condensed capitals.

Originally inspired by Optima, the initial design had flared stems and was to be used on IBM Selectric electric typewriters. The difficulty of designing typefaces for use on a typewriter is that every character's width and the space either side all have to be equal, so a 'w' has to fit into the same space as an 'i', causing a great degree of difficulty when designing the characters. Previously, Serifs were favoured for typewriters because the size of the serifs could be adjusted to fit the space available. Letter Gothic was different, however, in that it was conceived as a Sans Serif, making its design much more of a challenge. Roberson, who was an engineer at IBM, worked hard to achieve the balance between letter spacing and readability. The removal of all baseline serifs to create a Sans Serif resulted in a condensed character set – a characteristic more noticeable in the upper-case set, which always requires more room.

Supplied in two weights, both with italics, the monospaced Letter Gothic is ideal for tabular lining of numerals and also for use with technical data. Its engineered look has been much favoured by designers and typographers who wish for an unfinished, distressed quality to their designs and when set in paragraphs.

FF Meta

ERIK SPIEKERMANN · FONTFONT · 1991

A hugely influential typeface and one originally intended for use by Deutsche Bundespost, the German post office, FF Meta has often been dubbed the 'Helvetica of the nineties' and has over time expanded to include a huge range of weights and styles that meets every need and purpose.

In 1985, while renowned typographer, graphic and type designer **Erik Spiekermann** was working at design consultancy Sedley Place, a commission was given to rebrand Deutsche Bundepost. A requirement of the brief was the creation of a new, distinctive corporate Sans Serif typeface that could be read at small point sizes on low-quality paper stocks, in order to save space when employed. As one of the largest companies in Europe, much of Deutsche Bundespost's printing was done at local offices and invariably on laser printers, which made high-quality reproduction and economy important requirements of the design. In addition, it was requested that the new design should not be confused with other Sans Serif typefaces, notably Helvetica.

Working closely with the design team at Sedley Place, Spiekermann designed and produced a typeface titled PT55, although it was never taken up by the client for fear of 'causing unrest' and so lay dormant. Spiekermann, who by then had co-founded his own brand of fonts, **FontFont**, and the company FontShop International in 1989/1990, rescued the design, refined the typeface further and launched it in 1991 as FF Meta.

CATEGORY: Sans Serif

CLASSIFICATION: Humanist

COUNTRY OF ORIGIN: Germany

DISTINGUISHING MARKS: Slightly narrower than other Sans Serifs; large dot over 'i' and 'j'; bent tips on ascenders 'b', 'h', 'k', 'l' and 't'; hooked foot on 'l'; diagonal terminals on lower-case 'b', 'd', 'f', 't'; open bowl/loop on lower-case 'g'

FURTHER SIGHTINGS: Across the Berlin subway system

NOT TO BE CONFUSED WITH: Frutiger (p. 176); Interstate (p. 196); Knockout (p. 288)

OPPOSITE: FF Meta was one of FontFont's earliest releases and quickly garnered critical acclaim. It was one of the first digital typefaces to include Old Style figures and its legibility, humanist details, informality, economy and rapidly expanding family of now over 60 fonts have won many admirers. Shown here employed on a public transport map for Zurich, Switzerland.

FIELD FACTS_

FF Meta was named after a studio Erik Spiekermann headed up at the time, MetaDesign. The Deutsche Bundespost, the original client, never took up using Meta and went on to appoint an existing typeface for their communications – Frutiger – which they still use to this day (p. 176).

MacBook Pro

Apple Campus
One Infinite Loop

5,000

st successful Mac

Myriad

ROBERT SLIMBACH, CAROL TWOMBLY · ADOBE, LINOTYPE · 1992

CATEGORY: Sans Serif

CLASSIFICATION: Humanist

COUNTRY OF ORIGIN: USA

DISTINGUISHING MARKS: Round dot over letter 'i' and 'j' (Frutiger has square dots); minimal stroke contrast; large x-height; curved tail on upper-case 'R'; angled terminal on lower-case 'f' (Frutiger has a vertical terminal); angled uprights on upper-case 'M'

FURTHER SIGHTINGS: Adobe logo; Chevron; LinkedIn; Walmart; Gmail; Rolls-Royce; Cambridge University; Norwegian car licence plates

NOT TO BE CONFUSED WITH: Bliss (p. 150); Frutiger (p. 176)

Often compared to, and also often confused with, Frutiger, Myriad was commissioned by Adobe when they sought to create a new generic Sans Serif. Since its launch it has become popular globally for text and display typography.

In 1992, Myriad was launched. Its subtle humanist design led to its adoption by numerous designers as an alternative to the harder Swiss types that existed and as a change to the over-used Humanist and Geometric types such as Gill, Futura and Frutiger (which it borrows the most from). Thanks to its generic and friendly tone – not at all controversial in its appearance and so flexible with a mind-boggling 800-plus glyphs per font – it was selected by many global companies as a typeface that would work consistently across numerous languages in print and online.

Myriad was released by Adobe as part of their Adobe Originals series and produced as a Multiple master font (an Adobe font technology that allowed a typeface to be created in different styles and weights from the one font file). The original format was revolutionary as it gave the user the opportunity to create custom variations of Myriad based on weight, width and style, although this has been replaced by the OpenType version Myriad Pro.

Most notably, perhaps, Apple Computers employed Myriad (albeit with tweaks) as their corporate typeface in 2002, replacing their original Apple Garamond.

OPPOSITE: Now synonymous with the Apple brand, Myriad's approachable tone and flexibility have ensured its position as a modern classic.

Liebe
Angst
Sex
Trauer
Burg
Wut
Kampf
Gift
Huren
Blut
Frage
Beatles
Herz
www.burgtheater.at
IHRE SORGEN
MÖCHTEN WIR HABEN
WIENER STÄDTISCHE
Er
darf
Burg
kann
www.burgtheater.at
Wien hat eine neue Burg ach schön a so hm aha
Liebe
Angst
Trauer
Wut
Welt
Burg

Neutraface

CHRISTIAN SCHWARTZ · HOUSE INDUSTRIES · 2002

CATEGORY: Sans Serif

CLASSIFICATION: Geometric

COUNTRY OF ORIGIN: USA

DISTINGUISHING MARKS: Small x-height (Display version); low positioning of upper-case crossbars on 'A' and 'E'; long extenders; oversized bowl on 'P' and 'R'

FURTHER SIGHTINGS: Shake Shack restaurant chain, New York; *Quantum of Solace* movie; OHSU building, Portland; *Young Victoria* movie poster; Mikkeller Bar, Copenhagen

NOT TO BE CONFUSED WITH: Chalet (p. 154); Interstate (p. 196); FF Meta (p. 210)

OPPOSITE: For the Burgtheater Wien, a highly influential playwright theatre in Vienna, Austria, Raffinerie AG für Gestaltung developed a new corporate design based on an infinitely variable logo system that employed Neutraface at its core.

From leading American type foundry House Industries, the Neutraface typeface family was inspired by the typography employed on the modernist commercial buildings created by Austrian American architect Richard Neutra (1892–1970).

Richard Neutra's architecture is famed for its functional minimalism and clean, geometric lines and forms. House Industries' Christian Schwartz, working closely with colleagues Ken Barber and Andy Cruz, took the letterforms Neutra had employed on his architectural drawings and the signage on his constructions and developed them into complete alphabets. Schwartz also worked closely with Neutra's son and former practice partner, Dion Neutra, who assisted in the typeface's development. Inspired by Neutra's designs, it also draws heavily from other Geometric type designs, such as Futura. Schwartz was tasked with the challenge of creating a complementary lower-case design where none had existed before.

Since its release in 2002, the clean linear geometry of Neutraface has made it extremely popular and it is one of the foundry's biggest success stories to date. Although conceived as a headline and display face, a number of variations have been created including a text variant, a Condensed and a Slab Serif (p. 190).

New Rail Alphabet

HENRIK KUBEL, SCOTT WILLIAMS, MARGARET CALVERT, JOCK KINNEIR · A2-TYPE · 1965/2009

A revival of the British Rail alphabet created by design partnership Kinneir Calvert in the mid-1960s, this prodigious typeface first appeared in Britain's hospitals before being implemented across the country on the National Rail network and was later adopted by Danish rail stations and BAA (British Airports Authority).

In the UK in the 1960s, British designers Margaret Calvert and Jock Kinneir had a huge impact on the aesthetic of Great Britain with their typographic (Transport typeface) and information designs for the nation's motorway and road signage systems. This daunting project was followed up by the design of Rail Alphabet for the signage of rail stations, which was implemented across the country to replace the existing Gill Sans. Both typefaces were inspired by the clean and legible properties that Akzidenz Grotesk (p. 122) possessed.

In the 1990s, however, as British Rail was privatized and broken up into smaller companies, each with their own branding typographics, the sighting of the typeface became less commonplace and Railtrack, who owned the stations, replaced the typeface with 'Brunel' (*see* Foundry Types p. 198).

In 2005, Henrik Kubel and Scott Williams of A2-TYPE approached Calvert, with the idea of digitizing Rail Alphabet into a font. The typeface is now available in six weights with non-aligning numerals and italics.

CATEGORY: Sans Serif

CLASSIFICATION: Grotesque

COUNTRY OF ORIGIN: UK

DISTINGUISHING MARKS: Slightly narrower than other Grotesques such as Helvetica Neue; taller x-height; reduced stroke contrast over other Grotesques; horizontal terminal on lower-case 'a'

FURTHER SIGHTINGS: British Rail Stations; NHS Hospitals

NOT TO BE CONFUSED WITH: Helvetica (p. 194); Univers (p. 224)

OPPOSITE: New Rail Alphabet, in use at a UK rail station. The typeface's original designers Jock Kinneir and Margaret Calvert were responsible for designing the signing system, the lettering, and the relevant visual identity manual pages (working directly with British Rail, within specifications set by Design Research Unit, an early British design consultancy).

FIELD FACTS_

Calvert and Kinneir are noted for their groundbreaking designs for their Transport typeface and the graphical information systems which revolutionized Britain's road network signage. Their system of coordinated colours, shapes, symbols and consistent grids and coherent typographical hierarchies set the benchmark internationally and greatly influenced designers in other countries.

HAMMER
UCLA
MADE IN
L.A.
Westwood

HAMMER
MUSEUM
UCLA
ALL
OF
THIS
AND
NOTHING
JANUARY 30 — APRIL 24, 2011
HAMMER

ITC Officina Sans

ERIK SPIEKERMANN, OLE SCHÄFER, JUST VAN ROSSUM · ITC · 1990

CATEGORY: Sans Serif

CLASSIFICATION: Humanist

COUNTRY OF ORIGIN: Germany

DISTINGUISHING MARKS:
Slightly heavier stroke weight on book faces; slightly narrow; pronounced dots over lower-case 'i' and 'j'; standard lower-case 'g'; horizontal bar on upper-case 'J'; regular widths

FURTHER SIGHTINGS:
www.wawa.com

NOT TO BE CONFUSED WITH:
Bliss (p. 150); Letter Gothic (p. 208)

OPPOSITE: The Hammer Museum, Los Angeles, USA, employing ITC Officina Sans as its corporate typeface employed on its logotype to all branding and marketing communications.

Designed to be employed on office documentation and business communications, and therefore to withstand the perils of low-resolution devices such as laser printers and photocopying, ITC Officina Sans was released with a Slab Serif version with the same design solutions inherent in its forms.

Motivated by his work on the typeface for Deutsche Bundespost (*see* FF Meta, p. 210) and the designs of Letter Gothic and Courier, **Erik Spiekermann**'s Officina project incorporated similar objectives to those typefaces designed to work well on low-quality devices. Its heavier than normal stroke, large counters and regular widths and spacing allowed Officina to work at much smaller sizes while retaining legibility and readability in both the Serif and Sans Serif versions.

Despite both the Serif and Sans Serif initially being released together as only two weights, Regular and Bold (with italics), Officina soon gained sufficient popularity among designers to justify the creation of further weights. **Just van Rossum** had assisted in completing the Sans design with Spiekermann but then later **Schäfer** added additional weights post-launch in the mid-1990s. The range now includes Medium, Extra Bold and Black weights and matching italics for both Sans and Serif versions.

Optima

HERMANN ZAPF · LINOTYPE · 1958

Inspired by the plaques carved into Italian gravestones from the 1530s, the elegant Optima was Hermann Zapf's most successful design. It crosses the line between Serif and Sans Serif thanks to the elegant calligraphy-inspired tapering of his letter strokes.

Optima may have begun life as scribblings on the back of a 1,000-lire banknote, but its success can be attributed to its clean, simple, elegant strokes and its classical Roman proportions – qualities that make it an all-purpose face suitable for display, headline and text settings. The flared terminals act to replace serifs so it works well in both modern and classical contexts. It possesses a warmth and style that has proved appealing to many designers – it is a popular choice for the packaging of beauty and bathroom products. That said, its use has been widespread and varied, and its carved, classical presentation can be seen on many memorials and carvings.

The type was originally cut by renowned punchcutter August Rosenberger at the D. Stempel AG type foundry in Frankfurt. In 2002, 50 years after his first sketches, Zapf revisited his Optima design with Linotype's Akira Kobayashi, and the redesigned version was launched as Optima Nova. This new family featured additional weights (Light, Demi and Heavy) and also removed the Extra Black weight. Aided by the advantages of being able to work digitally, additional character sets were created along with a set of real italics, which replaced the original sloped Romans.

CATEGORY: Sans Serif

CLASSIFICATION: Humanist

COUNTRY OF ORIGIN: Germany

DISTINGUISHING MARKS: Tapering strokes; Roman proportions to upper-case characters; double-storey 'g'; high contrast; near vertical stress; prominent flaring on terminals; angled terminal on lower-case 't'; moderate x-height; moderate width

FURTHER SIGHTINGS: Estée Lauder; Aston Martin

NOT TO BE CONFUSED WITH: Albertus (p. 24); Friz Quadrata (p. 70)

OPPOSITE: Optima employed for America's participants and fallen of the Vietnam War at the Vietnam Veterans Memorial, Washington.

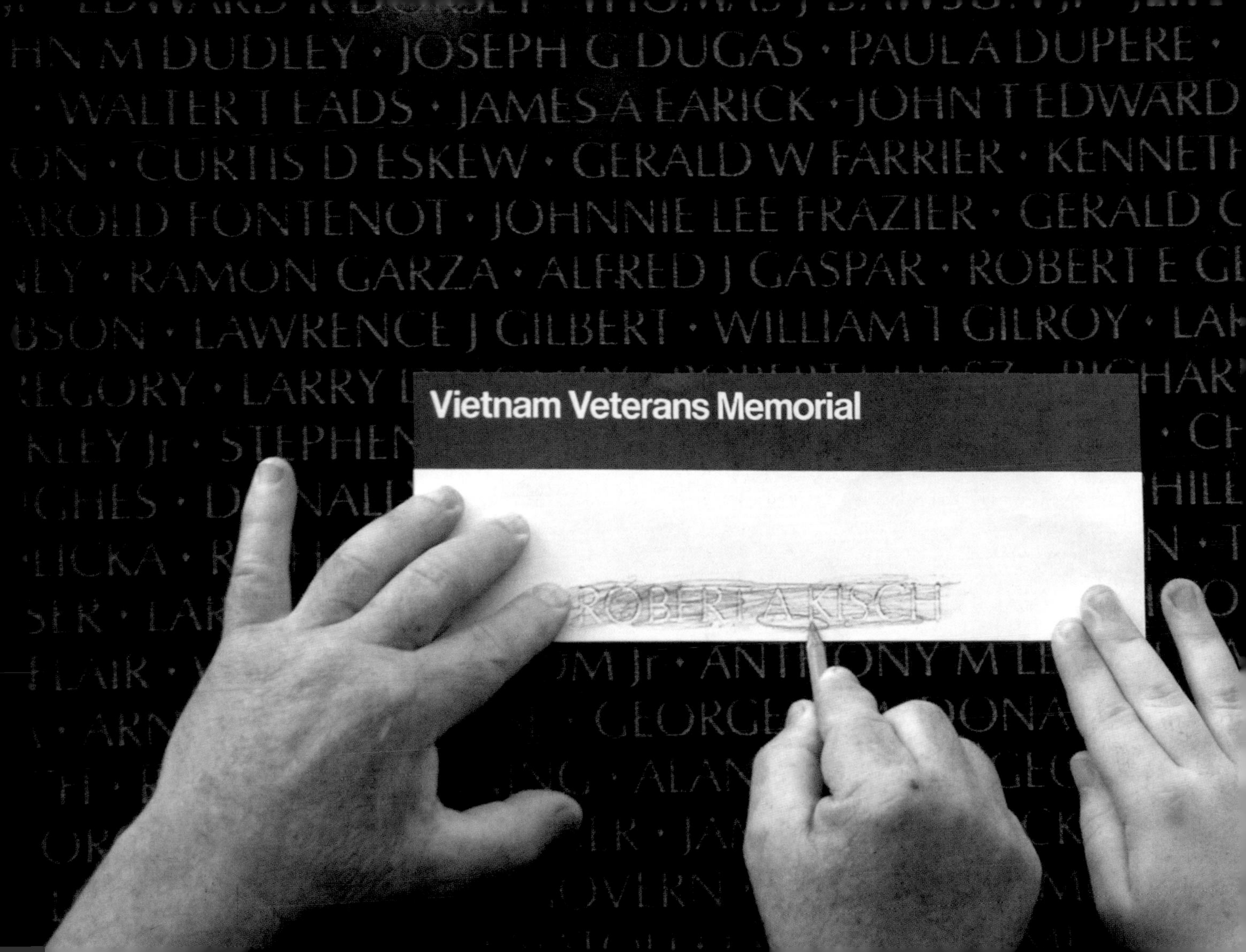

Vietnam Veterans Memorial

ROBERT A KISCH

FIELD FACTS_

Otl Aicher's Rotis is named after the small village in the Allgäu region of Germany where he has lived and worked since 1972. Aicher is also well known for his design for the 1972 Munich Olympic Games; as part of the commission he developed an international system of pictograms to identify sports and other activities and services, all of which contributed to its status as a design classic.

Rotis Sans Serif

OTL AICHER · MONOTYPE · 1989

CATEGORY: Sans Serif

CLASSIFICATION: Grotesque

COUNTRY OF ORIGIN: Germany

DISTINGUISHING MARKS: Condensed proportions; small bowl and raised bar on lower-case 'e'; flattened lower loop on 'c'; square dot over 'ı' and 'j'; arms of upper-case 'K' meet at stem; flattened tail on upper-case 'Q'

FURTHER SIGHTINGS: Foster Associates; Montreal city logo; Nokia; Bulthaup; Stellenbosch University, SA; Metro Bilbao; Manchester Metropolitan University; Accenture

NOT TO BE CONFUSED WITH: Frutiger (p. 176); Letter Gothic (p. 208)

OPPOSITE: Clean and precise, **Rotis Sans Serif** has often been allied with lifestyle, design and architectural products.

Otl Aicher's unified typeface family of Rotis for the Agfa foundry extends from a full Serif through a Semi Serif and Semi Sans to a full Sans Serif design. Aicher's intention was to create a typeface family that would maximize legibility across all styles and be interchangeable, fulfilling all typographic requirements under one roof.

The four families share similar weights, heights and proportions but evolve, almost morph, into the next family as serifs reduce and strokes vary. The revolutionary approach that Aicher took came under criticism (and still does) from some quarters, with traditionalists feeling that a coordinated approach in blending Serifs and Sans Serifs and modifying letterforms in such a methodical manner does not work for the better. However, the typeface has proved not only to work incredibly well in most applications but the whole family is an immensely popular choice for designers and typographers. A keynote indicator of Rotis is its distinctive lower-case 'c', where the bottom stroke flattens out along the baseline.

Univers

ADRIAN FRUTIGER · LINOTYPE · 1957

Possibly the most notable typeface of the twentieth century, Univers's beautiful, simple elegance and purity of form, partnered with its innovative cataloguing system for weights and styles, has made it one of the keynote typefaces of all time.

Adrian Frutiger began the Univers design as a student in Zurich. Later, while art director at Parisian foundry Deberny & Peignot, he was commissioned to create a Sans Serif for the foundry. Rather than develop and work from existing designs the foundry held, he referred back to his earlier studies and created a new Grotesque that would not only work in display and headline settings but, importantly, would also work in longer texts, a setting in which most Sans Serifs at that time struggled.

Univers was launched in 1957 as a family of 21 typefaces. Its cool, professional tone, neutral appearance and suitability as a text face meant it was widely used. Not only did its modular weights and styles work harmoniously together across the family, but its compatibility with many other fonts of differing styles was a huge boon for graphic designers and typographers.

Another major innovation was Frutiger's use of numerals rather than names to indicate weight, width and slope, and all organized within a 'periodic table' for reference. This was a revolutionary development that has been adopted in many instances for other typefaces.

CATEGORY: Sans Serif

CLASSIFICATION: Grotesque

COUNTRY OF ORIGIN: Germany

DISTINGUISHING MARKS: Moderate x-height; moderate descenders; low contrast; strokes terminate at 90° angles; monocular 'g'; closed apertures; large counters; mildly curving leg on upper-case 'R'; narrow body width

FURTHER SIGHTINGS: Frankfurt International Airport; Montreal metro system; Munich 1972 Olympics branding

NOT TO BE CONFUSED WITH: Arial (p. 128); Helvetica (p. 192)

OPPOSITE: Univers's cool and neutral forms provide any wayfinding system with a precise and clear presentation of directions and messages.

FIELD FACTS_

Adrian Frutiger's impact on modern typography cannot be underestimated. As the designer of the Univers and Frutiger typefaces (among many others), these designs shaped and influenced type design in the latter part of the twentieth century and remain influential today. Frutiger's work is also notable for the invaluable innovation of a two-digit numbering standard system (first seen when Univers was launched) for each typeface, whereby the first numeral indicates the weight and the second the width – for example, Univers 45 (4 = Light; 5 = Roman) and Univers 67 (6 = Bold; 7 = Condensed).

LPG-Bio Markt
20
LECKER · PREISWERT & GESUND
Eingang

VAG Rounded

VOLKSWAGEN AG · LINOTYPE · 1979

CATEGORY: Sans Serif

CLASSIFICATION: Geometric

COUNTRY OF ORIGIN: UK

DISTINGUISHING MARKS:
Even stroke weight; rounded terminals; no italics; circular forms; monoline bold stroke; closed apertures; short ascenders; moderate descenders; long extenders

FURTHER SIGHTINGS:
www.wayfaring.com

NOT TO BE CONFUSED WITH:
Comic Sans (p. 336)

OPPOSITE: VAG Rounded seen in a less than corporate environment. Alternative rounded font types include Helvetica Rounded, as used by Skype (Bold), and Arial Rounded, as used by MySpace (also a Bold variant). Both are companies that wish to strike a friendlier and more upbeat tone with their communications.

Designed as a corporate typeface for German car manufacturer Volkswagen AG (hence VAG), VAG Rounded's approach is a revival of nineteenth-century Grotesques but with the distinctive feature of rounded terminals, which create a softer and more approachable aspect to its appearance.

When the Volkswagen Group (VW) required a distinctive new corporate typeface it involved another carmaker, Audi, to initiate the design process. VW had purchased Audi, but with both companies having distinctive separate typographic identities (Audi at that time were using Times and VW Futura) a decision was made to create a new typeface for the dealerships that had to sell both brands. Given the collaboration between the two large auto companies, a number of individuals were involved in creating VAG Rounded and accreditation has since become confused, leading to conflicting accounts of who was responsible for the design. This didn't prevent the typeface from being employed in a number of contexts, including in some of the group's non-car activities, such as VAG Bank and VAG Leasing.

It was an unusual approach for a car manufacturer to go with such a 'fun' typographical aesthetic, but in order that VW associates and dealerships globally could use the typeface it was released into the public domain. In the late 1980s, VW rebranded and the typeface was dropped, but it still continues to be available and widely used.

Verdana

MATTHEW CARTER, TOM RICKNER · MICROSOFT · 1996

Intentionally designed for on-screen use, Verdana has been crafted for the restraints of pixel resolution rather than from the traditional approach of calligraphy or carving and can be seen as one of the best of the Web fonts.

Verdana was designed in 1996 by renowned type designer **Matthew Carter** for the **Microsoft Corporation**; the brief was to create a new typeface to work solely on screen and at small sizes. Carter's use of a large x-height, wide proportions, open letter spacing and large counters all enabled the font to be read at small sizes, even at 9 point. Another factor in the success of Carter's design was ensuring that characters that could appear similar had enough distinction between them as to not confuse, for example, '1' has a bar added to its baseline to separate it from a lower-case 'l'.

Carter worked closely with **Tom Rickner** on the end design for the hand-hinting of Verdana, the refinement of the type on screen at differing sizes (a painstaking and highly specialist task). When released as part of Microsoft's Windows operating system and in software such as Office and Internet Explorer it soon took off and was often employed in website design and online materials. The typeface is now bundled on all PCs and Apple computers.

CATEGORY: Sans Serif

CLASSIFICATION: Humanist

COUNTRY OF ORIGIN: USA

DISTINGUISHING MARKS: Large x-height; wide proportions; loose letter spacing; horizontal base on '1'; curved tail on 'Q'; horizontal bar on top of lower-case 'j'; double-storey 'a'; square dot over 'i'; upper-case 'R' has two variations, straight and curved tail

FURTHER SIGHTINGS: Finnish news site www.iltasanomat.fi

NOT TO BE CONFUSED WITH: Frutiger (p. 176)

OPPOSITE: The original Verdana, designed by David Berlow and David Jonathan Ross of the Font Bureau with Matthew Carter in consultation, predated **Verdana Pro**, which was released in 2011. This new version, available in OpenType, possessed many more typographic features such as true small capitals, ligatures, fractions, Old Style figures, and expanded and condensed ranges of weights.

FIELD FACTS_

In 2009, Swedish furniture maker and flat-pack aficionados IKEA changed their corporate typeface from their IKEA Sans (a customized Futura) to Microsoft's Verdana. IKEA's aim was to present a consistent presentation online and in print but the replacement of the typeface with what was deemed a Web font sent the type and design communities into passionate dismay.

With much press coverage, it even resulted in an online petition being created demanding the decision be reversed or anything but Verdana chosen. At the time of writing this has 7,081 signatures.

PATISSERIE VALERIE
Est. 192
EST. 1926
EST. 1926

Display

OPPOSITE: The organic and Art Nouveau qualities of **Arnold Böcklin** (p. 238) put to good use above a cake shop.

Aachen

COLIN BRIGNALL, ALAN MEEKS · ITC · 1969

Bold and powerful, Aachen's authority in visual communications is unmistakable, wherever it has been used. Its heavy forms were an immediate hit, making it a popular choice for display work that needed to make a statement.

It was designed at the end of the 1960s to be employed in large sizes on display and headline work. Despite drawing inspiration from the period in which it was designed, Aachen still feels remarkably contemporary, especially in view of the recent preference among many graphic designers for ultra-bold lettering in display and poster settings. The design also incorporated influences from earlier times, when wood-block lettering was used in posters and billboards.

Aachen was a co-production between chief designer **Colin Brignall** and his colleague at Letraset, **Alan Meeks**. The first release contained five styles and was offered as dry-transfer lettering sheets. Named after the German town of Aachen, where it was believed Johannes Gutenberg first used movable type, the family was expanded in 1977 to include a range of 15 styles and was also released as phototype fonts. It wasn't until the start of the 1990s that Aachen went digital. Aachen's effectiveness increases when tightly kerned, and when employed with close line spacing can provide considerable typographic impact to any design.

CATEGORY: Serif

CLASSIFICATION: Slab Serif/ Egyptian

COUNTRY OF ORIGIN: UK

DISTINGUISHING MARKS: Heavy appearance, medium contrast; vertical stress; short, bracketed serifs; narrow width; oval 'o' and 'O'; short tail on uppercase 'Q'; small counters

FURTHER SIGHTINGS: *The Departed* film poster; *Pulp Fiction* film logotype; *Machete* film logotype; Papa John's pizza; www.madfoods.com

NOT TO BE CONFUSED WITH: A2 Beckett (p. 244); ITC Machine (p. 298)

OPPOSITE: Bold and a tad brutal, just like the fictional movie character Rambo, Aachen's presence can never be ignored.

FIELD FACTS_

Colin Brignall first started out in work as a fashion photographer. It was in 1964 that he joined Letraset Type Studio (then leaders in graphic arts products) as a photographic technician. With a keen eye and an enthusiasm for type, he rose through the ranks; by 1974 he was working as a type designer and then later became type director, where he oversaw and designed a vast range of typefaces. His font designs include Countdown (1965), Premier, Lightline (1969), Revue (1969), Jenson Old Style (with Freda Sack, 1982) and Werkstatt (1999), to name just a few.

THE FANS

"REG LEWIS SERVED OUT IN THE RHINE DURING THE WAR, BUT WAS
DURING THE WAR MATCHES. HE'D TURN OUT IN THOSE GAMES PL
LANE AFTER HIGHBURY HAD BEEN DAMAGED BY THE LUFTWAFFE
CAREER AT ARSENAL AND

RECORD BOOKS SUGGES
REG SCORED MORE GOAL
ARSENAL SHIRT THAN A
ELSE IN THE CLUB'S HIST

IF YOU INCLUDE YOUTH, RESERVE AND WARTIME GAMES AS W
APPEARANCES. BUT STILL HE NEVER SCORED AS MANY AS HE
BECAUSE OF THE WAR. I GOT HIS AUTOGRAPH ONCE AND CON
A GOAL HE'D SCORED THAT DAY. 'IT DOESN'T FEEL RIGHT', HE
BE RIGHT UNTIL WE'RE BACK AT HIGHBURY WHEN ALL THIS I

HARRY GRAHAM

Agency Gothic

JASON CASTLE · CASTLETYPE · 1990

CATEGORY: Sans Serif

CLASSIFICATION: Square Gothic

COUNTRY OF ORIGIN: USA

DISTINGUISHING MARKS: Condensed squared forms; rounded corners; monoline; open counter on upper-case 'R'; arm and leg of 'K' meet at stem; diagonal strokes of 'M' meet above baseline

FURTHER SIGHTINGS: Arsenal Football Club, UK; *Shutter Island* movie

NOT TO BE CONFUSED WITH: Bank Gothic (p. 240); A2 Beckett (p. 244)

OPPOSITE: Agency Gothic used at the Emirates Stadium, London.

A revival of Morris Fuller Benton's 1933 titling face Agency Gothic for American Type Founders, Agency Gothic CT was undertaken by US type designer Jason Castle for a magazine commission. Over time the family has expanded to include a dynamic display face.

Commissioned by *Publish* magazine, Jason Castle of CastleType created a revival of this dramatic and dynamic display typeface for the journal in 1990, initially with the development of two styles, Agency Gothic Condensed and Agency Gothic Open (an outlined version with drop shadow). Over the years, CastleType have added more weights and styles to the pairing, including Agency Gothic Bold and the popular Agency Gothic Inline, which possesses a strong outer border stroke and hollow infill. The typeface collection now ranges from Light, Medium and Bold to an Inline version and the aforementioned Condensed and Open variants.

Agency Gothic's condensed and squared capital forms make it an appropriate choice when an authoritative and dramatic tone is required. Its 'hard' profile is reminiscent of letterforms employed in communist propaganda posters of the early to mid-twentieth century. All punctuation and numerals are included in the collection, as well as extensions for all European languages that use the Latin alphabet, plus Cyrillic letterforms.

Amelia

STANLEY DAVIS · LINOTYPE · 1965

Before man landed on the moon, Stanley Davis's futuristic typeface, named after his daughter Amelia, set the tone and style for the space race with its rounded organic structure and hi-tech appearance.

Stanley Davis's typeface reflected the zeitgeist at the time of early digital technology, space travel and science fiction. Influenced by 'liquid' MICR (Magnetic Ink Character Recognition) typefaces, characters to be read by magnetic readers and the human eye, its 'teardrop' counters and terminals form unusual shapes to create a distinctive and highly recognizable letterform structure.

Its 'space' aesthetic led to its use on the branding for Moon Boots, a popular fashion spin-off of the NASA astronauts' footwear, and also as the title logotype for The Beatles' *Yellow Submarine*. It is rarely used now due to its dated appearance and immediate 'space' and 'technology' references; you are more likely to find it employed on home-made signs and displays in Internet cafes rather than in a commercial context.

CATEGORY:
Ornamented/Novelty

CLASSIFICATION: Futuristic

COUNTRY OF ORIGIN: USA

DISTINGUISHING MARKS:
Teardrop counters and terminals; rounded organic forms; high stroke contrast

FURTHER SIGHTINGS: tmz.com; The Beatles' *Yellow Submarine*

NOT TO BE CONFUSED WITH:
OCR-B (p. 306)

OPPOSITE: Rounded and organic in form, Amelia's distinctive and quirky appearance makes for an eye-catching typeface and one that possesses a strong 'science-fiction' aesthetic.

FIELD FACTS_

The work of artist Arnold Böcklin was rooted in fantasy and tended to shun realism. His pieces depict a variety of mythical creatures, including sea monsters, nymphs, mermaids and centaurs. His most recognized work is *Die Toteninsel (Isle of the Dead)*, with several versions painted between 1880 and 1886.

Arnold Böcklin

OTTO WEISERT · OTTO WEISERT FOUNDRY · 1904

CATEGORY:
Ornamented/Novelty

CLASSIFICATION: Art Nouveau

COUNTRY OF ORIGIN: Germany

DISTINGUISHING MARKS: Floral, decorative ornamentation and organic character shapes; overlapping crossbars; bowls intersected by diagonal strokes; looped strokes connecting terminals on upper-case 'M'

FURTHER SIGHTINGS: *That '70s Show*; James Blunt's *Back to Bedlam* cover; Patisserie Valerie bakery chain

NOT TO BE CONFUSED WITH:
ITC Benguiat (p. 246)

OPPOSITE: Arnold Böcklin's organic appearance is an appropriate match for this wine bar-cum-shop.

Love it or hate it, Arnold Böcklin's unique visual properties make it a classic and perhaps the best-known example of Art Nouveau letterforms.

Designed in 1904 by the type foundry Otto Weisert in Stuttgart, Germany, the typeface was named in memory of Arnold Böcklin, a Swiss symbolist painter who died three years earlier.

Its ornamental style and hints of floral decoration in its letterforms found favour with graphic designers of the 1960s and 1970s, who used it widely in popular-culture designs, ranging from poster designs to album covers for rock bands.

When created, its decorative and ornate style was much more important than its legibility, hence its application as a display type rather than for reading texts.

Bank Gothic

MORRIS FULLER BENTON · 1930

Despite its contemporary and technological aesthetic, this typeface is well on the way to its centenary and in the face of many trends that have been and gone is still very popular today. Widely employed as a display face in films, books, television and video games, it is often seen in the science fiction genre.

Despite its age, the highly influential American type designer Morris Fuller Benton's (*see* Century p. 52) Bank Gothic has survived the test of time to remain one of the most popular display and titling typefaces available today. Originally with no lower case, the weights come with a small caps version instead. The distinctive element of Bank Gothic's design is its rectilinear form, which provides the typeface with a very clean, balanced and legible presentation.

There have been numerous cuts since the first release by ATF, with Bitstream and Linotype both offering versions. The most extensive range is offered by Fonthaus, who released their revival in 2010. Their version, Bank Gothic Pro, not only comes with the original additional Condensed version but also a family of lower-case characters for each of the three weights, Light, Medium and Bold.

CATEGORY: Sans Serif

CLASSIFICATION: Square Gothic

COUNTRY OF ORIGIN: USA

DISTINGUISHING MARKS: Rectilinear construction; monoline stroke weight; extended character width (non-Condensed only); angled terminals on upper-case 'C'; rounded corners; open counters

FURTHER SIGHTINGS: Television shows, including *24*, *ER*, *NCIS*, *Stargate SG-1* and *The Event*; films, including *X-Men* series, *Moon, Eagle Eye*, *Short Circuit*, *The International*, *I, Robot*, *Transformers*, *Lock Out*; *Call of Duty 4: Modern Warfare*; Hamburger Union

NOT TO BE CONFUSED WITH: Eurostile (p. 160)

OPPOSITE: Despite its heritage, London's oldest food market prominently displays its name above the traders in Bank Gothic.

BOROUGH MARKET
roast
OPEN EVERY DAY

ABOVE, RIGHT AND OPPOSITE: Arsenal Football Club's Emirates Stadium is awash with the use of Bank Gothic (and a dash of FF Meta here and there) as the typeface is employed across the site from large three-dimensional concrete letterforms to steel, engraved and screen-printed types.

MIRATES STADIUM
WILSON
HAPGOOD
GEORGE
11
ARSENAL
DAY
BOX OFFICE
position closed
THE ARMOURY

A2 Beckett

A2/SW/HK · **A2-TYPE** · 2009

Hard-edged and impactful, this contemporary Sans Serif is influenced by machine-cut era wood type. Its condensed forms and bold construction provide the typeface with authority and immediacy.

Designed in 2009–10 by London-based studio A2/SW/HK, A2 Beckett was employed initially on the covers of a Faber and Faber series of books by Samuel Beckett and was later released by them through their foundry A2-TYPE in 2011. Supplied in six weights – Extra Light, Light, Regular, Medium, Semibold and Bold – its hard edges create a confident and striking impression.

The original project came about when Faber and Faber planned to reprint Beckett's complete works. Faber art director Miriam Rosenbloom commissioned A2/SW/HK to create concepts that avoided pictorial clichés. As part of their research they looked at earlier Faber covers for Beckett titles designed by Berthold Wolpe, in which only his typeface Albertus (p. 24) and differing colour schemes had been employed. Following in Wolpe's footsteps, a bespoke typeface, A2 Beckett, was created for the project. The end designs featured the book titles in vertical arrangements and with contrasting sizes and colours. Despite each cover being different, they combine to form a visually striking and dramatic series of titles.

CATEGORY: Sans Serif

CLASSIFICATION: Grotesque

COUNTRY OF ORIGIN: UK

DISTINGUISHING MARKS: Double-storey lower-case 'g'; condensed structure; minimal stroke contrast; rounded corners; flattened stems; angled cut on horizontal terminals; no overshoot on rounded letters

FURTHER SIGHTINGS: A rare find, but with a range of weights and styles its flexibility makes it ideal for publishing and print solutions

NOT TO BE CONFUSED WITH: Aachen (p. 232); Knockout (p. 288)

OPPOSITE: A2/SW/HK's dynamic design for Faber and Faber's 80th-anniversary series of Samuel Beckett's books. The studio created A2 Beckett specifically for the project, now available through their foundry A2-TYPE.

Samuel Beckett
Murp
phy

Samuel Beckett
Watt

Samuel Beckett
Endga
m

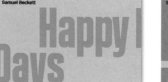

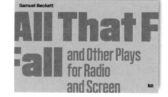

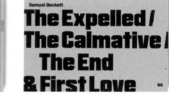

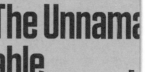

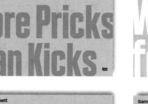

FIELD FACTS_

In recent years, American type foundry House Industries collaborated with Ed Benguiat to release the Ed Benguiat Font Collection in honour of his work and contribution to design. Consisting of five Benguiat-inspired typefaces – Ed Interlock, Ed Brush, Ed Gothic, Ed Roman and Ed Script – the suite of fonts was also accompanied by a set of humorous icons dubbed 'Bengbats'.

ITC Benguiat

ED BENGUIAT · ITC · 1977

CATEGORY:
Ornamented/Novelty

CLASSIFICATION: Art Nouveau

COUNTRY OF ORIGIN: USA

DISTINGUISHING MARKS: High x-height; multiple widths and weights; stress at top half of characters; strong Art Nouveau aesthetic

FURTHER SIGHTINGS: Display and advertising work; *Pulp Fiction* movie title sequence

NOT TO BE CONFUSED WITH:
Albertus (p. 24); Friz Quadrata (p. 70); Arnold Böcklin (p. 238)

OPPOSITE: ITC Benguiat has an unusual appearance due to its high-waisted letters, reminiscent of Art Nouveau typefaces. Here it is employed to great effect by London bead shop Beadworks.

Legendary type designer Ed Benguiat's self-titled typeface was inspired by the typefaces of the Art Nouveau period and was influential in the revival of the style. Distinctive and quirky, its visual association with the aforementioned art movement does limit its usages.

Graphic designer, typographer, type designer, teacher, jazz percussionist and pilot Ed Benguiat's extraordinary and prolific career has led him to design and contribute to well over 600 typefaces (more than any other designer) in addition to designing or redesigning many of the most iconic logos and logotypes that exist today, including AT&T, Coke, *Esquire* magazine, Ford, the *New York Times*, *Reader's Digest* and *Playboy* (and my personal favourite, the original *Planet of the Apes* movie logo).

An established big band jazz drummer who feared a career downturn in later life, he became an illustrator and in 1953 associate director of *Esquire* magazine. At the start of the 1970s he joined and became a leading figure at ITC (International Typeface Corporation) where he produced a wealth of designs as well as producing ITC's in-house journal, the revered *U&lc*, with his contemporary, Herb Lubalin. A Sans Serif variant of ITC Benguiat was also created, titled ITC Benguiat Gothic.

Henrik Kubel • A2-TYPE

LONDON, UK

A2-TYPE was formed in 2010, a type foundry set up by the London-based design studio A2/SW/HK whose founders are Scott Williams and Henrik Kubel. Established to release and distribute over a decade's worth of specially crafted typefaces, the foundry offers access to a unique collection of fonts, specially created for print, screen and environment.

A2-TYPE have also created bespoke typefaces for a range of clients including the Design Museum, London; Penguin Press, NYC; Ljubljana, capital city of Slovenia; Expedia; UK Government, gov.uk; Royal College of Art; *Wallpaper** and *Aperture* magazines in New York.

Q: You started off as a graphic designer founding the award-winning studio A2/SW/HK with Scott Williams. How did your work evolve to you both designing typefaces and setting up the A2-TYPE foundry in 2010?

A: As part of our design philosophy we have continuously designed typefaces for all of our commissions since we set up our design studio in 2000. We made a conscious decision not to use typefaces by other designers, and not to retail any of our fonts either. When we launched the New Rail Alphabet fonts in 2009, in collaboration with British design icon Margaret Calvert, we could see that there was a genuine interest in our type design. A year later we decided to establish A2-TYPE – a division of our design studio A2/SW/HK.

A2-TYPE deals solely with retail and custom type commissions.

Q: You have designed typefaces specifically for particular projects as well as designing typefaces solely for distribution via your A2-TYPE foundry. Are there technical or creative limitations for each way of working?

A: There are no technical limitations, all of our fonts are carefully crafted and have, depending on the usage, multiple weights and styles.

OPPOSITE: A2 Beckett, originally designed for a series of books by A2/SW/HK for publisher Faber and Faber (*see* p. 244).

A2 BECKETT IN 6 WEIGHTS!

ExtraLight
Light
Regular
Medium
SemiBold
Bold

HHHHHH hhhhhh AAAAAA aaaaaa
RRRRRR rrrrrr NNNNNN nnnnnn
SSSSSS ssssss OOOOOO oooooo

BBBBBB

IDEAL FOR BOOK COVERS AND MAGAZINE HEADLINES

r dettes, am
partage à fai
tenter de peu

Light
Light Italic
Regular
Regular Italic
Medium
Medium Italic
SemiBold
SemiBold Italic
Bold
Bold Italic

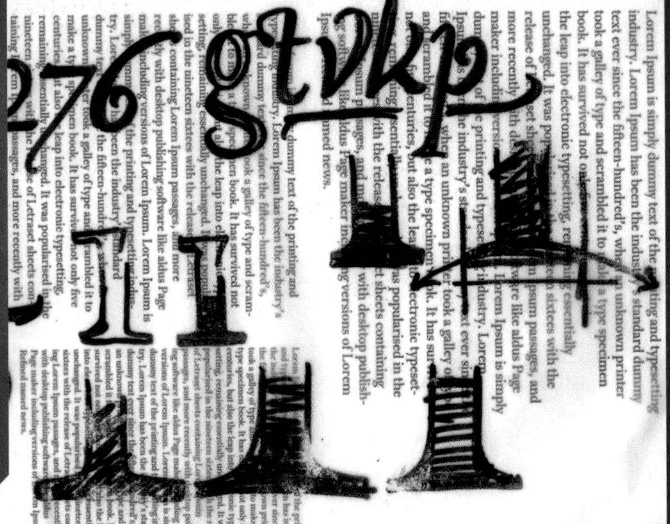

R
COMMUNICATION
aaaaa

a 16th-Century typeface with contemporary proportions — inspired by the Plantin Moretus Museum archives in Belgium. *To be released in 5 weights in Autumn 2012 by* London based type studio www.a2-type.co.uk

Antwerp
HAS BEEN
Designed in
five[5
weights plu
Accompanyin
ITALICS

Designed for *Books, Magazines & Newspape*

OPPOSITE FAR LEFT, TOP: Detail of an original printed sample from the Plantin-Moretus Museum in Antwerp, which served as the inspiration for Henrik Kubel's Antwerp typeface design with preliminary ideas sketched out bottom left.

MIDDLE TOP: Danish designer Henrik Kubel of A2-TYPE.

MIDDLE CENTRE: Ideas sketched out while visiting the Plantin-Moretus Museum in Antwerp.

TOP AND BOTTOM RIGHT: The Antwerp typeface completed, showing the five weights and the variations in letterform style.

BELOW: The A2-TYPE logo.

Q: How do you decide what to add to your portfolio of fonts?

A: Gut feeling!

Q: In 2010, you were awarded the prestigious three-year artist and designer working grant from The Danish Arts Foundation. How did this come about and how did this affect your studies and work in type design and development?

A: The grant enabled me to focus solely on type design, which was exactly what I needed to get to 'the next stage'. I used the grant to further my studies in type design and over the past three years completed type design courses at Reading, the Plantin-Moretus Museum in Antwerp and most recently at Type@Cooper in New York.

Q: As part of your continuing research and visits to the Plantin-Moretus Museum in Belgium, you created the 'sixteenth-century typeface' Antwerp (p. 28) inspired by the archives on display there. What was it that drew you to this particular period and approach in type design?

A: I designed Antwerp (five weights plus italics) because it was a particular style of font we had needed for some time in our studio for the book and magazine work we do. I wanted to design a 'soft font' with contemporary proportions, but rooted in history. For many years I have been looking at, and have drawn inspiration from, designers and punchcutters from the fifteenth and sixteenth centuries. The Plantin-Moretus Museum has great examples of books printed with these hot-metal fonts. However, my Antwerp typeface is not based on a specific model or style – it's more like a feel of the fonts from this era.

Q: In 2011, you launched a revival of the British Rail alphabet with New Rail Alphabet (p. 216). You collaborated closely with Margaret Calvert, its designer, on the typeface design and the creation of additional weights. How did this project and relationship come about?
A: We got permission from Margaret Calvert to revive the font back in 2005 for a project we were working on for the Hayward Gallery; in the end, the client decided on a Serif font and New Rail Alphabet was put in a drawer. Three years later Margaret called me and asked if I would be interested in finishing the font and to add multiple weights and italic styles... A collaboration started and we released New Rail Alphabet fonts, six weights plus italics (12 fonts in total), in the beginning of 2009.

Q: Your type designs have been very well received by the design community, winning numerous awards over the last few years. What would you say is the most satisfying aspect of designing type and what benefits does it bring to your wider graphic work?
A: The fact that we draw fonts for all of our studio's design work enables us to give our clients a unique voice. It is an exhaustive working method and always a long process, but an extremely rewarding one. We like to think it sets us apart as a design studio. The power of typography and bespoke fonts is incredible!

Q: What would you say are the characteristics of a good typeface or, alternatively, what do you look for in a typeface when considering a selection for your work?
A: It depends on the job. We craft all of our own fonts – that way, we can be very particular and design exactly what we need for any job and client.

Q: Have you ever witnessed your typefaces being employed in a surprising or unusual manner?
A: Yes, I am always encouraged and surprised!

Q: To anyone thinking of taking up designing their own typeface and creating a font, what advice would you give them?
A: Just do it, work as hard as you possibly can and remember that most typeface designers are self-taught!

OPPOSITE
TOP LEFT: Original sample of the British Rail alphabet used on the UK's rail network.

FAR RIGHT TOP:
The British Rail typeface was also adopted by the Danish, here seen in the DSB (Danske Statsbaner, Danish State Railways) corporate guidelines manual.

MIDDLE FAR RIGHT: Henrik Kubel discussing the typeface with Margaret Calvert, one of the original designers along with Jock Kinneir.

BOTTOM LEFT: The old design with New Rail Alphabet traced over the top with (far right) a comparison with Neue Helvetica.

Platform 3
Wimbledon
Kingston
Surbiton

bcdefghijk

yz ABCDEF

234567890

Comparison

Comparing New Rail Alphabet to Helvetica Neue

New Rail Alphabet has a larger x-height (increases legibility in smaller point), is more uniform, has a 'squarer' look, longer ascenders and descenders plus lighter Capitals — Light, Medium & Bold match in weight to Monotype Calvert — a Slab Serif font relating to British Rail Alphabet. At default setting our new design takes up less space, when compared to Helvetica Neue.

FF Blur

NEVILLE BRODY · FONTFONT · 1991

Embracing the advancing development of digital design technologies, renowned British designer Neville Brody's groundbreaking typeface FF Blur heralded a new age in graphic design and in typeface experimentation and development.

With the introduction of the Apple Macintosh computer in the creative industries in the 1980s, type design and development was made much simpler and easier than it had been in the past (although still by no means an easy task). By the early 1990s, Neville Brody had established himself as one of Britain's leading graphic designers and typographers. His FF Blur typeface exploited these new software and hardware capabilities and its appearance reflects this time of advancement and playfulness, epitomizing the digital aesthetic of much of the graphic design output of the period following its launch.

Brody's typeface is built around an existing Sans Serif Grotesque but, having been made into a greyscale bitmap, it was then taken through varying stages of Photoshop blurring to create three weights: Light, Medium and Bold. This simple process spawned many imitators and created a trend in graphic design for a time where much of the design created was employing blurred or abstract/soft typography. It is still popular today; its use, however, can display nostalgia for the 1980s.

CATEGORY: Sans Serif

CLASSIFICATION: Amorphous

COUNTRY OF ORIGIN: UK

DISTINGUISHING MARKS: Blurred outline; no hard edges or corners; organic contours to all letterforms

FURTHER SIGHTINGS: Natural Break fast-food restaurant chain; *The Graphic Language of Neville Brody 2* book

NOT TO BE CONFUSED WITH: VAG Rounded (p. 226)

OPPOSITE: Blur's amorphous profile was created with digital manipulation software and is representative of the typographical experimentation seen in the 1980s.

Circle

FIELD FACTS_

In 2011–2012, 23 digital typefaces were selected and admitted to the Museum of Modern Art's (MoMA) architecture and design collection. These fonts and families were put on display for the first time in an exhibition entitled Standard Deviations in New York. Brody's FF Blur was among the chosen few – a selection that also included Erik Spiekermann's FF Meta (p. 210), ATF's OCR-A (p. 306), Albert-Jan Pool's FF Din (p. 158) and Matthew Carter's Bell Centennial (p. 148), Galliard (p. 72) and Verdana (p. 228).

FIELD FACTS_

Soon after its appearance, the original Bodoni's impact on early nineteenth-century type design was being felt far and wide. In England, the employment of such contrasting thicks and thins was being adopted for the purpose of advertising, resulting in the term 'Fat Face'. Robert Thorne, an English type designer and foundry owner, was credited with the term's creation.

Bodoni Poster

CHAUNCEY H. GRIFFITH · 1929

CATEGORY: Serif

CLASSIFICATION: Modern/Didone

COUNTRY OF ORIGIN: USA

DISTINGUISHING MARKS: Extreme contrast with thick and thin strokes; ball terminals cut into stems on 'J'; heavy, bold and swollen appearance

FURTHER SIGHTINGS: Seen often used in applications where the subject matter is not taken too seriously and a lighter tone can be employed

NOT TO BE CONFUSED WITH: Didot (p. 66)

OPPOSITE: Bodoni Poster Condensed employed for the branding of the *Mamma Mia!* theatre production, seen on Broadway, New York.

Based loosely on the classic eighteenth-century typeface design from which it takes its name, Bodoni Poster's influences date back to a later time and that of the 'Fat Faces' that appeared in early advertisements and posters. For that reason, they very much resemble the bold wood-cut letterforms of the nineteenth and twentieth centuries.

Bodoni Poster certainly pushes the boundaries of contrasting stroke weights to the extreme and appears to have gorged itself on cake to attain its appearance. However, its distinctive, heavy and cheerful appearance has made it popular in advertising and display signage.

Because of its heavy appearance it is certainly not best employed as a text typeface; it is better used in larger print, and for this reason the range is limited to Regular, Italic and Compressed. There are other Bodoni-inspired heavyweights available, including Bodoni Ultra Bold, Bodoni Black, Sahara Bodoni and Bodoni Classic Ultra. In addition, a typeface called Fat Face exists which is a more stylized version (yet again) with extremely thin, vertically aligned spurs and serifs and a slight condensed quality to its appearance. All of these take their lead from the style of Giambattista Bodoni's more refined original.

Bottleneck

TONY WENMAN · ITC · 1972

Welcome to the 1970s. If any typeface could be said to wear platform boots, it would be Bottleneck. Reminiscent of the period, it immediately evokes memories of a time gone by when trousers were flared and so were the typefaces.

Bottleneck's very distinctive tongue-in-cheek appearance and structure is formed around the imbalance between the top serifs and the super-enlarged bottom serifs. It is almost as if the lower part of each character has been inflated or, as mentioned earlier, is wearing platform boots.

Its fun, wacky and nostalgic appearance means it is often seen on retro-styled print and advertising applications but never used seriously.

CATEGORY: Ornamented/Novelty

CLASSIFICATION: Slab Serif

COUNTRY OF ORIGIN: UK

DISTINGUISHING MARKS: Lower serifs greatly enlarged; small counters; slab serifs; high-contrast stroke weights; descender of lower-case 'p' curls backwards

FURTHER SIGHTINGS: Anything relating to the 1970s

NOT TO BE CONFUSED WITH: Aachen (p. 232); Arnold Böcklin (p. 238)

OPPOSITE: With its bulbous and flared lower half, Bottleneck's proportions strongly convey a nostalgic 1970s tone.

BiOND
SCHUH

VI
secolo a.C.
le prime mura di

Broadway

MORRIS FULLER BENTON · MONOTYPE · 1928

CATEGORY:
Ornamented/Novelty

CLASSIFICATION: Art Deco

COUNTRY OF ORIGIN: USA

DISTINGUISHING MARKS: High stroke contrast; geometric construction; strong vertical stroke weight; rounded terminals; large counters

FURTHER SIGHTINGS:
Broadway Inn Hotel, New York

NOT TO BE CONFUSED WITH:
Bodoni Poster (p. 256)

OPPOSITE: Reminiscent of the 1920s and 1930s graphic vernacular, Broadway is still a common sight today and can be seen around bars, restaurants and hotels.

Epitomizing a glamorous and sophisticated New York of the 1920s and 1930s, Broadway has become synonymous as a 'jazz'/showtime-themed typeface and is probably one of the most widely recognized designs to convey the Art Deco period.

Designed by **Morris Fuller Benton** (*see* Century p. 52) and first published by ATF and available in only the upper case (the lower case having been designed and introduced by Sol Hess in 1929), this typeface was widely adopted and gained enormous popularity in print and display – especially signage. By the 1950s, ATF had discontinued it but it was later rediscovered and is now often seen used in a 1920s and 1930s graphic vernacular. Its identification with the period is now so strong it can be employed for little else, which limits its use.

There are a number of variants now available to the original design, with a Broadway Engraved (Sol Hess Monotype, 1928) which incorporates a more graphic, decorative design where elements of the stems are split into two parts, one heavy and one thin. In addition, there is a Condensed and an ITC Manhattan, a copy that incorporates hairline strokes and has an even greater contrast in stroke weight as a result.

Cooper Black

OSWALD BRUCE COOPER · LINOTYPE · 1922

With its rounded, inflated forms and bulbous features, there's no mistaking Cooper Black. A perennial favourite among designers (the old adage being every designer has to use it at least once in their lifetime), its heavily weighted aesthetic has a jolly, friendly and timeless appearance to it.

Designed by Oswald Bruce Cooper, a partner in Bertsch & Cooper in Chicago, and first released by Barnhart Brothers & Spindler type foundry at the start of the 1920s, Cooper Black is in fact an Extra Bold version of his earlier design Cooper Old Style, a lighter standard weight. Popular since its release, it has enjoyed many revivals, noticeably in the 1970s and in recent years being used on corporate identities and advertising campaigns. Cooper famously said of the face that it was 'for far-sighted printers with near-sighted customers' in referring to its heavyweight design.

Despite its popularity and huge sales, conservative type designers were critical at the time, seeing it as vulgar. That didn't dampen the enthusiasm with which it was taken up and employed in everything from shop fascias to point-of-sale displays, packaging and advertising. Italic, Condensed and Outline versions are available, as is a HiLite version. Released by the Wordshape foundry in 2012, the latter features highlighted shading over the letterforms that lends a three-dimensional quality to its appearance.

CATEGORY: Serif

CLASSIFICATION: Old Style

COUNTRY OF ORIGIN: USA

DISTINGUISHING MARKS: Heavy stroke weight; moderate contrast in strokes; rounded bulbous serifs; tiny counters; non-aligning numerals; backward tilting counters on 'O' and 'Q'; elliptical dots on 'i' and 'j'

FURTHER SIGHTINGS: *Garfield*; *Pet Sounds* by The Beach Boys; *Brothers* by The Black Keys; *Modern Toss* logotype

NOT TO BE CONFUSED WITH: Bodoni Poster (p. 256)

OPPOSITE: The use of Cooper Black by the 'easyGroup' of companies has created a dynamic and fun brand, on land and in the air, as seen here on their budget airline easyJet branding.

easyJet
easyJet.com
G-EZGP
easyJet

SW17

W3 6H

–58: SE

8: SE1 2

, 68B: S

27: HA9 6DL 1969
17: W3 7LW
30: N19 3TN
1, 29: N4 2LQ
37: SW17 7DD
14: W3 6HF
54–58: SE1 3PH
188: SE1 2EE
30, 68B: SE1 4NU
7.43, 61: SE1 3BD
38, 24: SE15 2NZ
41: N2 2BX
41: N2 9QG
10B: SE22 8QB 2012

Foundry Fabriek

DAVID QUAY, FREDA SACK · THE FOUNDRY · 2006

CATEGORY: Sans Serif

CLASSIFICATION: Geometric

COUNTRY OF ORIGIN: UK

DISTINGUISHING MARKS: Stencil forms; angled corners; geometric design; small angled returns on stems of 'W'; small angled returns on diagonal of upper-case 'N'; crossbar on 'H' connects with only one stem; split top and bottom strokes on 'S'

FURTHER SIGHTINGS: Ideal for when an industrial and machined appearance is required in a design

NOT TO BE CONFUSED WITH: Glaser Stencil (p. 274); Foundry Gridnik (p. 278)

OPPOSITE: In a design by the author for the ISTD's My London, My City exhibition, the bold, geometric forms of Foundry Fabriek make a powerful statement explaining the locations he has resided at in London.

With its strong, constructed appearance formed of stencil characters, the inspiration behind Foundry Fabriek was industrial fabrication – the process of assembling components so that parts of materials or structures are united.

The idea for Foundry Fabriek started through a commission, from the architects Kho Liang Ie, to produce a version of Foundry Gridnik that could be laser-cut out of steel panels to be sited within a new building for Interpolis (a Dutch insurance company). Wim Crouwel was consultant on this project with David Quay, and the typeface was subsequently developed into a family and included in **The Foundry** typeface collection. The uniformity of the compact character widths are consistent with Crouwel's design philosophies. There are five weights to the family (Light, Regular, Medium, Bold and Extra Bold), giving the typeface great flexibility for a variety of applications.

What is most striking about this typeface is that, although it is based on stencil forms, the designers have introduced a great number of elegant design details into the letter structures, with angled returns on terminals, additional breaks in the strokes and diagonal corners all adding to a design that encapsulates its engineering inspiration.

Foundry Flek/Plek

DAVID QUAY, FREDA SACK · THE FOUNDRY · 2006

Complementary designs built around the same 5 x 9 dot matrix system lie at the core of the Flek and Plek typeface families. From this simple but precise arrangement of dots the alphabet variations are created.

Both typefaces are built around the same dot matrix arrangement in Light, Regular, Medium and Bold, Foundry Flek/Plek has an integral dot matrix grid as a background. Uniquely, the dot matrix grid in both families (and their weights) all align exactly when laid over one another. This creates stunning visual effects when lighter weights are on top of bolder weights as the designer can make different colour effects within the letterforms themselves. The success of the 5 x 9 grid even caters for capitals, lower case, ligatures, fractions, punctuation and typographic symbols to be incorporated into the fonts.

There are also auxiliary fonts of just grid patterns in varying multiples of dots formed from the grid, enabling the designer to create dot matrix arrangements which all align to the letterforms. The addition of these patterns also permits the designer to experiment and arrange complex patterns of dots with ease (horizontally and vertically), allowing for a rewarding and fun process working with the type. With designer **Quay** based in Amsterdam, the names were derived from the Dutch word *plek*, meaning 'spot', and *flek*, meaning 'fleck'.

CATEGORY: Ornamented/Novelty

CLASSIFICATION: Dot Matrix

COUNTRY OF ORIGIN: UK

DISTINGUISHING MARKS: Dot matrix construction; 5 x 9 grid system

FURTHER SIGHTINGS: 26 Letters exhibition at the British Library; Durham, UK; 41 Places: 41 Books

NOT TO BE CONFUSED WITH: n/a

OPPOSITE: The grid system of Foundry Flek/Plek was the basis for this illuminated art installation in the UK as part of the LUMIERE festival, Durham, designed by Richard Wolfströme. Projected coloured light was shown through a matrix of holes (3,640 drilled holes per side) to form words. The 'Lightwriting' cube told a story four faces at a time, changing every 20 seconds. Visitors ran around and followed the stories before all four sides changed to the next 'page'.

I went to go
to a football
match but a
volcano came
came. The
fireman had
ten pence!
Frightened
What if we
dig a big hole
to get the
CHIQUITO

Under Queen
Victoria's blank gaze,
Monika puts the brake
on the buggy and
sits on the ledge
that surrounds the
Clock Tower.
It has been a hard
morning for Ben. He
had to have his
injection. Here the
doctors are all so
stiff-upper-lip.
She just jabbed in
the needle.
41 Places
Instead, they started
to look around.
That's how they
found themselves
drinking tea in a
café in St James'
Street, looking at
each other and going:
This is great.
It's like a
relationship.
There aren't
necessarily
reasons why
it's going to
fantasised about
the rural life, a big
garden for Ben and
the dog. But the
reality, they
realised, would be
too... commuter-ish,
too claustrophobic.
She and her husband
Julian hadn't
intended to move to
Brighton. They hadn't
even wanted to come
back to England after
America, but his work
has brought him home.
To compensate they

OPPOSITE, ABOVE AND RIGHT:
41 Places: 41 Books was a city-wide installation across the coastal town of Brighton, in the UK. Foundry Flek/Plek were employed to tell a variety of stories about people who lived, worked and played in the area. A diverse range of printing and production techniques were used on a range of materials and surfaces by the designer Richard Wolfströme to create a treasure hunt of typography.

Futura Black

JOSEF ALBERS, PAUL RENNER · 1929

A heavy and strong display face, Futura Black represents the constructivist aspects of the Bauhaus movement and, despite its dramatic presence, its timeless, stencilled forms can be viewed in a wide range of environments, from architecture through to contemporary club scene graphics.

Renner's design follows on from the letterforms originally drawn by Josef Albers in 1926 at the Bauhaus which he (along with the Bauer design office) went on to compose as a typeface in 1929 and release as a part of the Futura series. Despite being called Futura, it has little to do with the family concerning its design, and as with Futura Display, they lumped together for marketing reasons due to the popularity of the Futura typeface family. The typeface is built around the core shapes of circle, triangle and square, yet Futura Black's geometric construction shares some characteristics with the likes of the bold Didone 'Fat Face' typefaces such as Bodoni Poster (p. 256), as a number of ball terminals are cut into the character shapes (see lower-case 'a' and 'f' as examples).

With a mix of curves and hard diagonals, what makes Futura Black such an interesting design is that, in the right hands and correctly treated, the typeface can be employed to convey a range of visual messages and interestingly reflect a variety of periods from the past and the future, despite its hard and heavy appearance.

CATEGORY: Sans Serif

CLASSIFICATION: Stencil

COUNTRY OF ORIGIN: Germany

DISTINGUISHING MARKS: Heavy, bold appearance; Stencil, geometric construction; rounded terminals on lower-case 'a', 'f', 'c' and 's'; leg of 'R' and extenders on 'E' formed of triangles

FURTHER SIGHTINGS: Boston public safety departments; Au Bon Pain branding; *The Love Boat* title sequence; Andrews & Dunham Nepal Tea

NOT TO BE CONFUSED WITH: Foundry Fabriek (p. 246); Glaser Stencil (p. 274)

OPPOSITE: A public restroom at 14th Street in the South Beach area of Miami Beach displays Futura Black prominently, complementing the Art Deco characteristics of the architecture and design in the area.

14th STREET

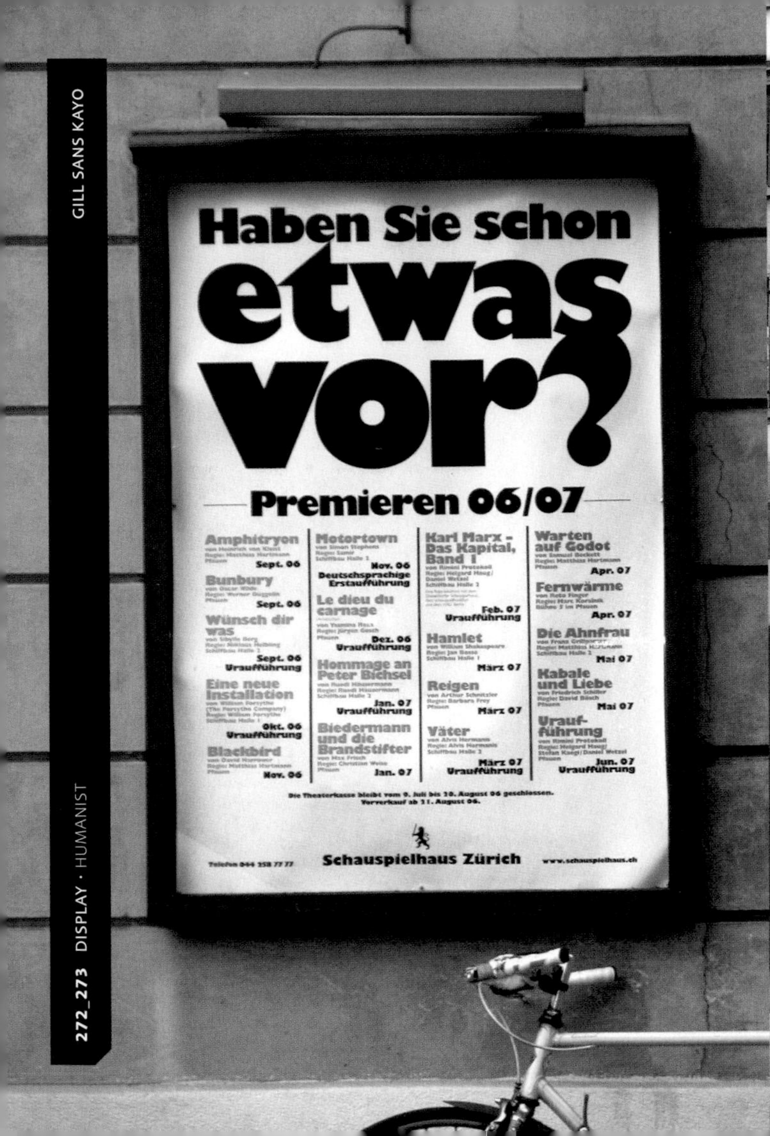

Haben Sie schon
etwas
vor?

Gill Sans Kayo

ERIC GILL · MONOTYPE · 1936

CATEGORY: Sans Serif

CLASSIFICATION: Humanist

COUNTRY OF ORIGIN: UK

DISTINGUISHING MARKS: Ultra-bold stroke weight; horizontal oval counter on upper-case 'C'; pronounced stem and terminal on double-storey 'a'; imbalanced stroke contrast; inverted curve at top of stems on 'i' and 'j'; circular terminal on lower-case 'r'; offset circle on lower-case 'i' and 'j'

FURTHER SIGHTINGS: *Toy Story* and *Shallow Hal* films; Schauspielhaus, Zurich; Foto Woehl; City Circle Sightseeing Berlin

NOT TO BE CONFUSED WITH: Cooper Black (p. 262)

OPPOSITE: Designed by Raffinerie AG für Gestaltung with Studio Achermann, the striking branding and posters for the Schauspielhaus theatre in Zurich have at their core Gill Sans Kayo.

Gill Sans Kayo, also known as Gill Sans Ultra Bold, creates strong opinion among designers and typographers – 'ugly', 'overinflated' and 'cartoonish' are some of the terms used to describe Kayo. It's hard to believe this awkward and brash design came from the same hand that created Gill Sans and Perpetua.

Termed *Kayo*, as in a 'knockout' in boxing terminology, this heavyweight typeface was commissioned as a rival to the German Futura Extra Bold. Eric Gill was reticent about designing extra bold weights for display typefaces and certainly for his Gill Sans family of types. In his own book on the subject of type design, *An Essay on Typography*, he decries the use of super-heavy designs over practical and aesthetic ones. Knowing full well that his designs were not working on an aesthetic level, he went on to accept the commissions despite his own views.

The peculiarity with the Gill Sans family is, when sat next to each other, the weights are at odds with one another in terms of their proportions; for example, between capital heights, stroke and character widths. They also lack consistency of weight and form from lighter to heavier weights. When compared to other typeface families that retain a sense of progression, the Gill family can almost come across as not even related.

Glaser Stencil

MILTON GLASER · LINOTYPE · 1970

An all-capitals font created by legendary US graphic designer Milton Glaser, Glaser Stencil possesses a geometric design that reflects a trend of that time towards Sans Serif typefaces such as ITC Avant Garde Gothic and Futura. However, its distinction lies in its dynamic stencil construction.

Milton Glaser's contribution to US graphic design and illustration, and to the craft globally, cannot be underestimated. Probably best known for his 'I love NY' logo (1973) and before that his Bob Dylan poster for CBS Records (1966), over his long career he has worked on every conceivable form of graphic communication.

Despite having originated over 40 years ago, Glaser Stencil feels remarkably modern and fresh in its design. Its stencil form is intuitive and imaginative, with the breaks in the letter strokes not where you would perhaps expect to see them, creating unusual letter shapes and remarkably interesting word forms when placed together. It is ideal for technology or industrial type messaging, and its distinctive appearance and legibility also make it perfect for wayfinding and other display purposes. Other typefaces by Glaser include Babyfat, Babycurls, Baby Teeth and Houdini.

CATEGORY: Sans Serif

CLASSIFICATION: Stencil

COUNTRY OF ORIGIN: USA

DISTINGUISHING MARKS: Rounded and geometric stencil forms; stroke breaks under bowl of 'R', diagonally on 'S' and on stem of 'A'

FURTHER SIGHTINGS: *Phaidon Design Classics*; Brixton Splash, London; Epigram lanterns; *Buster* movie

NOT TO BE CONFUSED WITH: Foundry Fabriek (p. 264); Futura Black (p. 270)

OPPOSITE AND OVERLEAF: Nick Kapica/SV Associates' wayfinding system for the art museum *Dieselkraftwerk* in Cottbus, for the city council, employs Glaser Stencil in a range of colour palettes and typographic hierarchies. Its industrial look is a perfect marriage with the site's architecture and its previous use, as a power station.

BLACK
BOX

SCHALTHAUS
CAFETERIA
AUFZUG
WC

S1 S2 S3
AUSSTELLUNGSRÄUME
MASCHINENHAU
SCHALTHAUS
CAFETERIA
WC
GARDEROBE
AUFZUG

AUSSTELLUNGSRÄUME
MASCHINENHAUS
SCHALTHAUS
CAFETERIA
WC
GARDROBE
AUFZUG

VIDEOTECHNIK

5.10.
[MÄRKISC
SAND
SPUREN
ZWISCHEN
SUJET,
WERKSTOFF
UND
LANDSC AFTS
RAU

Foundry Gridnik

WIM CROUWEL · THE FOUNDRY · 1974 (FONT FAMILY CREATED 1996)

Named after legendary Dutch graphic designer Wim Crouwel's nickname 'Mr Gridnik' (for his love of using grids), this Geometric typeface is based on an earlier design of Crouwel's from 1974 for Olivetti typewriters.

In 1974, international typewriter manufacturer Olivetti commissioned Wim Crouwel to create a new and bespoke typeface to be used on their electric typewriters. Crouwel's solution was a geometric design, possessing 45° angled corners to the characters and a monoline stroke weight. The resultant typeface was called Politene but sadly it was never used for its original application as the use of typewriters declined and the project was shelved. All was not lost, though, and Politene did make an outing soon after for the Dutch Post Office, PTT, where it appeared in slightly modified form on their postage stamps up to 2002.

In 1996, British type designers **The Foundry** worked with Crouwel to create a digitized version of Politene. This was initially released as part of the Architype Crouwel collection and then developed into a family of four weights: Light, Regular, Medium and Bold. Within The Foundry collection are also other Crouwel typefaces including Architype Stedelijk (p. 314) and Architype Fodor.

CATEGORY: Sans Serif

CLASSIFICATION: Geometric

COUNTRY OF ORIGIN: The Netherlands/UK

DISTINGUISHING MARKS: Monoline stroke weight; strong geometric appearance; 45° angled corners; squared structure to letterforms; open counters; closed apertures; long horizontal strokes

FURTHER SIGHTINGS: Fogg Mobile; Cooper Union academic building, New York; Dutch postage stamps; onedotzero.com; Radio Barcelona

NOT TO BE CONFUSED WITH: Bank Gothic (p. 240); Architype Stedelijk (p. 314)

OPPOSITE: **Foundry Gridnik** employed as signage and interior wayfinding on the Cooper Union building, New York.

FIELD FACTS_

Wim Crouwel, graphic/type designer and typographer, is one of the world's leading exponents of communication and visual design. He was one of the founders in 1963 of Total Design, a groundbreaking design studio, and is renowned for his love and use of grids in his work. Among his most recognized works are the innovative and distinctive typographic designs of posters, catalogues and exhibitions he produced for the Dutch Stedelijk Museum in Amsterdam. His work remains highly influential today.

Headline 2012

GARETH HAGUE · ALIAS (BESPOKE) · 2012

CATEGORY: Sans Serif

CLASSIFICATION: Geometric

COUNTRY OF ORIGIN: UK

DISTINGUISHING MARKS: Oblique only; monoweight stroke; no curves; hard, jagged, angled letterforms; diagonal bar on lower-case 'e'; single line weight

FURTHER SIGHTINGS: All around the London 2012 Summer Olympics

NOT TO BE CONFUSED WITH: n/a

The London 2012 Summer Olympic Games' official typeface, Headline 2012, was seen worldwide by an audience of billions. Love it or hate it, this oblique, jagged typeface is distinctive, immediately identifiable and remarkably legible when viewed across the myriad of applications it was designed for.

It was Gareth Hague's 1997 typeface Klute, a contemporary Blackletter, that helped influence and inspire the controversial and widely despised (and that's putting it lightly) London 2012 Olympics logo by Wolff Olins. The logo was designed to evoke the impression of graffiti so as to motivate and inspire the youth demographic to get involved. The esteemed branding agency turned to Hague and his type and graphic design studio **Alias** to create the official games typeface and complement the jagged and broken appearance of their '2012' design.

Hague's Headline 2012 bespoke typeface design met with mixed reviews. However, in the context of the games it was one of the few elements of the branding that was a success. Used in the main as a display and headline face at events during the games, its slanted characters and simple 'scratched' letterforms made for a typeface that was legible, distinctive and recognizable – more so when used on directional and wayfinding signage, thus creating a distinction between the games communications and the wealth of other typographical styles that confronted visitors to the games in and around London.

OPPOSITE: London was a sea of Headline 2012 for the summer games and its distinctive jagged forms were far better received than the official logo by designers and the general public alike.

Kade Letter Fabriek

DAVID QUAY · RE-TYPE.COM · 2008

Emigrating to Amsterdam at the start of the millennium, British type designer David Quay travelled around the harbours of the Dutch port on an old bicycle, noting the many steel-cast, welded and hand-painted types, which would later be the inspiration behind Kade Letter Fabriek.

Upon settling in the Netherlands, Quay wished to create a typeface that reflected the impressions he had of his new home country: 'pragmatic, direct and honest'. He also wanted it to incorporate his observations of the city, and his experiences as a type designer.

The resultant Display/Semi-display typeface was named Kade – the Dutch for 'quay'. The end design has an industrial and 'hard' quality to its appearance but despite this, serves to be warm and friendly, possessing many of the handcrafted and engineered features and quirks that one would expect to see within the original source of inspiration.

The six distinct styles are published in OpenType format, featuring small caps and multiple numerals (proportional Old Style, tabular Old Style, proportional lining and tabular lining), as well as two complete sets of fractions.

CATEGORY: Sans Serif

CLASSIFICATION: Geometric

COUNTRY OF ORIGIN: The Netherlands

DISTINGUISHING MARKS: Horizontal crossbar on apex of upper-case 'A'; unbracketed serifs on 'I'; flattened apex and point on diagonal strokes of 'M' and 'W'; leg and arm of 'K' intersect on crossbar connected to stem; minimal stroke contrast; flattened curves on 'C' and 'D'

FURTHER SIGHTINGS: VIVID Gallery, Rotterdam

NOT TO BE CONFUSED WITH: Bank Gothic (p. 240); Foundry Gridnik (p. 278)

OPPOSITE: The steel-cast and hand-painted types located around the port of Amsterdam and (far right), Quay's early sketches for the design of Kade Letter Fabriek.

FIELD FACTS_

For Kade, designer David Quay took an unusual but highly effective approach to creating the italics. In discussion with a draughtsman at a ship engineering company, it was explained to him that the lettering on a ship's bow is rotated left or right depending on whether it is on the port or starboard side. Rather than slanting the letters and correcting any distortions, as one would do with a Geometric typeface, Quay rotated the characters 8° and left rounded letters and elements untouched, correcting only the horizontals.

ABOVE AND RIGHT: From original inspiration, to digitally drawn type, and then employment on an exhibition catalogue for the Zuiderzeemuseum in Enkhuizen, clear illustration is provided of the evolution of many typefaces today. David Quay's industrial typeface reflects the heritage of marine letterforms in the Netherlands and the resultant Display/Semi-display typeface is named *'kade'* – the Dutch term for 'quay', a happy coincidence for the designer.

KLF
JOL
TJOTTER
SCHOUW
BLAZER
AAK
TJALK
BOTTER
KLIPPER
KLF Haven Collectie designed by David Quay
at the Kade Letter Fabriek Amsterdam
www.davidquaydesign.com
d.quay@planet.nl
TypeSheet 02

HACIENDA SAN LUCAS

FIELD FACTS_

The Maya civilization existed in one form or another for close to two millennia until its ultimate demise in the late seventeenth century. The Mayans created and used one of the most beautiful and intelligent logographic languages seen, employing hieroglyphs that were both ideographic (a graphic symbol that represents an idea or concept) and syllabographic (a graphic symbol that represents the syllables of a word). The New Maya Language is a redesign of certain ideographs that achieves a contemporary feel by employing modern-day subjects and topics (p. 360).

Kakaw

FRIDA AND GABRIELA LARIOS · LATINOTYPE · 2013

CATEGORY:
Ornamented/Novelty

CLASSIFICATION:
Rationalized Script

COUNTRY OF ORIGIN:
El Salvador

DISTINGUISHING MARKS:
Condensed letterforms; rounded serifs and terminals; extended ascenders and descenders on lower case; raised positioning of crossbar and spines on upper case

FURTHER SIGHTINGS:
Hacienda San Lucas eco-lodge, Honduras; Gaia 2012 spirituality centre; SapoSerpiente photography and design studio, Copán/San Salvador

NOT TO BE CONFUSED WITH: n/a

OPPOSITE: Kakaw employed for the logotype and branding for the Hacienda San Lucas, an environmental resort in Honduras.

This unusual and distinctive Central American-styled typeface was developed to work in conjunction with a set of pictograms called the 'New Maya Language' (p. 360), a logographic language of Mayan-influenced hieroglyphs. The typeface has intentionally long ascenders and descenders, and peculiarly edged characters that echo the pictograms' distinctive organic forms.

The letterforms' design concept was created by Gabriela Larios as part of her undergraduate degree work, which centred on the creation of a logotype for the revival of the harvesting and dyeing processes of natural blue indigo. These initial characters were then developed into a full Display typeface by Frida. Cuban-based designer Alexis Manuel Rodríguez Diezcabezas de Armada designed the upper case, launched in 2013 through LatinoType, a font foundry based in Chile whose aim is to design and launch typefaces that possess influences relating to the 'Latino' identity. LatinoType's Miguel Hernández designed the family's remaining fonts: Light Italic, Regular, Italic, Bold and Bold Italic.

The typeface was used by Ideas Frescas, the San Salvador/London design studio that the Larios sisters ran (2000–2007), as their company typeface. It's also employed on several Central American corporate identities that the consultancy has undertaken. A set of fun and lively dingbats has also been created to accompany the typeface (p. 358).

Knockout

JONATHAN HOEFLER, TOBIAS FRERE-JONES · HOEFLER & FRERE-JONES · 1994

Containing a huge array of combinations within the one collection, Knockout punches other Sans Serif Gothic display types firmly out of the ring. This highly versatile family possesses nine widths and four weights, allowing for great variety and flexibility within a single typeface.

Inspired by wood block typefaces of the nineteenth century, this large family possesses a collection of 32 Sans Serifs. The careful design and planning process means that a number of the weights and widths work as display faces and at smaller sizes as text faces.

Knockout references historical forms of categorizing type by having a much more organic and looser system for sorting, rather than modernism's more structured cataloguing arrangements. Instead of employing typical signifiers, such as Regular and Bold, the typefaces are packaged in 'series' much as nineteenth-century wood block types. They are intended as individual designs whose qualities are suited to specific applications rather than being derivatives of a central master whose core principles remain largely unchanged.

The boxing metaphor continues, with weights echoing boxing's classification system for fighters – Junior Flyweight, Junior Bantamweight and so on up to Ultimate Heavyweight (and even Sumo). Lighter weights start out in Series A with the heavier weights in Series F and G.

CATEGORY: Sans Serif

CLASSIFICATION: Gothic

COUNTRY OF ORIGIN: USA

DISTINGUISHING MARKS: Bold Sans Serif family ranging from Super Condensed to Extra-bold Wide; individual refinements to all fonts

FURTHER SIGHTINGS: 7th Zagreb Jewish Film Festival, 2013; Lincoln/New York exhibition, New York Historical Society; Holzer Kobler Architekturen identity; griplimited.com; Salt River Fields baseball training facility; The Public Theater, NYC; *The Fighter* film titles

NOT TO BE CONFUSED WITH: Franklin Gothic (p. 174); Gotham (p. 188); Helvetica (p. 192)

OPPOSITE: Knockout employed by Artur Rebelo and Lizá Ramalho of the design studio R2 as a typographical wall on a chapel in Lisbon, Portugal.

DEUS
ME
LIVRE
POR
AMOR
DE DEUS
VÊ
O QUE O DIABO
ESCONDE
DEUS DÁ O
FRIO
CONFORME
A ROUPA
U
DEUS
ZURROS
DE
BURRO
NÃO
CHEGAM
AOS
CÉUS
AOS
POBRES
EMPRESTA
A DEUS
DEUS
NÃO
DORME
PARA
BAIXO
TODOS
OS
NDE
DEUS QUANDO FECHA UMA PORTA ABRE A JANELA
VOZ D

Jason Smith • Fontsmith

LONDON, UK

Fontsmith is a leading and established boutique type foundry known for creating fonts that are distinctively human and full of character. Founded in 1997 by Jason Smith, Fontsmith today represents a truly international team of designers working from a London studio.

The Fontsmith library includes an extensive collection of typefaces – elegant and traditional, contemporary and quirky – suitable for a range of applications. In addition, the team design and create bespoke typefaces for global brands, as well as design and advertising agencies.

Q: You started off as a graphic designer working on corporate identities. How did this evolve to designing typefaces and setting up the Fontsmith foundry?

A: I actually started off as a lettering artist and calligrapher. I desperately wanted to do graphics but I never studied it so my background in calligraphy and lettering led me to become a typeface designer. I became the in-house lettering artist for a company called Wagstaffs. My job was to come up with the lettering styles to match product or brand: Quavers, Jaffa Cakes, Flake, Hovis, Ready brek… they were all mine. There were also loads of cheeses, crisps, pickles, cereals, chocolates and so on. I was dealing with questions like '*How do you make a word look fizzy for a fizzy drink?*' That was great fun. I remember walking around supermarkets only buying products I had done the lettering for.

I had worked with other type designers such as David Quay and Freda Sack at The Foundry and all back in the day before computers (not that long ago, actually). I would draw the type or logos by hand and ink the artwork on Polydraw. Later on I learnt how to digitize lettering and type to the computer and then make digital fonts. The craft was the same but the tools were just different. I was the youngest lettering artist in London and I was giving clients artwork digitally. Word spread and I got very busy. A few clients commissioned some typefaces for brand work they were doing. I had always wanted to work on TV identities and film titles and got a couple of good breaks from taking my

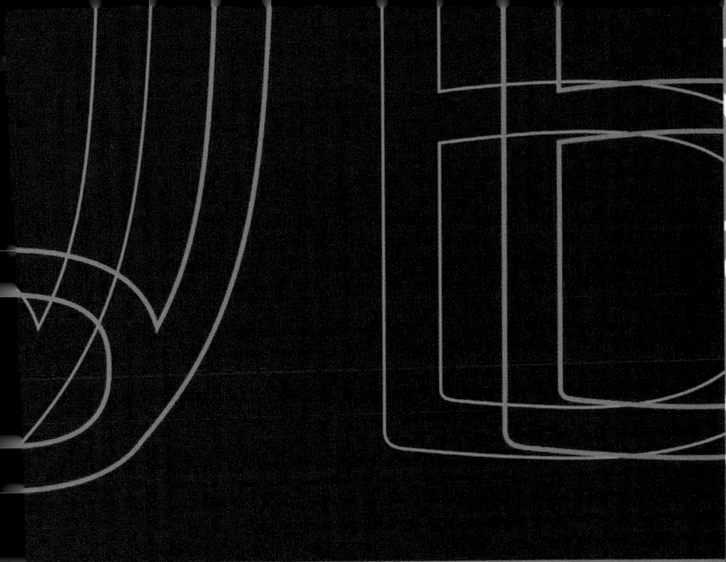

ABOVE AND RIGHT: Fontsmith's designs for FS Joey. Originally designed for a new video on-demand online service, its weights are finely tuned for use both on screen and in print. Designed by Jason Smith and Fernando Mello.

FAR RIGHT: Fontsmith founder and type designer Jason Smith.

FS Jack
Fontsmith
FS Jack Poster
abcdefghijklmn
opqrstuvwxyz
ABCDEFGHIJKLMN
OPQRSTUVWXYZ
1234567890

LEFT: FS Jack, a humanist Sans Serif design, described as 'confident, cool, good-looking and enthusiastic'. Designed by Jason Smith and Fernando Mello portfolio around and introducing myself and my work. I won a couple of jobs at Channel 4 and did the Post Office typeface. I branded myself as Fontsmith and set up a small studio and employed Phil Garnham, whom I taught how to draw and design type and be a support for me. The work kept coming in but I wanted to design and sell my fonts on the internet so everyone could use them and the website was born. Haven't looked back since, really. There are now seven of us and we have a pretty good reputation for innovative and beautifully crafted fonts.

Q: You have designed a wealth of bespoke typefaces commissioned by commercial organizations. How does the design and production process differ to typefaces that you create and market yourself? Are there technical or creative limitations for each type of working?
A: Every commission is different. However, the one thing that remains the same is that we approach the typefaces we design for customers from a pure design point of view; our work is never sold for technical reasons, it's all about adding value to the branding and building a strong identity. The technical side of things is easy and a given; every type foundry should be able to problem solve and produce technically sound fonts. You wouldn't go and commission a brand identity from a brand agency based on how good their artworkers are; you win commissions based on your portfolio of ideas and the design skills you have.

Q: You have designed corporate typefaces for the majority of Britain's key TV channels including BBC One, ITV, Channel 4 and Sky1. Does designing a typeface for primarily screen-based presentation require a differing approach?
A: It certainly influences the design, but not in a technical way, in a functional way. Type for broadcast screen is very different from type for computer screen. It's an entirely different set of problems. TV identity is about engaging your brand for a particular remit or demographic. Colour, music, images, language and immediacy are the important things here. The fonts we design are like a glue that holds all that together.

Investing in a typeface designed for you will create a unique, consistent identity for your brand. More than 40 million people see our fonts every day – but they don't see us. They see our clients. They see brands whose *typeface* is as familiar and identifiable as their names.

Q: How do you go about creating typefaces that embody a company's brand values?
A: At Fontsmith we have many years' experience in creating typefaces that work with the most visible, best-known brands in Britain. We know that what we design has to fit with who you are. We believe in collaboration. You know who you are; we know how to turn that into a uniquely appealing, customized typeface. With the clients' feel for their brand and our expertise in design, we can create a typeface that gives them a whole new layer of branding and of market impact.

Once I have an idea of the design brief I can understand what is required for the client. Things usually go back and forth a few times so everyone is in agreement on the rough design.

Q: Where do you get your ideas for starting a new design or in choosing a typeface to revive?

A: The first typeface I designed was a student project. I was 17 at the time and drew it all by hand and inked it in on drawing film. Many years later I digitized it. It is now known as FS Rome. Caps only, classic Roman alphabet. It sells about 30 copies a year. Fontsmith has never, ever done a revival, we have been influenced by the past and it inspires us at times, but everything is drawn, evaluated and crafted from a fresh point of view. It's the toughest thing to come up with your own brief for a new design to bring to market. You simply never know if it'll be a hit. Investing six months or a year on new work for retailing is a massive investment so we take our time to really think about what we want to add to the library.

Q: Many of your typefaces possess people's names. How do you go about ascribing a 'personality' and then choosing a name for your typeface designs?

A: From the shapes of cars and buildings. From colours and from words. I find that the older I get, the more I realize how instinctive I am. It doesn't take me ages to conclude that what I am designing is the right thing for the market. I guess people pay me to be instinctive, that's the point. I should have a wealth of inspiration and knowledge. I think the inspiration itself to give the type a name and a personality simply comes from a conversation with my colleagues. People and Places is the tool we find easiest to sum up a personality… or a face (pun intended)!

Q: To anyone thinking of taking up designing their own typeface and creating a font, what advice would you give to them?

A: Create a mood board with lots of visuals. Try and create a vibe, match a colour and photographs. Look through as many design books and find shapes that you like. Then start to sketch shapes, serifs, letters... draw an 'a', an 'n', a 'g', a 'b' and a 'k'. These are your fun letters. Enjoy it, nothing you do will be wrong. The skills of a type designer really come when you craft your letters, but you need to start somewhere, so don't be afraid.

RIGHT: Fontsmith's Serif typeface, FS Sally, going through the exhaustive processes of creating a new typeface from initial sketches – created digitally using font creation software – through to specimen sheets where every element is inspected and refined to perfection before release.

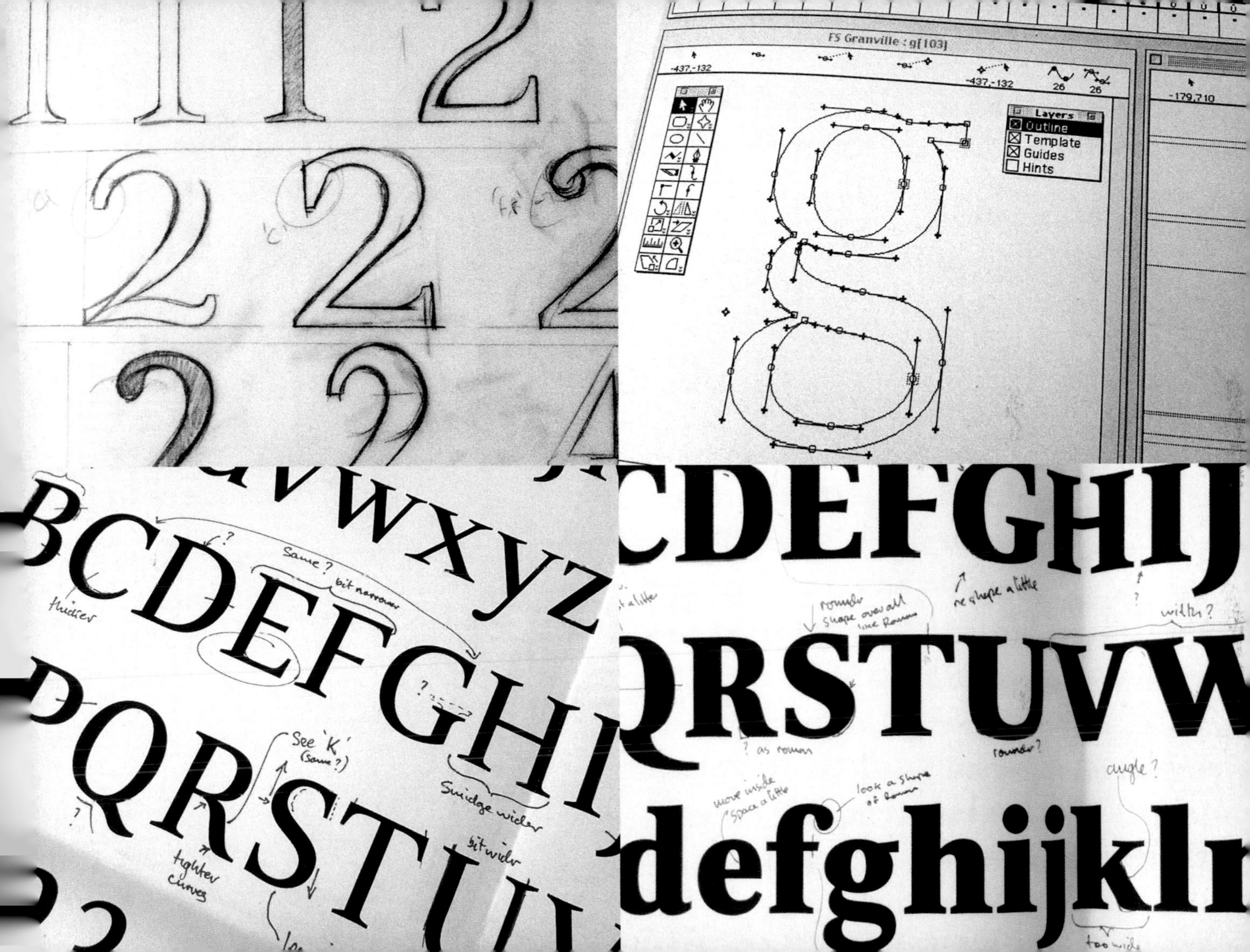
FS Granville : g[103]
-437,-132
-437,-132
26
26
-179,710
Layers
Outline
Template
Guides
Hints
Same?
bit narrower
thicker
See 'K' (Same?)
Smidge wider
bit wider
tighter curves
re shape a little
width?
? as roman
rounder?
angle?
look a shape of Roman
too wide

LCD

ALAN BIRCH · LINOTYPE · 1981

The technological innovation of the 1970s spawned digital watches and clocks, and with it the now ubiquitous LCD display. This typeface conveys the digital presentation of liquid crystal displays and its characteristic upper case segmented construction.

Recognized the world over, this distinctive typeface comes only in upper case and is constructed from regular-sized consistent module components to form variations in characters. Each stroke is angled at the ends by a 45° oblique to abut an adjoining section and form an even stroke.

There are a number of LCD-style types available from other foundries. Linotype's LCD is notable because it is designed as an italic; Quartz is available from earlier Letraset designs and comes in Light, Regular and Bold.

CATEGORY: Ornamented/Novelty

CLASSIFICATION: Futuristic

COUNTRY OF ORIGIN: UK

DISTINGUISHING MARKS: Modular construction; distinct LCD appearance; seven-stroke construction

FURTHER SIGHTINGS: Most digital alarm clocks and digital watches

NOT TO BE CONFUSED WITH: Foundry Gridnik (p. 278)

OPPOSITE: The mechanics of time pieces such as shown contributed to LCD's construction from simple stroke components built around a fixed arrangement.

8:46

ITC Machine

RONNIE BONDER, TOM CARNASE · ITC · 1970

CATEGORY: Sans Serif

CLASSIFICATION: Geometric

COUNTRY OF ORIGIN: USA

DISTINGUISHING MARKS: Heavy monostroke; angled corners and returns; absence of any curves; all upper case; slightly condensed; narrow counters

FURTHER SIGHTINGS: Blockbuster Video; American football; *Top Gun* and *Battleship* films

NOT TO BE CONFUSED WITH: Aachen (p. 232); Bank Gothic (p. 240)

OPPOSITE: ITC Machine's heavy and bold appearance makes it appropriate for messages and display typography where it needs to impose its authority in a dynamic manner. The example shown possesses much the same structure in design.

With not a curve in sight, this bold and industrial typeface has often been a good choice for maximum impact display and advertising work when the message needs to be SHOUTED!

Created back in the 1970s in just two weights, Medium and Bold, this upper-case alphabet has a heavy presence, with its brutish, beveled geometric letters and total lack of curves creating an impactful and hard aesthetic. As such, it's most often seen when the subject matter is of a similarly high-impact or forceful nature and notable uses are bold display and signage applications.

More often seen in the United States, the **ITC Machine** typeface has become synonymous with a lack of subtlety and it is commonly used in graphics and clothing for contact sports, especially American football, where its bold and heavy presence reflects the sport's serious intent and hard demeanour.

Mahou

JASON SMITH, EMANUELA CONIDI · FONTSMITH/MAHOU · 2012

Creating a typeface for Spain's largest beer brand was the task set for London type foundry Fontsmith (*see* p. 290) by branding consultancy Interbrand Madrid. The challenge was to create a new title font that complemented the existing Mahou logo yet retained the Latin personality of the brand.

As part of Interbrand's launch of the Mahou beer brand in the UK, Paul Marshall, senior designer at Interbrand Madrid, approached Fontsmith to explore the concept of a new typeface for the long-established beverage. As with all Fontsmith's type designs, an exhaustive process began with the sketching out of a number of ideas and designs for the new typeface collection. The letterforms were to be used as a title font in several weights, all of which not only had to complement and in some way reflect the almost Blackletter aesthetic of the existing Mahou logotype, but also work independently on advertising and display materials.

The new design is a modern Sans Serif with humanist qualities and echoes of the Mahou wordmark, with a mix of angled terminals, curved forms with delicate returns on tails, and a monoweight construction. A particularly distinguishing highlight in the design is the crossbar on the 'A', which possesses a refined curve to its line, creating a warmer character aesthetic and evoking a Latin tone. The new design was a great success in communicating the values of a modern-day, stylish brand that has not lost touch with its heritage.

CATEGORY: Sans Serif

CLASSIFICATION: Humanist

COUNTRY OF ORIGIN: UK/Spain

DISTINGUISHING MARKS: Monoweight appearance; curved letterforms; angled terminal on mid-bar of 'E'; return on tail of 'R'; curved junction on 'L'; curved crossbar on 'A'; oval letterforms; rear-facing return on first stem of 'M' and 'I'

FURTHER SIGHTINGS: Bespoke typeface created for Mahou

NOT TO BE CONFUSED WITH: FS Albert (p. 126); Bliss (p. 150); Foundry Sterling (p. 170)

OPPOSITE: Fontsmith's bespoke Mahou typeface employed on promotional and launch items for the Spanish beer brand.

MADRID
MOLA
SABE A MADRID
COPA MAHOU

GRUUT
GENTSE STADSBROUWERIJ

Mason

JONATHAN BARNBROOK · EMIGRE · 1992

Esteemed British designer Jonathan Barnbrook's Mason typeface was groundbreaking when released in the early 1990s. Its ecclesiastical aesthetic proved popular and it was employed in a number of contexts, from TV graphics to publishing and packaging.

Mason's ingenious and distinctive design was a long time in development, with the initial idea coming from many years of sketching by Barnbrook, and extensive research into ancient manuscripts and Russian letterforms. The typeface was initially released by the **Emigre** type foundry (*see* Profile p. 56) and called Manson – after the serial killer Charles Manson – but such was the uproar generated by this unfortunate titling that it was renamed Mason.

Despite its religious manuscript overtones, Mason displays a contemporary approach to its design, with a highly constructed and uniform consistency to its letterforms. Its character set possesses many details suggestive of its influences: the 't's are crucifixes, the 'V's and 'W's appear like heraldic shields and the 'M's have angled top bars in the style of a castle's portcullis. With these many elegant touches, Mason is often employed in fantasy and historical genres to create a 'medieval' aesthetic. Alongside the Serif release, Barnbrook created a Humanist Sans Serif version that reflects Eric Gill's (p. 186) and Edward Johnston's (p. 204) typeface designs, both of which influenced Barnbrook during his design education.

CATEGORY: Serif

CLASSIFICATION: Roman Inscribed

COUNTRY OF ORIGIN: UK

DISTINGUISHING MARKS: Ornate letterform construction; double horizontal bar on upper-case 'H'; extended tails on upper-case 'Q' and 'R'; diamond on top of 'i'/'I' and 'j'/'J'; crossbar on 'Z'; no lower case, just capitals and small capitals

FURTHER SIGHTINGS: Philip Pullman's *His Dark Materials* books and subsequently *The Golden Compass* film

NOT TO BE CONFUSED WITH: Shàngó Gothic (p. 108); Trajan (p. 112)

OPPOSITE: Mason employed for the identity and livery for Gruut, a beer brand from Ghent, Belgium.

Namco

AKIHIRO OYA · FREEWARE · 1998

Created from the classic logotype for the Japanese video game developer and publisher Namco, Oya's design expands on the futuristic, extended letterforms of the Namco logo to create a range of letterforms that build on the distinctive design features of the marque.

The Japanese corporation Namco was best known for its innovation with video and arcade games such as *Pac-Man* – its greatest success – along with other classic games such as *Tekken* and *Ridge Racer*. The company's identity reflected the visual zeitgeist within the video games industry of technology, innovation and a certain science-fiction aesthetic. As such, Namco's letterforms reflect this technological innovation and pioneering freeform spirit in their appearance.

It was Japanese graphic designer Akihiro Oya who took the logo and developed the design further into a typeface, although it's a rather incomplete character set only available with a lower-case design (which incorporates several upper-case designs as small case) and numbers. The distinctive corners of the characters provide a hi-tech aesthetic, mixing rounded with sharp 90° angles. The typeface also includes logo designs redrawn from early Namco games including *Rally-X* and *Xevious*.

CATEGORY: Ornamented/Novelty

CLASSIFICATION: Futuristic

COUNTRY OF ORIGIN: Japan

DISTINGUISHING MARKS: Extended letterforms; lower case only; heavy monostroke appearance; rounded and 90° corners; squared letterforms; small counters; no descenders/ascenders; hi-tech appearance

FURTHER SIGHTINGS: Seen in amusement arcades globally; Namco Museum; Xbox 360; Namco X Capcom soundtrack

NOT TO BE CONFUSED WITH: Bank Gothic (p. 240); Foundry Gridnik (p. 278)

OPPOSITE: As dynamic and dramatic as the games they made: the Namco logotype, the basis for the **Namco** typeface, by Japanese designer Akihiro Oya.

namco®

MANCHESTER
UNITED

Sat 09 Apr 2011
Kick Off 3pm
Fulham
Barclays Pr

MANCHESTER
UNITED

Sat 09 Apr 2011
Kick Off 3pm
Fulham
Barclays Premier League

South Stand Upper

Block
STH221
Row
U
Seat
187
Entrance
C 2
Europa Suite
09237242

MANUTD.COM
0161 868 8000

OCR-B

ADRIAN FRUTIGER/AMERICAN TYPE FOUNDERS · LINOTYPE · 1966/1968

CATEGORY:
Ornamented/Novelty

CLASSIFICATION: Machine Readable

COUNTRY OF ORIGIN: USA

DISTINGUISHING MARKS:
OCR-A: Monospaced appearance; monoline stroke weight; rounded terminals; angled curves and corners
OCR-B: Monospaced appearance; minimal contrast in stroke weight; rounded curves; more grotesque appearance

FURTHER SIGHTINGS:
The Matrix film

NOT TO BE CONFUSED WITH:
Channel 4 (p. 156); DIN 1451 (p. 158)

OPPOSITE: A global standard, OCR-B seen here employed on a ticketing application.

With the dawn of the computer age in the 1960s, a new typographical approach had to be created to enable machines, rather than the human eye, to read typed letters. OCR-A was the first of its kind to be designed to be machine-readable.

In the early days of computing, creating a typeface that was OCR (optical character recognition) and therefore readable by machine, yet also legible to the human eye, was no mean feat. As computers scanned and 'read' more documents for organizations such as banks and governments, the need for an accurate typeface was crucial. A combination of simple, clean strokes and a monospaced arrangement of the letters helped to achieve this, leading to a solution that worked for both recipients (albeit imperfectly for people, for whom the process of reading was more laboured).

The original OCR-A was created by **American Type Founders** and was the first to meet the requirements laid out by the US Bureau of Standards. Very soon afterwards, **OCR-B** was designed by **Adrian Frutiger** to improve on the original design. This OCR typeface had increased legibility to the human eye over its counterpart and had more traditional letterforms. In 1973 it was made the world standard for OCR applications and is still very much in use.

As a result of their technological look and feel, both OCRs have often been used by designers to impart a 'techno' feel to their work and are often seen employed in the science-fiction genre.

FRANKLIN & MARSHALL
FRANKLIN & MARSHALL
FRANKLIN & MARSHALL

Princetown

DICK JONES · **ITC** · 1981

CATEGORY: Serif

CLASSIFICATION: Geometric Slab

COUNTRY OF ORIGIN: UK

DISTINGUISHING MARKS: Heavy border and monoweight construction; angled corners and returns; absence of any curves; all upper case; slightly condensed; narrow counters

FURTHER SIGHTINGS: Franklin & Marshall

NOT TO BE CONFUSED WITH: ITC Machine (p. 298)

Princetown is perhaps most readily identified as nearly always being seen on US college sweatshirts and sports garments. Its bold geometric forms and slab serifs make it easy to spot.

Designed in 1981 for the Letraset dry transfer library by Dick Jones, Princetown's heavily outlined appearance makes for a striking alphabet. Created in capitals only and with no curves in the design, the typeface was inspired by US college and university sportswear and as such is nearly now always seen within a sporting reference.

Continuing the sports/fashion association, a modified Condensed variation of the Princetown typeface is employed by fashion clothing company Franklin & Marshall, who in fact license their name from the US school.

OPPOSITE: The typeface of choice for casual university wear the world over, Princetown possesses a strong American college aesthetic seen here employed by US fashion label Franklin & Marshall.

Pump

PHILIP KELLY · **ITC** · 1975

With its rounded forms and geometric appearance, Pump evokes memories of the 1970s. Inspired by, and adopting a similar form to, the 1900s influenced ITC Bauhaus (p. 140), the typeface has remained popular thanks to its fun, retro appearance.

Designed originally in the Letraset studio by British designer and typographer **Philip Kelly**, Pump's success lies in its simplicity – it was designed primarily around curves and geometric forms. Pump is available in upper and lower case in Light, Medium, Demi and Bold. Its most imaginative treatment is as a tri-line design, where the letterforms are created from three parallel lines running together to form the letter shapes. With a particularly strong sporting connotation, it (or a close imitation of it) is often seen on the back of a footballer's or other sportsperson's shirt.

Because of the nature of its appearance, Pump is most successful when the characters are set closely together, creating a circular flow through the letter strokes.

CATEGORY: Sans Serif

CLASSIFICATION: Geometric

COUNTRY OF ORIGIN: UK

DISTINGUISHING MARKS: Circular motif and highly rounded aesthetic; open counters on numerous letters; monoweight stroke; diagonal crossbar on lower-case 'e'; closed counter on lower-case 'e' (whereas they are open in the ITC Bauhaus typeface)

FURTHER SIGHTINGS: Rare

NOT TO BE CONFUSED WITH: ITC Bauhaus (p. 140)

OPPOSITE: Pump's rounded forms make for a fun, lively and striking display signage.

note

TOMORROW'S SHOW:

TONIGHT'S SHOW:

Small £2.00
Regular £3.50
TEXAN
PHILADELPHIA
½ POUND BURGER
CALIFORNIAN
NEW YORKER
NACHOS
LOUISIANA
CHIPS
FRESHLY MADE
HOT DOGS

Rosewood

KIM BUKER CHANSLER, CARL GROSSGROVE, CAROL TWOMBLY · ADOBE · 1994

CATEGORY:
Ornamented/Novelty

CLASSIFICATION: Tuscan

COUNTRY OF ORIGIN: USA

DISTINGUISHING MARKS: Ornate infill; drop shadows; slab serifs; narrow letterforms

FURTHER SIGHTINGS: Delights of Sweden crispbread

NOT TO BE CONFUSED WITH:
Clarendon (p. 54); Aachen (p. 232); Bottleneck (p. 258)

OPPOSITE: Chromatic printing of type allowed for the use of two or even three colours, in precise register, to make up the full letterform. It was often employed in the late 1800s on posters and billboards to create impact and a more striking design. Here it is teamed up with Comic Sans to shout about hot dogs on Brighton Pier, UK.

Roll up, roll up! All the fun of the fair is to be had with this playful yet intricate revival of a nineteenth-century wood letter Slab Serif face. Rosewood is available in two variants: Regular is an ornate, decorative design with a drop shadow; Rosewood Fill allows for a second colour to be employed as a background tone.

Released in 1994 by **Adobe** as part of its Wood Type collection, Rosewood's inspiration is taken from a chromatic (*see* caption) design by William Page in 1874, then a leading designer and manufacturer of wood type for letterpress printing in the US. As many of the wood types of the second half of the nineteenth century were based on Clarendon type letterforms, Rosewood follows suit and possesses a strong Slab Serif design. Where it differs from the norm is that its infill contains a detailed decorative design in the top half of the characters, reminiscent of 'Wild West' ornamented wood type.

Rosewood also pays homage to the chromatic printing process by possessing a second font that can appear behind the main typeface as a background colour – a feature that allows the designer, when aligning the elements of the full typeface and the variant, to employ two colours in the setting of the type, thus creating a lively and striking impression. However, the background 'infill' works just as well on its own as a typeface on its own merit.

Architype Stedelijk

WIM CROUWEL · THE FOUNDRY · 1968 (FONT CREATED 1997)

Architype Stedelijk first appeared in legendary Dutch designer Wim Crouwel's poster *Vormgevers*, commissioned by the Stedelijk Museum in Amsterdam in 1968.

In the *Vormgevers* design, Crouwel created a rigid grid system across the poster in which the typeface was built using the various arrangements of the grid to create each letterform. The top half of the poster was constructed out of 57 vertical lines and 41 horizontal lines, and despite the highly technological appearance of the type, it was all drawn lovingly by hand to create a seminal and striking black and white solution. This was of course long before the advent of the Apple Mac in design. In 1997, the typeface was redrawn and expanded into a full font alphabet by London type foundry **The Foundry**.

Crouwel's most recognized work is for the Van Abbemuseum and the Stedelijk Museum (between 1956 and 1972) in which he established his reputation for experimental typefaces and innovative design using grid-based solutions. Crouwel still is one of the leading graphic designers and typographers in the world. Born in 1928, he designed his first poster back in 1952 and to this day is still working, acting as a consultant and touring the globe giving lectures.

CATEGORY: Sans Serif

CLASSIFICATION: Geometric

COUNTRY OF ORIGIN: The Netherlands/UK

DISTINGUISHING MARKS: Rigid grid structure to letterforms; monoline weight; slight rounded corners; appearance of bitmap construction

FURTHER SIGHTINGS: *Vormgevers* poster; Stedelijk Museum Amsterdam

NOT TO BE CONFUSED WITH: Foundry Gridnik (p. 278); OCR-A (p. 306)

RIGHT: Wim Crouwel's classic *Vormgevers* poster employing his Architype Stedelijk typeface. Its letterforms are constructed directly from a grid formation synonymous with Crouwel's typographic experimentation.

FIELD FACTS_

Wim Crouwel's exploration and use of grid systems and his creation of geometrical typefaces in his work earned him the nickname of 'Mr Gridnik' from his friends. In later years, when his typeface Politene (an unused commission in 1974 by typewriter manufacturer Olivetti) was digitized by London type foundry The Foundry, it was renamed Foundry Gridnik (p. 278) in celebration of his alternative title.

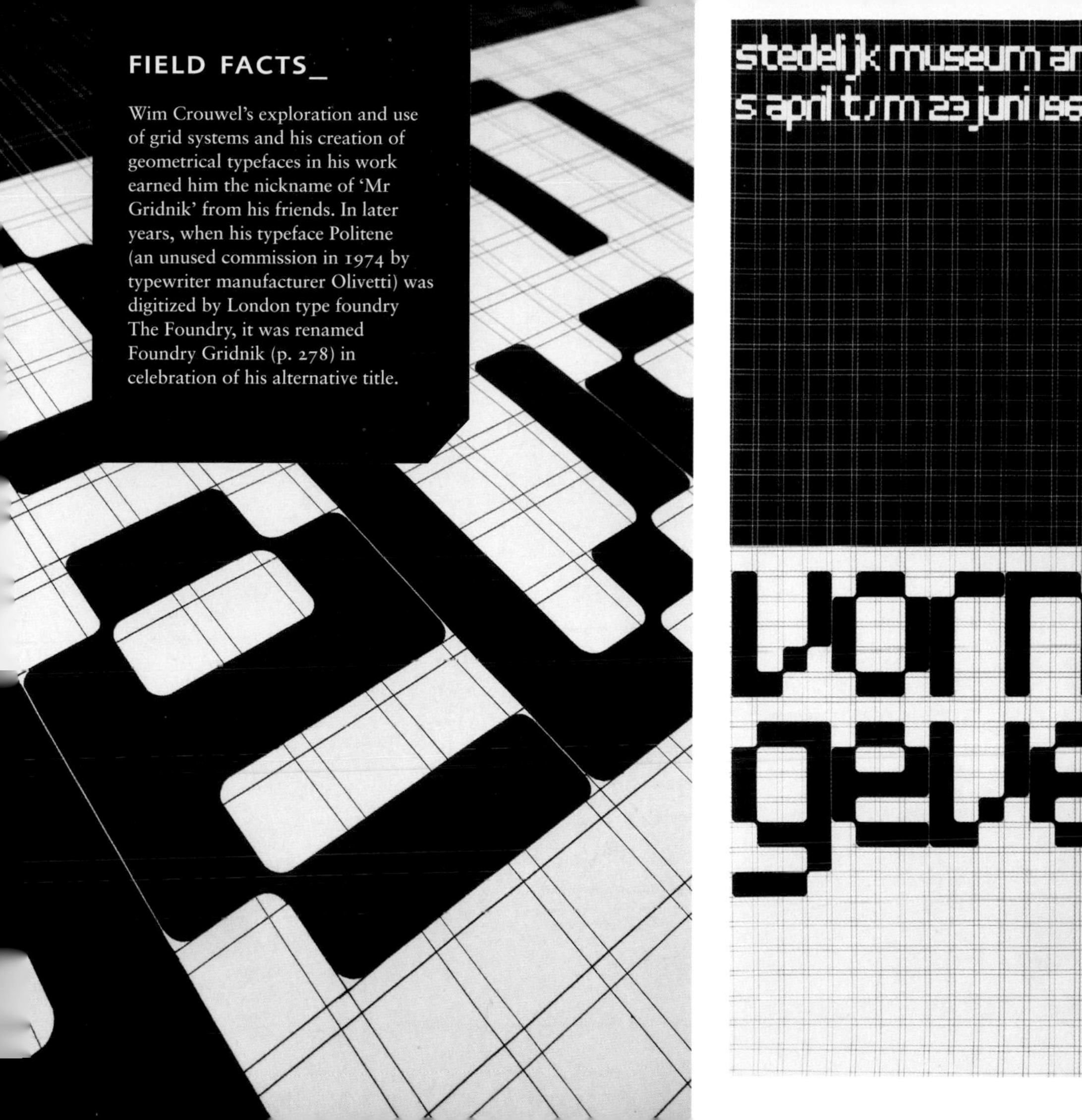

stedelijk museum amsterdam
5 april t/m 23 juni 1968

vorm
gevers

THE HOME DEPOT
Enter
Enter

Stencil

GERRY POWELL · ADOBE/LINOTYPE · 1938

CATEGORY: Serif

CLASSIFICATION: Stencil

COUNTRY OF ORIGIN: USA

DISTINGUISHING MARKS: Bold letterforms; rounded and bracketed serifs; stencil appearance; high stroke contrast; vertical stress; short extenders

FURTHER SIGHTINGS: Public Enemy logo; The Home Depot; World War II military vehicles and planes; *The A-Team* logo (film and TV series); *M*A*S*H* TV series; Disney's *Recess*

NOT TO BE CONFUSED WITH: Bodoni Poster (p. 256); Glaser Stencil (p. 274)

Often seen on packing crates and old military vehicles, Stencil is an ideal choice for an earthy, tough font for those who need to roll their shirt sleeves up, ignore the niceties of typographic craft and just get on with the task ahead.

Stencil was designed for American Type Founders in 1938 by American designer Gerry Powell, who drew his inspiration from the sprayed and painted stencil lettering one would find on packing cases and crates. The typeface employs just the one weight and possesses rounded corners and serifs, with no lower case. Surprisingly legible, even when used in crude stencil formats, it has often been copied and imitated, with a number of foundries offering their own versions. Stencil is ideal for graphics that denote a transportation or military tone, or for designs that need a rough and tough image.

OPPOSITE: Loud and proud, Stencil assists in flying the flag at The Home Depot.

FF ThreeSix

HAMISH MUIR, PAUL MCNEIL · FONTFONT · 2011

This experimental typeface system has been created with six typefaces in four weights. Its principled geometric construction exploits the restrictions of adhering to geometry in its design.

Created by Paul McNeil, a type and information systems designer in London, and Hamish Muir, founding principal of design studio 8vo (1985–2001) and independent graphic design consultant, the FF ThreeSix typeface explores the boundaries of legibility within its letterform construction. By employing key principles and consistent forms in the typeface design, optical tricks are played on the reader when viewing texts set in smaller sizes and despite letter strokes being broken, legibility is maintained as these breaks 'disappear' and an evenness in the type occurs. Upon application at large display sizes, the broken forms become apparent and create a distinctive and coordinated system of letters, retaining their readability but projecting further the typeface's distinctive appearance.

The consistency in design is highly mathematical. The system is constructed from a grid of 36 unit squares. These are then subdivided into nine units. Each letter is formed using only vertical and horizontal straight lines and circular arcs. The cap-height, x-height, ascender and descender measurements are also consistent across all fonts and weights, all providing a rigid yet highly flexible typeface system.

CATEGORY: Ornamented/Novelty

CLASSIFICATION: Geometric

COUNTRY OF ORIGIN: UK

DISTINGUISHING MARKS: Formed from a grid of 36 unit squares, only horizontal/vertical lines and circular arcs are employed to form the letters

FURTHER SIGHTINGS: *Contemporary Australian Architecture*, Outcast Editions interactive digital books

NOT TO BE CONFUSED WITH: Foundry Gridnik (p. 278); Architype Stedelijk (p. 314)

OPPOSITE: FF ThreeSix 072 Regular cast in concrete and used for a typographic installation as part of Nick Kapica/SV Associates' wayfinding system in New Zealand's Massey University *Te Ara Hihiko* College of Creative Arts.

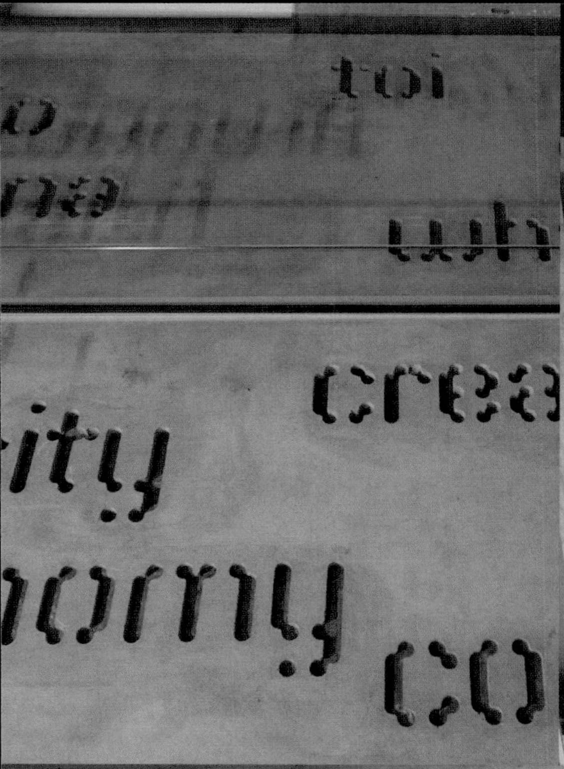

toi
mātauranga
whanaungatanga
creativity
virtuosity
understanding
autonomy
connectedness
EXIT

FIELD FACTS_

In 2008 van Blokland revisited the design of FF Trixie (FF Trixie HD) to increase the level of intricacy within the typeface. A problem with earlier distressed type is that coarse detailing looks blobby when big, so more detail was introduced by adding further points to the vector outlines making up the font and in addition creating alternatives for each character for variation.

FF Trixie

ERIK VAN BLOKLAND · FONTFONT · 1991

CATEGORY: Serif

CLASSIFICATION: Distressed

COUNTRY OF ORIGIN: The Netherlands

DISTINGUISHING MARKS: Broken-up typewriter font

FURTHER SIGHTINGS: *Capote* and *Atonement* film posters; *The X-Files* television series; US Girl Scouts advertising; cover of *So-Called Chaos* by Alanis Morissette

NOT TO BE CONFUSED WITH: American Typewriter (p. 26)

OPPOSITE: The broken forms of Trixie (paired with American Typewriter at bottom right) can clearly be seen in this detail of a shop sign. Due to limitations in its construction, the forms of the glyphs clearly show the bezier outline construction in this early version. A later version was created including more points, for a more refined and distressed appearance when used large (*see* Field Facts).

How does a printed sheet typed out on a decrepit typewriter at a friend's house in Berlin become one of the most recognizable distressed typefaces globally? Answer: all thanks to a starring part in the hit television show *The X-Files*.

In the early 1990s, Dutch designer Erik van Blokland experimented with turning scanned images into fonts and writing samples – one could describe it as an 'instant font'. In discussion with colleague Just van Rossum, the concept of degraded typewriter letterforms was suggested and months later while van Blokland was visiting a friend, Beatrix Gunther (or Trixie, as her friends called her), he found a suitable typewriter at her house. With a typed up sample sheet in hand he soon developed it into a font, which was then published by FontShop International under their FontFont brand. The actual original typeface on the typewriter was called Triumph Durabel, and was created in 1930s Nuremberg.

Its decayed and broken-up letterforms mirror a typewriter's often inconsistent strike upon the paper and the overall effect is one of a 'bureaucratic environment', as van Blokland describes it. It was adopted soon after by *The X-Files* television programme, whose global audience brought huge success to a typeface with very modest beginnings.

Umbra

ROBERT H. MIDDLETON · LINOTYPE · 1935

Defined only by its shadow, these elegant Sans Serif forms are reminiscent of a light-weighted Sans such as Gill.

Originally designed to be a second-colour drop shadow printing for the typeface Tempo Light, Umbra was developed to be used as an unusual singular display typeface on its own. Its name refers to its construction from the shadowed part of its form.

British-born Robert H. Middleton emigrated to the US when he was a young boy. Initially, he had wanted to be an artist, but after encountering the work of German designer Ernst F. Detterer decided to work as a type designer at the Ludlow Typograph Company of Chicago, famous for their Ludlow Typograph ('The Ludlow'), a machine that combined hand assembly with hot metal casting of type for lines of text that was used widely in newspapers and the rubber stamp industry at the time. In later years he founded The Cherryburn Press, where he continued to design typefaces.

CATEGORY: Ornamented/Novelty

CLASSIFICATION: Geometric

COUNTRY OF ORIGIN: USA

DISTINGUISHING MARKS: No actual form; defined only by shadow; no serifs; upper case; one weight

FURTHER SIGHTINGS: Used in contemporary design applications, its striking appearance makes it ideal for more 'avant-garde' usages

NOT TO BE CONFUSED WITH: Futura (p. 180); Glaser Stencil (p. 274)

OPPOSITE: Umbra's classical yet contemporary aesthetic makes it ideal for a more fashion-led approach to graphic design.

FALL
COLLECTION
13/14

Zebrawood

CARL CROSSGROVE, CAROL TWOMBLY, KIM BUKER CHANSLER · ADOBE · 1994

CATEGORY:
Ornamented/Novelty

CLASSIFICATION: Tuscan

COUNTRY OF ORIGIN: USA

DISTINGUISHING MARKS:
Scalloped edges; drop shadow; ornate and decorative infill; three graduated dots stacked in lower half of stems; small flared serifs

FURTHER SIGHTINGS: Its ornate detailing allies it closely with the visual references associated with funfairs and circuses

NOT TO BE CONFUSED WITH:
Rosewood (p. 312)

OPPOSITE: Waxing lyrical. Zebrawood's fun and kitsch appearance used to full effect in this retro-designed waxing and tanning boutique in London.

Derived from an American Wells & Webb type company specimen catalogue published in 1854, this recreation of an Antique Tuscan style of letterform possesses all the hallmarks of ornate nineteenth-century wood type.

The Antique Tuscan style of wood type in the nineteenth century features scalloped, contoured edges and upturned serifs with points. Thanks in part to its capacious letterforms, it encouraged the addition of embellishments and ornate infills and decoration. **Zebrawood** employs many of those styles, with a filled upper half containing a decorative infill and an open lower half employing a dot motif in the stems, tails and curved strokes. Add to that a deep drop shadow and you have a typeface that possesses a large sense of occasion and nostalgia.

As with Rosewood (p. 312), Zebrawood is intended to be used as a chromatic design and an alternative version is available for multicolour printing where the printing of type allows the use of two or three colours overlaid in precise register. This striking effect was put to good use on handbills and posters for subject matter such as the circus or fairgrounds and can still be seen today employed in a similar manner.

Sublime
IT'S
SALE
TIME
UP TO 70% OFF
OUR WOMENSWEAR +
ACCESSORIES

Script

OPPOSITE: Bickley Script (p. 330) employed outside a fashion boutique with a modern-day attempt at a 'script' chalked onto the blackboard below.

ALIMENTARI
30

Balloon

MAX R. KAUFMANN · 1939

CATEGORY: Script

CLASSIFICATION: Brush Script

COUNTRY OF ORIGIN: USA

DISTINGUISHING MARKS: Appearance of broad-nibbed pen- or brushstrokes; incomplete joining of strokes; upper case only; crossbar of 'A' not fully connected to stem

FURTHER SIGHTINGS: Former Nickelodeon TV channel logotype

NOT TO BE CONFUSED WITH: Bruno (p. 332); Brush Script (p. 334)

OPPOSITE: Balloon's informality provides a cheeky tone to signage and display messaging.

With the appearance of being scrawled by a hurried broad-nibbed pen, Balloon's handwritten yet clear form allows it to work well as a display typeface when a lighter, informal approach is needed and is reminiscent of the lettering that would appear in comic books.

Designed in 1939 by American lettering artist **Max R. Kaufmann**, Balloon has proved popular – near-identical cuts are offered by a majority of foundries. Available in three weights (Light, Bold and Extra Bold), there is also an outlined version, complete with drop shadow, that can be obtained from foundry Elsner+Flake. Typefaces with a similar aesthetic design to Balloon include House Slant (House Industries) and Flash (Edwin W. Shaar), also created in 1939.

Bickley Script

ALAN MEEKS · ITC · 1986

This light, flowing calligraphic script is based on the handwriting forms that were evident towards the close of the nineteenth century. Its large open capitals and joined-up lower case create a flamboyant stroke path, combining elegance with a human touch.

Originally commissioned and released by Letraset in the mid-1980s, Alan Meeks's elegant, romantic Script font draws its appearance from the forms of late nineteenth-century handwriting called copperplate or English round hand. This style of calligraphic writing was produced by using a sharpened nib rather than flattened. The weighting of the strokes and the contrast within each letterform were determined by the amount of pressure applied to the nib rather than the angle at which a flattened nib edge was held. The term 'copperplate' comes from the reference copybooks with which students learned and practised their writing – the name deriving from the fact that the books were printed using copper plates.

In order to maintain a handwritten appearance, Bickley Script is designed so that the lower case joins up when set, with the oversized capital letters bestowing an ornamental touch to the start of a sentence. Its feminine and informal nature provides an elegance to most presentations; however, because of its thin stroke weight and ornate detailing, it is best used at larger point sizes, for example on display work or the packaging of more luxurious consumer items such as chocolate boxes.

CATEGORY: Script

CLASSIFICATION: English Round Hand

COUNTRY OF ORIGIN: UK

DISTINGUISHING MARKS: Thin stroke weight; loose handwritten construction; open counters; horizontal bar through upper-case 'Z'; overlaying of strokes; flamboyant tails and curves

FURTHER SIGHTINGS: Ideal for display and titling application where a more 'feminine' tone is required

NOT TO BE CONFUSED WITH: Brush Script (p. 334); ITC Edwardian Script (p. 338)

OPPOSITE: The flowing lines and open elegance of Bickley Script used above a fashion boutique.

Sublime

men's and ladies'
activewear
& team
merchandise

$9.99 – $24.99

$20-$50

Bruno

JILL BELL · ADOBE, MONOTYPE · 1999

CATEGORY: Script

CLASSIFICATION: Handwriting

COUNTRY OF ORIGIN: USA

DISTINGUISHING MARKS: Loose, handwritten quality; irregular letter shapes between shared features such as counters; repeat strokes on upper-case stems; monoweight stroke

FURTHER SIGHTINGS: Used when requiring an informal and light-hearted tone to communications

NOT TO BE CONFUSED WITH: Balloon (p. 328); Brush Script (p. 334); Macmillan Headline (p. 348)

OPPOSITE: Jill Bell's Bruno typeface employed on in-store advertising. Its loose, informal style makes it ideal for friendly promotional messages.

Named after the largest of her three cats, Bruno was created by Los Angeles-based lettering artist Jill Bell from a scrawled note reminding her to buy cat food. It was her first font for Adobe.

From a shopping list scrawled in haste comes this scratchy and loosely structured typeface, which has all the hallmark irregularities of handwritten text. With a rough and ready structure, it is an ideal choice for those who are after a looser aesthetic. A number of the upper-case characters have repeat strokes on their stems for emphasis, as if the writer needed to make sure the character was written down correctly. It is available in Regular and Bold weights; Bell's aim was to create an 'informal version of an artist's hand-printing'.

Jill Bell, prior to setting up her lettering and typography studio over 20 years ago, worked as a calligrapher, as a sign painter and as a production artist for esteemed graphic designer Saul Bass. She has not only received font design commissions from ITC, Adobe, Agfa/Monotype and Linotype but also judged type design contests for both the TDC (Type Directors Club in New York) and Linotype. Her commercial lettering project clients include Disney, Pillsbury and Ralph Lauren.

Brush Script

ROBERT E. SMITH · LINOTYPE · 1942

A successful and highly popular font since its release and much imitated and copied over the years, Brush Script has proven itself to be the 'leader of the pack' when it comes to a casual script typeface. However, it is not to everyone's taste, and is rarely employed by professional designers or typographers. Perish the thought!

Despite its global popularity and widespread use, Brush Script is more often found in more quotidian contexts, such as in a shop window or on a poorly laid-out menu, on the side of a burger van, or laser-printed and flyposted onto a hoarding. To many (myself included) it exposes a lack of taste on the part of the user. Yet despite this hostility from modern design communities, it was loved in the past, particularly with advertisers and retailers in the 1940s and 1950s. Its exuberant and dynamic brushstrokes were an eye-catching alternative to contemporary designs, with its irregular lower case and unaligned baseline imitating the flow of classical handwriting while retaining a formal regularity. Representing a more impactful option, Brush proved popular among designers who wanted to strike a warmer note in their messages and the selling of wares.

As time passed and tastes developed, particularly with the advent of the 'International Typographic Style' (otherwise known as the Swiss Style), a cleaner, more minimal and modern approach to graphic design and typography found favour. As a result, in professional circles Brush has become largely obsolete.

CATEGORY: Script

CLASSIFICATION: Brush Script

COUNTRY OF ORIGIN: USA

DISTINGUISHING MARKS: Strong contrast on strokes; heavier, bolder strokes than most scripts; small returns on broad brushstrokes; letters formed of single strokes; connecting lower-case characters

FURTHER SIGHTINGS: *Neighbours* TV series (original)

NOT TO BE CONFUSED WITH: Balloon (p. 328); Gigi (p. 344)

OPPOSITE: Brush Script is useful in those contexts where a retro or ironic tone is required (for instance this light box display in Rome, Italy). It is very hard to imagine a popular revival ever occurring but who knows? Watch this space...

FIELD FACTS_

In his bestselling book *Just My Type* (2010), Simon Garfield cites a survey carried out by Anthony Cahalan on designers' favourite and least favourite typefaces. In it, Brush Script ranked third in the 'hated' category with Times New Roman at number one and Helvetica/Neue Helvetica coming second.

Der Burgplatz, historisches Zentrum Braunschweigs,
bildet mit der Burg Dankwarderode, dem
Dom St. Blasii und dem Vieweghaus ein Ensemble
von hoher geschichtlicher und kultureller Bedeutung.
Welfenherzog Heinrich der Löwe ließ um 1166 als
Zeichen seiner Macht auf der Mitte des Platzes den
Braunschweiger Löwen als erste freistehende
Großplastik nördlich der Alpen errichten und
stiftete den Dom St. Blasii. Die Burg
Dankwarderode wurde Ende des 19. Jh.
rekonstruiert.
Dieses Stadtmodell aus Bronze wurde im
Jahre 2008 von den fünf Lions Clubs gestiftet:
LC Braunschweig, LC Braunschweig Alte Wiek,
LC Braunschweig Dankwarderode, LC Braunschweig
"Die Leoniden" und LC Braunschweig Klinterklater.

Comic Sans

VINCENT CONNARE · MICROSOFT · 1995

CATEGORY: Script

CLASSIFICATION: Handwriting

COUNTRY OF ORIGIN: USA

DISTINGUISHING MARKS: Handwritten appearance; primitive letter strokes

FURTHER SIGHTINGS: *The Sims* video game; Las Rocas wine; war memorial in Geffen, the Netherlands; Microsoft PCs

NOT TO BE CONFUSED WITH: Balloon (p. 328); Bruno (p. 332)

OPPOSITE: Despite lacking the precision and refinement of other typefaces, the real issue with Comic Sans is its use out of context. Here it is seen on a plaque in the city of Braunschweig, Germany. In 1999, two Indianapolis designers, Dave and Holly Combs, set up the website bancomicsans.com after one of their employers requested they use the typeface in a museum exhibit aimed at children. The site is still running and there exist many other sites, online petitions, satirical pieces and even games dedicated to the eradication of Comic Sans.

Comic Sans is probably the most hated and perhaps the most controversial typeface (after Helvetica?) among designers and type aficionados, with petitions, campaigns and hate sites created to lambaste it. While its popularity among the wider public cannot be denied, it is the nature of its employment that is problematic.

Inspired by lettering from comics, Comic Sans was developed by **Microsoft** type engineer **Vincent Connare** in the mid-1990s. Initially for use within Microsoft applications (specifically the package 'Microsoft Bob'), it ended up being included in their Windows operating system and as such was shipped out on PCs all over the world. As the 'fun font', its use rapidly widened from DIY invites to the school fête flyer before being adopted by commercial organizations for use in professional communications. It is at this point that the typeface became vilified. It was the context in which it was being employed that was the issue; a serious message should be presented in a typeface that provides the appropriate tone. Comic Sans fails to provide any fitting tone other than frivolity.

There are those who *do* benefit from Comic Sans. Despite its casual appearance, the typeface is in fact highly legible, working well as a display face and also for on-screen text purposes, thanks to its even spacing and primitive recreation of character shapes. As such, dyslexia associations recommend the use of Comic Sans. So at the end of the day, Comic Sans isn't *all* bad.

ITC Edwardian Script

ED BENGUIAT · ITC · 1994

This elegant, swirling copperplate Script has all the romance and passion that one would expect from a calligraphic script. Its refined curves and intricate details combine to form the impression of handwriting from a bygone age.

Designed by the renowned and prolific New York lettering artist and designer Ed Benguiat, ITC Edwardian Script possesses a great number of considered and elegant design details within its letterforms. Its lower case is tightly controlled in its structure, with each of the characters designed so that it can join with any other to form unbroken lines of joined-up text. However, it is in the upper case that ITC Edwardian Script's real personality comes to the fore. Benguiat's skill and expertise as one of America's foremost typographers is evident in a series of highly ornate capitals whose flamboyant forms are embellished with multiple loops and curls. The intricacy of these characters and their perfect balance and beauty makes ITC Edwardian Script ideal for any display work where perhaps a nostalgic and romantic tone is required.

Sadly, a lack of imaginative use means it is more often seen on the default wedding invite, greetings card and engraved trophy.

CATEGORY: Script

CLASSIFICATION: French Round Hand

COUNTRY OF ORIGIN: USA

DISTINGUISHING MARKS: Looped descenders on lower-case 'g', 'j', 'y' and 'z'; ornate upper case with multiple flowing strokes; descenders on upper-case 'G', 'J', 'Y' and 'Z'; strong calligraphic quality to strokes; high stroke contrast; multiple loops at the end of terminals on upper case and also within counters

FURTHER SIGHTINGS: Ideal for classical applications for those needing a regal air

NOT TO BE CONFUSED WITH: Bickley Script (p. 330)

OPPOSITE: Classical overtones make ITC Edwardian Script ideal for more upmarket presentations, here seen above a store in the Netherlands.

The Jack Stafford Collection
POPUPSTORE

CLOSED
67

ELEONORE
DE
RUUK

FIELD FACTS_

Although associated with the Nazi party in the mid-twentieth century, the use of Blackletter typefaces in Germany was actually outlawed by the fascist regime in January 1941 after typically hysterical denunciation of Jewish involvement in their development. It was decreed that Antiqua Roman would from then on be the standard.

Fette Fraktur

JOHANN CHRISTIAN BAUER · 1875

CATEGORY: Blackletter

CLASSIFICATION: Fraktur

COUNTRY OF ORIGIN: Germany

DISTINGUISHING MARKS: Broken appearance; mix of rounded, angled and stroke elements; broad, bold calligraphic strokes; hard, angled terminals; exaggerated flourishes on upper case

FURTHER SIGHTINGS: Breweries; newspaper mastheads; hip-hop and heavy metal graphics

NOT TO BE CONFUSED WITH: Old English (p. 350)

OPPOSITE: Fette Fraktur has been employed more of late, featuring in media aimed at youth culture, the heavy metal and hip-hop music scenes and in the design of fashion labels. Here, however, it is shown in its more familiar environment as a street sign in Berlin.

One of the most widely used examples of Blackletter (also known as Gothic Script) typefaces available today, this nineteenth-century typeface epitomizes the broken-letter style of the Gothic Fraktur types. Intended as an advertising face in the 1800s, it is still popular today and is employed in the music, fashion and publishing industries.

'Black letter' refers to a style of calligraphy that was used across Europe from the Middle Ages onwards. It was first used by Gutenberg and is perhaps best known thanks to its continued use in Germany right up until the twentieth century, where it was so common as to be used as the text face in books. There are a number of sub-classifications for Blackletter types, denoting the style of the strokes, with the most common being Fraktur, implying 'broken' strokes. **Fette Fraktur**'s bold and impactful design is credited to German type designer and punchcutter **Johann Christian Bauer**, later founder of the Bauer Type Foundry. A version of this typeface was published in 1875 by the C. E. Weber foundry.

Fette Fraktur is a powerful, dramatic typeface that is often used in advertising and communications to project a traditional Bavarian/Austrian tone. It does possess negative connotations for many, who associate it with the visual language and propaganda of Nazism throughout the 1930s and 1940s. However, the typeface, along with other Blackletter designs, has in recent years enjoyed a bit of a renaissance.

Fette Fraktur vs Old English

[p. 340] [p. 350]

Though **Fette Fraktur** and **Old English** both belong to the broad clan of handwriting styles called 'blackletter' they are really quite distant cousins. Fette Fraktur is a Fraktur, a subclass of Blackletter type that is characterized by sweeping curved strokes and forms that are quite unfamiliar to contemporary readers. Old English is a Textura, a genre typified by narrow letters with straight sides and a very regular texture overall. Because it is easier for modern audiences to digest, you'll usually see Old English whenever legibility is a concern, but Fette Fraktur has that rich flavour associated with things that are antique or German.

Fette Fraktur has a single-storey 'a'. The Old English 'a' is double storey.

Fette Fraktur's 's' has a long, sweeping stroke at its top.

Fette Fraktur's capitals, particularly the 'A', 'V', 'S' (above) and 'Z' are typical of nineteenth-century Frakturs. English is a Textura with upper-case forms closer to Roman type.

The Fette Fraktur 'g' has a ball terminal.

Sags O fi 123	Fette Fraktur
Sags O fi 123	Old English

Fette Fraktur's 'f', 'p' and 'q' descend to a sharp point. The Old English 'f' does not descend.

The interiors of the Old English caps have ornamental strokes.

Fette Fraktur's dots are nearly circular. Old English has triangular dots.

Fette Fraktur has figures derived from an unrelated Roman style. Old English's figures appear to be drawn with a broad-nibbed pen in the same manner as the rest of the typeface.

Gigi

JILL BELL · **ITC** · 1995

With its floral and ornate flourishes of loops and curls, Gigi's feminine appearance and touches of Latin style have made it a popular script the world over with a range of applications, from greetings cards to corporate identities.

Handcrafted by renowned US font designer **Jill Bell**, Gigi's first incarnation was as a logo for an American performance group hailing from Los Angeles, entitled 'Los Vatos and the Cholo Girls' – an all-Hispanic cast – where the men dressed up as women, the women as men. Gigi was the feminine typeface and a masculine font was also created (later turned into the 'Carumba' typeface). Bell titled the font Gigi, which was her daughter's nickname but which also included references to the 1958 American musical romantic comedy *Gigi* starring Maurice Chevalier and Leslie Caron.

With its light and playful aesthetic, Gigi's use has been widespread and it is one of Bell's most successful and adaptable fonts. Despite its Hispanic connotations the typeface has not only been used for Spanish food outlet branding on a global scale but has been employed on book and CD covers, fashion label branding, greetings cards, textile and ceramic designs, company logos and even a children's book written by pop star Madonna.

CATEGORY: Script

CLASSIFICATION: Handwriting

COUNTRY OF ORIGIN: USA

DISTINGUISHING MARKS: Loose, handwritten quality; irregular letter shapes; ornate curls, loops and twirls on all characters; looped stems; varying stroke weights

FURTHER SIGHTINGS: Its ornate and swirled appearance has seen it being employed on a huge range of applications, from 'chick-lit' fiction to Tex-Mex food outlets

NOT TO BE CONFUSED WITH: Brush Script (p. 334)

OPPOSITE: For this woman's fashion boutique in Seal Beach, California, Gigi's ornate script reflects perfectly the 'D'Vine' fashions on offer in-store.

D'Vire
Boutique
Apparel & Shoe Salon

Kuenstler Script

D. STEMPEL AG FOUNDRY · 1902

CATEGORY: Script

CLASSIFICATION: English Round Hand

COUNTRY OF ORIGIN: Germany

DISTINGUISHING MARKS: Thin stroke weight; loose-flowing, handwritten construction; rounded terminals on stems; open counters; horizontal bar through upper-case 'Z'; overlaying of strokes; flamboyant tails and curves

FURTHER SIGHTINGS: Employed when elegance and sophistication are required with a classical tone

NOT TO BE CONFUSED WITH: Bickley Script (p. 330); ITC Edwardian Script (p. 338)

OPPOSITE: Kuenstler Script employed above a gentlemen's barber projects a sophisticated message to passers-by.

Released at the start of the twentieth century, this delicate and flowing copperplate script is distinctive for its rounded terminals appearing on the upper-case stems, ascenders and descenders, and for the fact that it's also, unusually for a delicate script, available in a bold, heavier weight.

Originally titled Künstler Schreibschrift, meaning 'artistic handwriting', the typeface was created by the in-house team at the Stempel foundry in Germany in 1902 and was inspired by the designs of nineteenth-century English copperplate scripts (*see* Bickley Script p. 330). As with other cursive scripts, there is a formality to the lower case to allow for the characters to link together as if it were handwriting. This intricacy, married with the delicate line strokes, makes for a refined and romanticized presentation when used.

In 1957, German typographer Hans Bohn developed and created the heavier weight of **Kuenstler Script** while working at the Stempel foundry. It is still quite unusual for a formal script to possess such an alternative, and it creates a greater opportunity for the typeface to be used in a display or headline scenario where a classic and period feel is required.

Macmillan Headline

MILES NEWLYN · MACMILLAN CANCER SUPPORT · 2006

Although not available as a commercial font, this intriguing typeface has been seen widely across the UK in print, adverts and television adverts for one of Britain's leading cancer charities. Unique in its appearance, its groundbreaking design revolutionized the way in which not just Macmillan but all charities communicated.

British type designer **Miles Newlyn** was appointed by leading branding specialists Wolff Olins to design a bespoke typeface for British cancer charity **Macmillan Cancer Support** as they underwent a major rebranding exercise. Known for their cancer nursing services, the charity wished to provide a much broader role in offering support for all cancer-related needs and also to be a force for change in cancer care.

The radical **Macmillan Headline**, created only in upper case, is a bold Brush Script design with a warm, dynamic and approachable attitude to its forms. Each character possesses three letterform variations, allowing for a more random and hand-drawn appearance, minimizing the repeat use of commonly used characters. However, its informal presentation still holds authority and used in simple but key statements also has sincerity. In addition, it is employed in the logotype for the charity with the overall effect being a distinctive and active presence on Britain's streets.

CATEGORY: Script

CLASSIFICATION: Brush Script

COUNTRY OF ORIGIN: UK

DISTINGUISHING MARKS: Broad and loose letter strokes; no sharp edges; irregular terminals; varying counters; broken edges to some strokes

FURTHER SIGHTINGS: Exclusive licence to Macmillan Cancer Support charity

NOT TO BE CONFUSED WITH: Balloon (p. 328); Bruno (p. 332); Comic Sans (p. 336)

OPPOSITE: For leading UK cancer charity Macmillan Cancer Support the bold decision to employ an informal and irregular Script for all headlines and advertising messages was groundbreaking and marked a sea change in how charities presented themselves.

005302

FOR CANCER SUPPORT
EVERY STEP OF
THE WAY

WE ARE
MACMILLAN.
CANCER SUPPORT

Call the Macmillan team free on
0808 808 00 00
(Monday to Friday, 9am–8pm) or visit macmillan.org.uk

Full of Love
Jamie Oliver
BOTTOMS UP
Cheers
imperia

Old English

WILLIAM CASLON · 1760

CATEGORY: Blackletter

CLASSIFICATION: Old English

COUNTRY OF ORIGIN: UK

DISTINGUISHING MARKS: Bold calligraphic appearance; use of rounded, circular strokes; exaggerated flourishes and ornamentation on upper case; finessed terminals

FURTHER SIGHTINGS: Public houses and tattoo parlours

NOT TO BE CONFUSED WITH: Fette Fraktur (p. 340)

OPPOSITE: Old English employed in a contemporary application for a kitsch designer retail outlet.

For centuries the 'Old English' Blackletter style has been prevalent across Britain, developed from the calligraphy of around the time of the Norman Conquest and adopting European mainland Blackletter styles as time passed. This particular version by Monotype is based on William Caslon's own Blackletter design, Caslon Black, which was created in around 1760.

This approach in the design of Blackletter falls under the classification of Textura, which is the more calligraphic of the types of Blackletter styles that exist. In comparison with the popular German Blackletter Fraktur types (p. 340), what is generically referred to as 'Old English' does differ greatly in tone and construction (*see* p. 342 for comparison chart). In this instance, lower-case types possess a simpler, cleaner structure than their German cousins but their upper case is also different, with the approach of Textura counters often detailed with ornamentation, the addition of twin strokes of varying contrast on vertical stems and an added degree of detailing on terminals with additional adornments, adding to its distinction.

Whereas other Blackletter designs can appear sinister and gothic, Textura designs are generally a lighter and more popular typeface of this style and are often employed where a regal air of authority and trust is required, or equally, can be seen swinging overhead in the form of a sign fixed outside the local public house.

Owned

RAY LARABIE · TYPODERMIC · 2005

For that freshly 'tagged' appeal, look no further. Owned's urban graffiti scrawl takes as its source of inspiration the subway and railway 'art' commuters see when taking their morning train to the workplace.

With its broad-stroke characters and hurried appearance, Owned comes straight off the newly vandalized wall or side of a train. As if written with a fat-nibbed marker, its urban appearance mirrors the 'tagging' one sees applied to walls and street furniture in every town and city around the world.

Owned was designed by Canadian type designer **Ray Larabie**, who has created for the font a huge variety of ligatures and character variants in order to provide the letterforms an immediacy and variety when setting passages of text to provide that 'just tagged' look. Just don't get caught using it!

CATEGORY: Script

CLASSIFICATION: Handwritten

COUNTRY OF ORIGIN: Canada

DISTINGUISHING MARKS: Handwritten, broad-nibbed scrawled letterforms; appearance of that of graffiti tagging; glyphs formed mainly from single-stroke paths

FURTHER SIGHTINGS: Used in applications where a 'street', hip-hop, youth tone is needed

NOT TO BE CONFUSED WITH: Balloon (p. 328); Brush Script (p. 334); Macmillan Headline (p. 348)

OPPOSITE: It's 'street', and it's 'Owned'. This urban typeface reflects the increasing use of tagging seen in towns and cities across the globe.

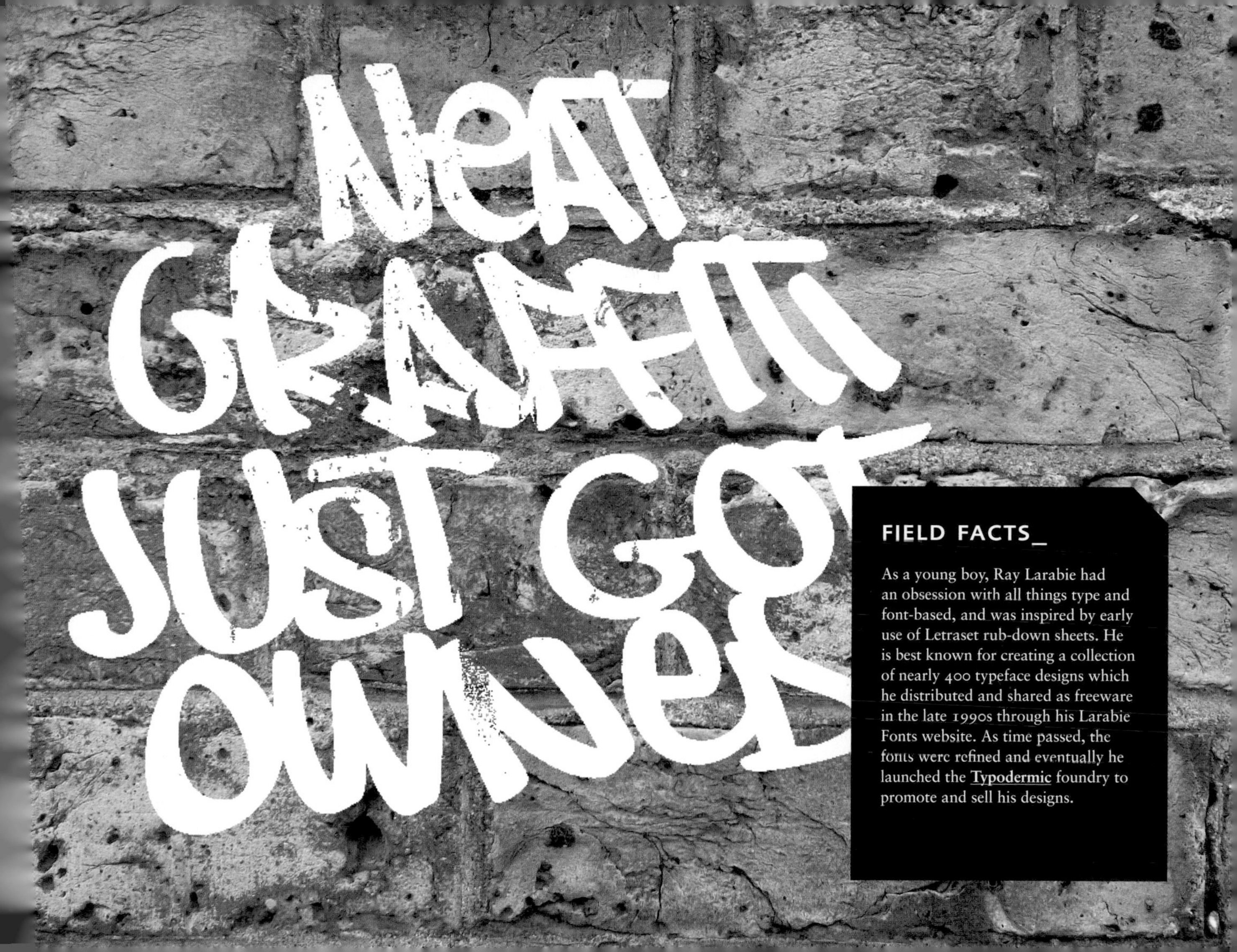
NEAT
GRAFFITI
JUST GOT
OWNED

FIELD FACTS_

As a young boy, Ray Larabie had an obsession with all things type and font-based, and was inspired by early use of Letraset rub-down sheets. He is best known for creating a collection of nearly 400 typeface designs which he distributed and shared as freeware in the late 1990s through his Larabie Fonts website. As time passed, the fonts were refined and eventually he launched the **Typodermic** foundry to promote and sell his designs.

SECTION FIVE

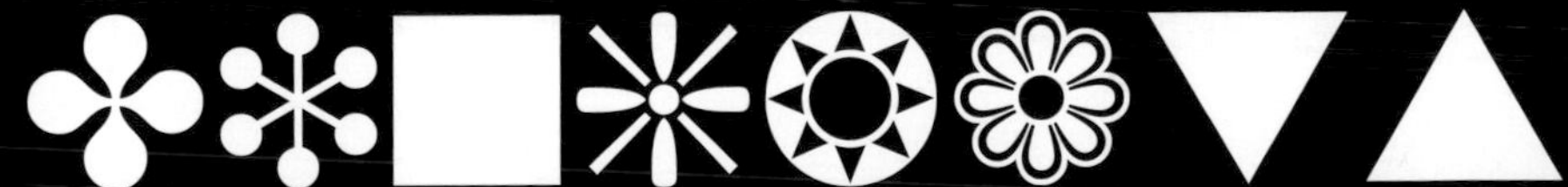

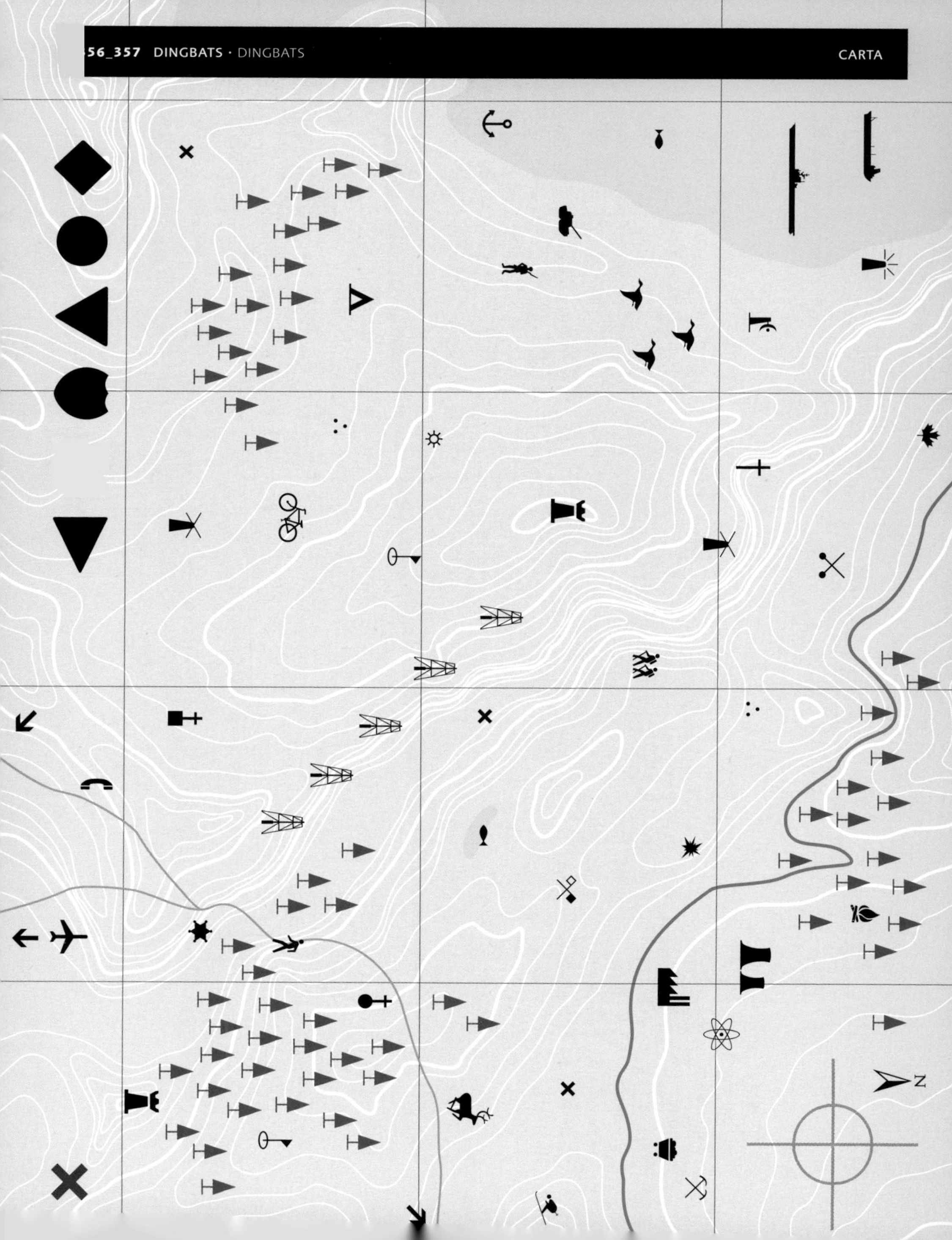

Carta

LYNNE GARELL · ADOBE · 1986

CATEGORY: Non-alphanumeric

CLASSIFICATION: Dingbats

COUNTRY OF ORIGIN: USA

DISTINGUISHING MARKS: Cartography-themed icons

FURTHER SIGHTINGS: Used extensively in cartography and urban-planning graphics

NOT TO BE CONFUSED WITH: ITC Zapf Dingbats (p. 370)

An all-encompassing map font, possessing a range of cartographic symbols inspired by maps and references from sources such as the US Geological Survey and *National Geographic*. Its range of icons covers the spectrum of land, sea and air.

Designed by US designer Lynne Garell, Carta's range of pictograms allows the designer to include an array of symbols commonly seen on maps in their work. Having studied under Hermann Zapf (*see* ITC Zapf Dingbats p. 370) at the Rochester Institute of Technology, Garell went on to work for **Adobe** in the type department, working as a 'type evangelist' to promote typographic awareness among audiences across the States. It was while she was at Adobe, working with type designers, calligraphers and graphic designers, that Garell developed Carta, an Adobe Original typeface.

Carta's comprehensive map icons range from pictograms of buildings through to shipping icons and a host of dingbats, making the font ideal for use in urban planning and mapping.

OPPOSITE: Carta's cartographic glyphs make it ideal for maps and urban-planning usages.

Kakaw Dingbats

FRIDA AND GABRIELA LARIOS · LATINOTYPE · 2013

Following Frida Larios's New Maya Language hieroglyphs system (*see* p. 360), and the accompanying typeface that she developed with her sister Gabriela to partner it, Kakaw (p. 286), the Larios sisters went on to create a fun and distinctive set of Kakaw Dingbats to accompany their letterforms.

With the successful design and development of Kakaw, the Chilean-based type foundry LatinoType who released the font suggested the idea of creating a set of dingbats that would work with their new typeface. Moving on from Frida's successful and innovative creation of the New Maya Language, a set of Mayan-influenced hieroglyphic pictograms, a lighter and more humorous approach was applied to the design of the dingbats to incorporate simpler but highly graphic illustrative forms.

Influenced by Gabriela's background in children's storytelling, the pictograms were originally intended to be recognizable animals. As the project developed, however, so did the 'animals', resulting in the creation of a number of quirky and humorous creatures. Frida Larios added her own designs and developed the rest of the range to include many everyday objects and some more extraordinary items such as rocket ships and UFOs. The 52 simple, organic icons possess great character and humour and are remarkably distinctive and contemporary while retaining a Central American feel.

CATEGORY: Non-alphanumeric

CLASSIFICATION: Dingbats

COUNTRY OF ORIGIN: El Salvador

DISTINGUISHING MARKS: Contemporary Mayan culture-themed icons ranging from animals to UFOs

FURTHER SIGHTINGS: n/a

NOT TO BE CONFUSED WITH: n/a

OPPOSITE: Frida and Gabriela Larios's Kakaw Dingbats font contains a number of familiar and not-so-familiar creatures and items.

~!#%*

Frida Larios

WASHINGTON DC, USA

Hailing from El Salvador, Frida Larios is an INDIGO (International Indigenous Design Network) ambassador and is the creator of the multi-award-winning New Maya Language pictograms: a symbol-based alphabet based on the principles of early Mayan hieroglyphs.

Her work has been exhibited at the National Taiwan University of Arts, Taipei, Taiwan and the Central Academy of Fine Arts Museum in Beijing, China. She has solo-exhibited at the Embassy of Mexico, Guatemala; the Museo para la Identidad Nacional, Tegucigalpa, Honduras; Canning House and the Embassy of El Salvador, London. Frida also won a beach volleyball gold medal at the 2001 Central American Games.

Q: You have been widely acclaimed and won many awards for having created a system of 'New Maya Language', which is a pictorial hieroglyphic typeface. Could you explain how this came about and the principles behind it?
A: I was inspired to reinterpret and redesign a selected logo-vocabulary from the dead Maya hieroglyphic language, while I was living in London. Being far away from my own Central American culture, and at the same time, being so close to a mecca of contemporary art and design, brought me close to my own roots. Central Saint Martins College of Art and Design (where I developed the project as my MA in Communication Design) was two blocks away from the British Museum in Holborn, which holds some of the most beautiful carved pieces in the Maya world. Thousands of years old, on par to avant-garde, art expressions, gave life to the concept behind New Maya Language. The Maya art and design is full of organic character in both content and style; it is based on the forms of the mythological plant, animal and spiritual worlds. In the development of the collection of pictograms (which grows year by year!), the symbolism and meaning behind the standardized Mesoamerica script, and its intricate style, are highlighted.

Q: What benefits does the New Maya Language have over more letter-based forms of communication?
A: The idea is to be able to 'read' the logograms without knowing a letter-based alphabet language, like Spanish. Roman letterforms are graphic elements, but they are abstract and not

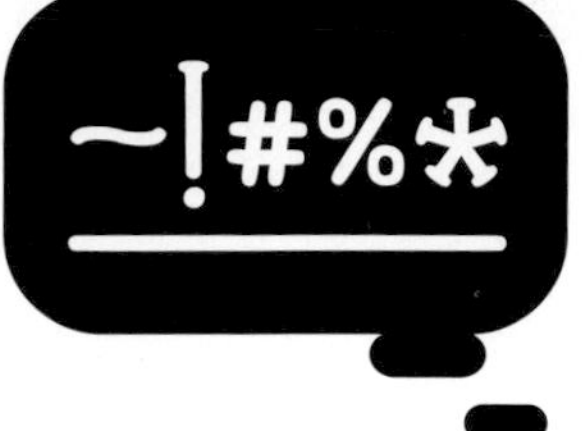

ABOVE LEFT: Design for iPhone case employing a **New Maya Language** 'skull' pictogram.

ABOVE MIDDLE TOP: Frida Larios, creator of the New Maya Language.

ABOVE MIDDLE AND RIGHT: A range of examples of the New Maya Language hieroglyphic 'alphabet'. Each pictogram tells a story and is constructed from the findings of Larios's extensive research and the reinterpretation of the original Maya hieroglyphs and symbolic art.

MUYAL

LEFT AND BELOW: Frida Larios's identity and packaging for MUYAL, an ecological and socially sustainable line of beauty products for the body and hair with all ingredients coming from Honduras. The word 'MUYAL' means cloud in Mayan and the pictogram has been created in line with the principles of the New Maya Language that Larios developed.

connected naturally to our cognitive system. They are foreign – especially to *campesinos* (farmers) who live off the land in rural areas, following the natural rhythm of seasons, and waking up at sunrise and going to bed at sunset. My New Maya Language vocabulary intends to speak the language of the ecosystem. The system is direct and to the point: harvesting is represented by a hand, a seed is represented by an oval, smoke is represented by a flame tongue – all in the spirit of the Maya artists' form and content. For the pictography to be recognizable and friendly to any language-speaking audience, it uses contemporary visual canons to decode a picture. The No Smoking and the New Maya Skull pictograms are the best examples from the series, as they are almost instantly recognizable. For the rest of the pictograms, my book is a didactic introduction to how the New Maya Language system works. The first chapter introduces the original Maya hieroglyphic system, the second chapter supplies the 'formula' behind each pictogram, and the third chapter shows field applications.

Q: You have taken the concepts behind the New Maya Language and applied it to contemporary identity and visual communication projects. Can you explain how the process works and what benefits (and if any disadvantages) using the system brings?

A: There has been a tendency for a good majority of southern hemisphere designers to imitate northern graphic styles. Like in many design disciplines, the norm is to look into what is fashionable in the Western world, rather than sourcing from a native background for innovation. Globalization has brought monoculture, as well as a revival of locality as a point of differentiation. In this sense, I believe graphic identities can be based on visual content that has relevance to the context in which the works are applied. My system can serve that purpose – why have an ISO standardized No Smoking pictogram if you can have a vernacular one that tells a unique and real story of the people who live in the region of application? It can even help reduce CO_2 emissions, as the system expands towards facilitating sustainable applications that rescue heritage craft and traditional production methods. This is the case of the Los Sapos archaeological site wayfinding system in Copán, Honduras. A single, simple pictogram was used in the signposting that means Path To in both the old and the New Maya Language. It was then carved on to large-scale local river rocks by an indigenous Maya-Chortí stone crafter. The rock posts embed with the landscape, are intuitively read and are self-sustainable.

Q: To accompany the system you have created a 'Roman' typeface. Could you explain the thinking behind it? What influenced its unique design? What, if any, were the issues in designing it?

A: It was a challenge to design a typeface that complemented, and at the same time contrasted, the pebble-shaped New Maya hieroglyphs. It couldn't be too round because the pictograms, or glyphs, are already based on a rounded square grid. An exaggerated ascender and descender seemed like a good contrast to a perfect circle x-height. For that reason, the lower case was created first. Luckily, my sister Gabriela had done the conceptual work of designing the lower-case letters 'b' and 'g' a few years ahead. The upper case was created to aid readability in the design of signs in public spaces. The upper case had to comfortably follow the rhythm of the extremely long lower-case ascenders. Narrowness was a constraint, but the result was pleasing enough to the eye, without bordering on the absurd and illegible. The design of the symbols and punctuation marks resulted in peculiar shapes that almost seemed like dingbats in their own right. And this is why the dingbats ended up having the same serifs as the glyphs: to give birth to creatures and UFOs with a very quirky personality. The Light version is very elegant-looking and has room for other applications, like water for chocolate (packaging) – especially as Kakaw means chocolate in Mayan!

Q: The New Maya Language system has been applied to a number of items, including ceramics and fashion. What are the challenges in working in other media, and are there further applications you still wish to do?

A: In my opinion the Maya artists were renaissance men comparable to Leonardo, Raphael, Michelangelo, who were not only fine artists, but also architects, sculptors, interior designers, poets, and even engineers – in other words, liberal innovators. And so were the Maya artists who were royal scribes and bookkeepers. In being so they held the knowledge of what they had to write about: history, politics, astronomy, mathematics, and art in general. No artist today can claim to master all these disciplines, but their talent is surely my source of inspiration.

It has been eight years now since I conceived the New Maya Language, and it has certainly developed into a multiple-avenue project that has life in sign, typography, surface, fashion, accessories, and educational toy design. My next project is to design an iPhone app that teaches children about the Maya language and helps their storytelling abilities. The system has no limits – it can even be reinterpreted into other script forms. I am willing to expand it as far as my imagination takes it, with the intent of making a part of my culture known to the world, to my fellow Mesoamerican citizens, and to the living Maya themselves.

OPPOSITE, TOP LEFT AND MIDDLE: Larios's New Maya Language adapted for a fashion range showing a ceramic vessel containing beans and beach-ware with an erupting volcano motif as a design.

FAR RIGHT TOP AND MIDDLE: Ceramic accessories and belt buckle both featuring distinctive pictograms.

BOTTOM LEFT AND RIGHT: Carved pictograms used as a wayfinding 'sign' hewn from a boulder.

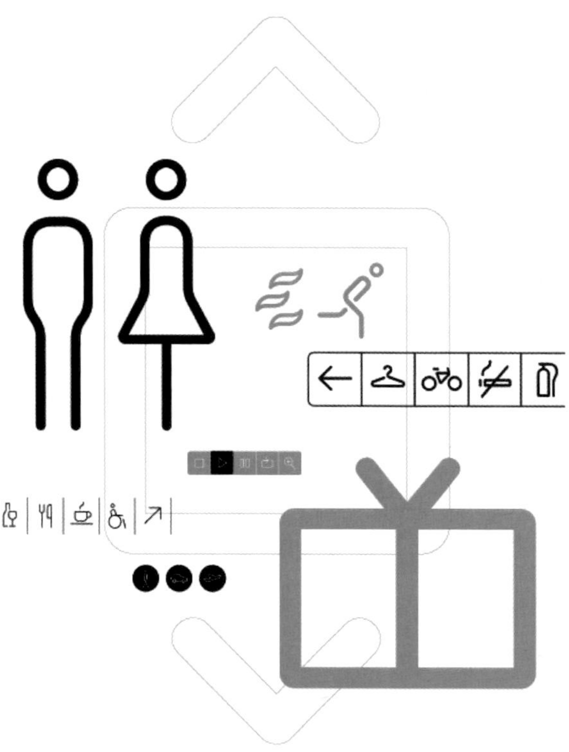

restaurant
second floor
gift set

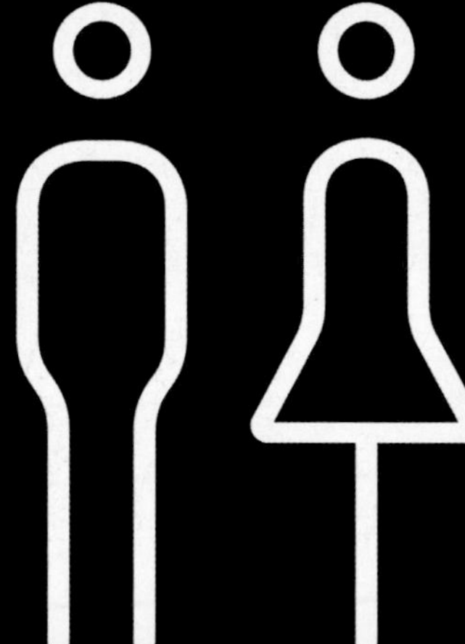

FF Netto Icons

DANIEL UTZ · FONTFONT · 2008

CATEGORY: Non-alphanumeric

CLASSIFICATION: Dingbats

COUNTRY OF ORIGIN: Germany

DISTINGUISHING MARKS: Keyline pictograms; rounded terminals; evenly spaced setting; Light, Regular and Reversed Bold options

FURTHER SIGHTINGS: Ideal for wayfinding and signage applications in public spaces and transport hubs

NOT TO BE CONFUSED WITH: Carta (p. 356); ITC Zapf Dingbats (p. 370)

OPPOSITE: The clean, elegant forms of the FF Netto Icons collection are designed to complement the FF Netto typeface also designed by Daniel Utz.

To accompany his geometric and pared-down Sans Serif typeface design, FF Netto, German designer and digital typography teacher Daniel Utz created a broad range of icons, from paper clips to aeroplanes, that can be employed with the typeface for a wide array of wayfinding and signage usages, from travel to dining and domestic applications.

These distinctive, contemporary and elegant pictograms cover a wide range of subject matter and appear in a monoweight stroke in three weights to pair up and work seamlessly with Utz's FF Netto Sans Serif family. The Light and Regular versions of the icons are simple keyline designs with the stroke weight matching the corresponding typeface weights. The bold designs have been created reversed out of individual squares with rounded corners, providing greater impact, as one would expect, when married with the bolder weights of the collection.

FF Netto Icons also matches the FF Netto typeface in width and size so is ideal for use in text and icon combinations where tabular alignment may be required. The Light and Regular pictograms are also supplied with border elements and separator lines so as to be enclosed in squares or rectangles of even spacing or combinations of both to create a variety of options for the designer. The rounded terminals on all icons help soften the icons' keyline construction and provide it with a very modern and clean appearance.

Wingdings

CHARLES BIGELOW, KRIS HOLMES · MICROSOFT · 1990

A comprehensive and wide range of icons is included in Microsoft's Wingdings dingbats collection. Initially named 'Lucida Icons, Arrows and Stars', the original collection was created to accompany the designers' Lucida text font collection created by US design partnership the Bigelow & Holmes foundry.

The extensive range of dingbats in Wingdings includes a diverse set of geometric shapes, gestures and internationally recognized symbols, including the Star of David, Zodiac and Yin-Yang symbols, with even the Microsoft logo itself included. A key and recognizable characteristic of the icons in this collection is their connection to the graphical user interfaces of personal computers, with elements such as a monitor, floppy disk and mouse design included as well as characters for files, folders and documents.

The full collection of Wingdings is organized into three fonts (Wingdings 1 to 3), with numbers 1 and 2 being pictogram-based and font 3 providing a range of arrow and directional icons, ideal for complex flow and directional information graphics.

CATEGORY: Non-alphanumeric

CLASSIFICATION: Dingbats

COUNTRY OF ORIGIN: USA

DISTINGUISHING MARKS: n/a

FURTHER SIGHTINGS: Microsoft applications

NOT TO BE CONFUSED WITH: Carta (p. 356); ITC Zapf Dingbats (p. 370)

OPPOSITE: Wingdings's collection of IT and personal computer icons makes it an ideal choice for infographics and flow diagrams for network planning and similar.

FIELD FACTS_

Even a Dingbat font can cause controversy. Soon after Windows 3.1 was released in 1992 the character sequence 'NYC' when set in Wingdings was deemed anti-Semitic as the letter-forms were represented in Wingdings by a skull, Star of David and thumbs up. An unfortunate setting coincidence, which Microsoft vehemently denied was intentional, explaining that the arrangement of characters in the font was more or less random.

ITC Zapf Dingbats

HERMANN ZAPF · ITC · 1978

CATEGORY: Non-alphanumeric

CLASSIFICATION: Dingbats

COUNTRY OF ORIGIN: USA

DISTINGUISHING MARKS: n/a

FURTHER SIGHTINGS: Microsoft applications

NOT TO BE CONFUSED WITH: Carta (p. 356); Wingdings (p. 368)

OPPOSITE: In 1994, experimental and often controversial US graphic designer and art director David Carson (noted for his highly experimental magazine design) employed ITC Zapf Dingbats in an interview with Roxy Music's Bryan Ferry in his publication *Ray Gun*. It wasn't used merely as an ornamentation detail; the entire double-page spread interview was set in the Dingbats font. Carson's explanation for this illegible setting was that the interview with the rock star had been so 'incredibly boring' that he hoped to make it interesting by using ITC Zapf Dingbats.

One of the most recognized and widely used Dingbat typefaces today, ITC Zapf Dingbats became popular when supplied as one of the first of Apple's PostScript fonts. It was created by eminent and prolific type designer Hermann Zapf, who also created the Palatino and Optima (p. 220) typefaces.

The collection of ITC Zapf Dingbats consists of a vast array of icons and it was Zapf's intention to create a family of pictorial elements that work with, and complement, contemporary typeface designs and to enhance visually communications and graphic design. As one of the early font releases with Apple Macintosh computers, it soon gained popularity and was often employed by designers in their work.

Initially, Zapf drew up over 1,000 different icon designs and, working with American foundry ITC, whittled this down to a subset of 360. The current ITC font contains 204 glyphs, including a large range of stars and floral motifs, exaggerated punctuation symbols, directional arrows and numerical symbols. In 2002, Hermann Zapf designed and produced Linotype Zapf Essentials, a modernized version of his existing typeface, with over 372 characters and symbols included in six fonts. The new collection draws on many of the unused symbols he created along with more contemporary subject matters such as email and mobile phone pictograms.

FURTHER READING_

20th-Century Type
Lewis Blackwell
Laurence King Publishing, 2004

30 Essential Typefaces for a Lifetime
Imin Pao (Editor), Joshua Berger (Editor)
Rockport Publishers, 2006

Anatomy of a Typeface
Alexander Lawson
David R. Godine, 1991

An A-Z of Type Designers
Neil Macmillan
Yale University Press, 2006

The Elements of Typographic Style
Robert Bringhurst
Hartley & Marks Publishers, 2013

Encyclopaedia of Typefaces: The Standard Typography Reference Guide
W.P. Jaspert, W. Turner Berry, A.F. Johnson
Cassell Illustrated, 2009

The Geometry of Type: The Anatomy of 100 Essential Typefaces
Stephen Coles
Thames & Hudson, 2013

Graphic Design before Graphic Designers: The Printer as Designer and Craftsman 1700–1914
David Jury
Thames & Hudson, 2012

Just My Type: A Book About Fonts
Simon Garfield
Profile Books, 2011

New Modernist Type
Steven Heller, Gail Anderson
Thames & Hudson, 2012

Stop Stealing Sheep and Find Out How Type Works
Erik Spiekermann, E.M Ginger
Adobe Press, 2003

Signs: Lettering in the Environment
Phil Baines, Catherine Dixon
Laurence King, 2003

Typography Sketchbooks
Steven Heller, Lita Talarico
Thames & Hudson, 2011

Type: v. 1: A Visual History of Typefaces and Graphic Styles
Cees de Jong, Jan Tholenaar, Alston W. Purvis
Taschen, 2009

USEFUL WEBSITES_

www.fontfeed.com
Daily news feed on fonts, typographic techniques and examples.

www.fontsinuse.com
An indexed public archive of typography.

www.myfonts.com
World's largest collection of fonts online to preview, sample and buy, plus information on typefaces and designers.

www.typepedia.com
Online community website to classify typefaces and provide educational information on type and typography.

www.typographica.org
Typographica is a review of typefaces and type books, with commentary on fonts and typographic design by Stephen Coles.

www.typophile.com
Internet discussion forum on all things type and typography.

Font Designers and Foundries

A2-Type _ www.a2-type.co.uk
Alias _ alias.dj
Berthold _ www.bertholdtypes.com
Bitstream _ www.bitstream.com
CastleType _ www.castletype.com
Commercial Type _ commercialtype.com
Dalton Maag _ www.daltonmaag.com
Daniel Utz _ www.danielutz.de
David Quay _ davidquaydesign.com
Elsner + Flake _ www.elsner-flake.com
Erik Spiekermann _ spiekermann.com
Erik van Blokland _ letterror.com
Emigre Fonts _ www.emigre.com
FontFont _ www.fontfont.com
Fonthaus _ www.fonthaus.com
Fontsmith _ www.fontsmith.com
Foundry Types _ www.foundrytypes.co.uk
Frida Larios _ www.fridalarios.com
Hoefler & Frere-Jones _ www.typography.com
House Industries _ www.houseind.com
Jeremy Tankard Typography _ typography.net
Jill Bell _ jillbell.com
Jonathan Barnbrook _ www.barnbrook.net
Just van Rossum _ www.letterror.com
LatinoType _ latinotype.com
Linotype _ www.linotype.com
Matthew Carter _ carterandcone.com
Microsoft _ www.microsoft.com/typography
Miles Newlyn _ newlyn.com
Monotype _ www.monotype.com
Neville Brody _ www.researchstudios.com
Ray Larabie _ typodermicfonts.com
Retype _ re-type.com
Timothy Donaldson _ timothydonaldson.com
Typotheque _ www.typotheque.com

INDEX_

Ausgang
exit
TAXI

controlled by the

PICTURE CREDITS_

a = above • b = below • l = left • r = right • c = centre

2al: © Peter Dawson • 2ac: Courtesy Nick Kapica/SV Associates • 2ra: © Peter Dawson • 2rc: © Peter Dawson • 2bl: Courtesy Gardiner Richardson • 2bca: © Peter Dawson • 2bcb: © Peter Dawson • 2br: Courtesy Fontsmith Ltd • 3al: © Peter Dawson • 3ar: Courtesy Intégral Ruedi Baur and Andreas Körner • 3bl: Courtesy Nick Kapica/SV Associates • 3br: © Peter Dawson • 9: © Stephen Coles • 11 © gagliardifoto/Shutterstock.com • 12al: Courtesy R2 Design • 12ar: © SeanPavonePhoto • 12bl: © Massimo Catarinella • 12br: © Peter Dawson • 22: © Peter Dawson • 24: © Peter Dawson • 27: © River North Photography/istockphoto • 28: Courtesy A2-TYPE • 31: photos © James Evans • 32al: © wdstock//istockphoto • 32ar: © Peter Dawson • 32bl: © Peter Dawson • 32br: © Peter Dawson • 36: © James Evans • 39: © Tom England/istockphoto • 40: © Andrew Cribb/istockphoto • 42: © Pepe Gimeno Proyecto Gráfico • 43al: © Florian Hardwig • 43ar: © Peter Dawson • 43br: © ChristosV • 44: © Tempura's lightbulb/istockphoto • 47–49 Courtesy Gardiner Richardson • 50: Library of Congress, LC Control No: 2003576546 • 53: © ZekaG/istockphoto • 54al: © Jeffrey M. Frank • 54ar: © Peter Dawson • 54bl: © Carterdayne Inc/istockphoto • 54br: © Peter Dawson • 57–61 Courtesy Emigre Inc • 63: © Peter Dawson • 64: © Peter Dawson • 67: © Peter Dawson • 68: Courtesy Grade Design Consultants Ltd • 71: © James Evans • 72: © Carterdayne Inc/istockphoto • 75: © Stephen Coles • 76: © Peter Dawson • 79: © Grade Design Consultants Ltd • 82: © Rossella De Berti/istockphoto • 85: Photos © Peter Dawson • 86: © Dwight Nadig/istockphoto • 89 Courtesy Emigre Inc • 90: Courtesy R2 Design • 93–97: Courtesy CastleType • 99: © James Evans • 100: © Peter Dawson • 103: © Peter Dawson • 106: © Stephen Coles • 109: Courtesy togetherdesign.gr. • 110al: © Peter Dawson • 110ar: © Peter Dawson • 110bl: © Peter Dawson • 110br: © VanHart/shutterstock • 113: © Peter Dawson • 114: Courtesy Ralf Herrmann • 117: Courtesy Coralie Bickford-Smith • 118: © Peter Dawson • 121: Courtesy Nick Kapica/SV Associates • 122: Courtesy Nick Kapica/SV Associates • 124a: © Pepe Gimeno Proyecto Gráfico • 124bl: © Stephen Coles • 124br: Courtesy Nick Kapica/SV Associates • 125: Courtesy Nick Kapica/SV Associates • 126: © Raw Design Studio/SM2 • 129: © Louise Evans • 132: © Marcus Lindström/istockphoto • 134 © Peter Dawson • 135al: © mm88/istockphoto • 135ar: © track5/istockphoto • 135br: © James Evans • 137: © imantsu/Shutterstock.com • 138: Courtesy of David Quay • 141: © Peter Dawson • 143–146: Courtesy of ATF • 149: © Bob Aufuldish • 150: © Peter Dawson • 155: © Cr-Management GmbH & Co. KG/istockphoto • 156: Courtesy Fontsmith Ltd • 159: © Colman Lerner Gerardo/shutterstock • 160: © Florian Hardwig • 163: © Stephen Coles • 164–167: Courtesy Intégral Ruedi Baur and Andreas Körner • 170: Courtesy Jeremy Tankard Typography • 171: Courtesy Nick Kapica/SV Associates • 172–173: Courtesy Nick Kapica/SV Associates • 174al: © Hande Yüce/istockphoto • 174ar: © pio3/Shutterstock.com • 174bl: © PP+C Creative Studio/istockphoto • 174br: © Erika Cross/Shutterstock.com • 177: © Peter Kirillov/shutterstock.com • 178al: © Oleg V. Ivanov/shutterstock.com • 178bl: © Peter Dawson • 178br: © Peter Dawson • 179: © Jordan Tan/shutterstock.com • 180: © Peter Dawson • 182: Courtesy of R2 Design • 183: Photos © Peter Dawson • 187: © Peter Dawson • 188: © Action Sports Photography/Shutterstock.com • 193al: © Gregory James Van Raalte/Shutterstock.com • 193ar: © Peter Dawson • 193bl: © Ben Bryant/Shutterstock.com • 193br: © Peter Dawson • 194al: © Andrea Gingerich/istockphoto • 194ar: © eddtoro/Shutterstock.com • 194bla: © seewhatmitchsee/istockphoto • 194blb: © Peter Dawson • 194br: © Peter Dawson • 195al: © Peter Dawson • 195ac: © whitemay/istockphoto • 195ara: © Peter Dawson • 195arc: © Peter Dawson • 195bl: © OnFilm/istockphoto • 195br: © Adam Korzekwa/istockphoto • 196: © Sorbis/shutterstock.com • 199–203: Courtesy Foundry Types Ltd • 204: © Peter Dawson • 205: © NoDerog/istockphoto • 208: © Louise Evans • 210: © Zürcher Verkehrsverbund/PostAuto Region Zürich, • 212al: © Drbouz/istockphoto • 212ar: EdStock/istockphoto • 212bl: Joe Ravi/istockphoto • 212br: EdStock/istockphoto • 214: Courtesy Raffinerie AG für Gestaltung • 216: © Adrian Lindley/Shutterstock.com • 218l: King of Hearts / Wikimedia Commons / CC-BY-SA-3.0 • 218r: @ Paolo Scarlata/ istockphoto • 220: © Shutterstock.com • 222: © Peter Dawson • 225: © Christopher Ames/istockphoto • 226: © James Evans • 229: © Giancarlo Malandra/istockphoto • 230: © Peter Dawson • 233: © Peter Dawson • 234: © Peter Dawson • 236: © Peter Dawson • 238: © Peter Dawson • 240–243 © Peter Dawson • 245: Courtesy of A2-TYPE • 246: © Peter Dawson • 249–253: Courtesy of A2-TYPE • 256: © magnez2/istockphoto • 259: © Florian Hardwig • 260: © Peter Dawson • 263: © Bikeworldtravel/Shutterstock.com • 264: © Peter Dawson • 267: © Matthew Andrews • 268–269: © Kenny Laurenson • 271: © Matthew Ragen/ istockphoto • 272: Courtesy Raffinerie AG für Gestaltung • 275–277: Courtesy Nick Kapica/SV Associates • 279: © Ben Bryant / Shutterstock.com • 280: © Peter Dawson • 283–285: Courtesy David Quay • 286: Courtesy Frida Larios • 289: Courtesy R2 Design • 291–295: Courtesy Fontsmith Ltd • 297: © Shih-Hao Liao/istockphoto • 298: © Filo/istockphoto • 301: Courtesy Fontsmith Ltd • 302: © Daniel Rivera • 305: © Peter Dawson • 306: © Freddi Boulton/istockphoto • 308: © Peter Dawson • 311: © J. G. Park • 312: © Peter Dawson • 315: © Peter Dawson • 316: © Ken Wiedemann • 318: Courtesy Nick Kapica/SV Associates • 320: © Peter Dawson • 323: © Grade Design Consultants Ltd • 324: © Peter Dawson • 326: © Peter Dawson • 328: © Peter Dawson • 331: © Peter Dawson • 332: Courtesy Jill Bell • 335: © Peter Dawson • 336: © Florian Hardwig • 339: © Florian Hardwig • 340: © Florian Hardwig • 345: Courtesy Jill Bell • 346: © Peter Dawson • 349: © Peter Dawson • 350: © James Evans • 353: © Grade Design Consultants Ltd • 354: © long8614/shutterstock.com • 356: © Grade Design Consultants Ltd • 359: © Grade Design Consultants Ltd • 361–365: Courtesy Frida Larios • 366: © Daniel Utz/FontShop • 369: © EDHAR/shutterstock.com / Grade Design Consultants Ltd • 370: © Grade Design Consultants Ltd 379: Courtesy Intégral Ruedi Baur and Andreas Körner • 380: © Peter Dawson • 383: © Peter Dawson.

ACKNOWLEDGEMENTS_

A huge thank you goes first to James Evans of Quid Publishing, who came up with the idea and invited me to write and design the book. The countless emails and conversations we have shared to pull this title together have been inestimable, and when I was in danger of drowning with the workload midway through the project, he safely steered it towards calmer waters. For that, James, you have my thanks. Medal of Honour also goes to James for finding the Bell typeface in use after our many months of searching – and all those trips to the Craft Beer Co. to get the right shot were worth it! To my editors, Richard Webb and Lucy York, who made sure my words were in the right order and made sense: thank you again for such diligence. Thanks also to Karen Levine at Prestel and Natalie Evans at Thames & Hudson for their constructive and positive feedback on the book's content.

Special gratitude to Stephen Coles, who kindly went out of his way to write up the typeface comparison spreads and the Foreword. The images he contributed were all much appreciated, and his input and insight into the book's text have been very welcome.

Of course, this book would be nothing without the skill and creativity of the many designers who have created such beautiful work over the years (and in doing so inspired and motivated myself and many others), as well as the individuals and organizations that have contributed to this book with their time, generous donation of their work, images for publication and/or generally running around for me upon request. I must thank, in no particular order: Jill Bell, David Quay, Jeremy Tankard, Mauro Gimeno at Pepe Gimeno - Proyecto Gráfico, Florian Hardwig at Kaune & Hardwig, Darren Richardson at Gardiner Richardson, Lizá Ramalho, Artur Rebelo and Filipa Namora at R2 Design, Christos Tsolerides at togetherdesign.gr, Ralf Herrmann, Coralie Bickford-Smith, Nick Kapica (extra gratitude to Nick for supplying such a range of wonderful creations) and Andrew Lawrence, Tom Heaton at Raw Design Studio, SM2 Studio, Liz Calvert at Thompson Brand Partners, Dian Hulse at Foundry Types, Eva Kubinyi and colleagues at Intégral Ruedi Baur Paris & Zürich, Peter Bilak, Andreas Körner, Raffinerie AG für Gestaltung, Antony Rathbone, Daniel Rivera, Richard Wolfströme, Kenny Laurenson and Matthew Andrews, J. G. Park and Morag Myerscough.

And an extra special thanks to those designers who agreed to allow me to pester them in asking questions about their work and hassle them endlessly for visual material. A very appreciative thank you goes to Jason Castle of CastleType, Henrik Kubel of A2-TYPE, Frida Larios, Freda Sack of Foundry Types, Jason Smith of Fontsmith, Wayne Thompson of ATF, and last but not at all least Rudy Vanderlans and Zuzana Licko of Emigre.

To research, write, photograph and then design one's own book has been a massive undertaking, and I could not have done it alone. Gratitude goes to my colleagues at Grade. Louise Evans, whose patience and enthusiasm never wavered in the many months, despite my constant interjections and changes of mind and to Paul Palmer-Edwards for his support during this trial by design.

Finally, thank you to my parents, friends and supporters, who have provided constant support and encouragement over the many, many months it has taken to create the book and put up with me and my typographic obsessions and distractions. I would promise to stop, but the love of type is a vocation. I hope that passion is conveyed within these pages, and shared.

T A

ABOUT THE AUTHOR_

Peter Dawson has over 20 years' experience within the design industry following his graduation from Kingston University in 1992. Having worked as a designer and then creative director at a number of design consultancies, he went on to co-found in 2000 his London-based studio Grade (www.gradedesign.com). Peter has worked for a diverse and extensive range of clients over the years from The British Museum to Walt Disney and specializes in branding, typographic and publishing design, having designed a large number of best-selling and award-winning illustrated book titles. Awards have included British D&AD annual inclusion, several ISTD Certificates of Excellence and 'Best Jacket' and 'Best Series' at the British Book Design and Production Awards. Peter is a Fellow, and a former Chair and board member, of the International Society of Typographic Designers and has been a visiting typography and design lecturer at a number of universities in the UK and overseas. In 2012 he co-authored *Graphic Design Rules*.